RETHINKING
JAPANESE HISTORY

The John Whitney Hall Book Imprint
commemorates a pioneer in
the field of Japanese Studies
and one of the most respected
scholars of his generation.
This endowed book fund
enables the Center for
Japanese Studies to publish
works on Japan that
preserve the vision and
meticulous scholarship of a
distinguished and beloved historian.

RETHINKING
JAPANESE HISTORY

Amino Yoshihiko

Translated and with an Introduction by Alan S. Christy
Preface and Afterword by Hitomi Tonomura

Center for Japanese Studies
The University of Michigan
Ann Arbor   2012

NIHON NO REKISHI O YOMINAOSU by Yoshihiko Amino
Copyright © 1991 by Yoshihiko Amino
ZOKU NIHON NO REKISHI O YOMINAOSU by Yoshihiko Amino
Copyright © 1993 by Yoshihiko Amino
Japanese original edition of both titles published by
Chikuma Shobo Publishing Co. Ltd., Tokyo
English translation rights arranged with Chikuma Shobo Publishing Co. Ltd., Tokyo,
through Japan Foreign-Rights Centre

Published by
Center for Japanese Studies, The University of Michigan
1007 E. Huron St., Ann Arbor, MI 48104-1690

Michigan Monograph Series in Japanese Studies
Number 74

Library of Congress Cataloging-in-Publication Data

Amino, Yoshihiko, 1928–2004.
    [Nihon no rekishi o yominaosu. English]
    Rethinking Japanese history / Amino Yoshihiko ; translated and with an introduction
by Alan S. Christy ; preface and afterword by Hitomi Tonomura.
      p. cm.
    Includes index.
    ISBN 978-1-929280-70-4 (cloth : alk. paper) — ISBN 978-1-929280-71-1
(pbk. : alk. paper)
    1. Japan—History—To 1600.   I. Christy, Alan S.   II. Tonomura, Hitomi.
III. Amino, Yoshihiko, 1928–2004. Zoku Nihon no rekishi o yominaosu. English.
IV. Title.

DS850.A4513 2012
952—dc23

                             2011044356

This book was set in Minion Pro.

This publication meets the ANSI/NISO Standards for Permanence of Paper
for Publications and Documents in Libraries and Archives (Z39.48–1992).

Printed in the United States of America

CONTENTS

BOOK ONE
Circuits of the Sea and Nonagricultural Production

BOOK TWO
Sacred Space and the People on the Margins of History

ILLUSTRATIONS

FIGURES

TABLES

PREFACE

The decision to publish translations of *Nihon no rekishi o yominaosu* and *Zoku Nihon no rekishi o yominaosu* was made during the summer of 1996. Funded by the Japan Foundation, Professor Amino was coming to the United States in the fall of that year to offer lectures and seminars at four institutions: the University of California, Berkeley, the University of Chicago, Princeton University, and the University of Michigan. At the University of Michigan, Professor Amino was going to offer a three-day mini-course on "Outcastes and Boundaries: Social History of Premodern Japan." Accompanying Professor Amino as translator was Alan S. Christy. Discussions about publishing the lectures and chapters of *Zoku Nihon no rekishi o yominaosu* quickly evolved into an agreement to publish both of Amino's books. The details were finalized and contracts were signed in the summer of 1997.

Here we are fourteen years later, and I can say for certain that this translation project would not have begun without the visit of Professor Amino to the United States, and the project would never have come to fruition without the dedication and perseverance of a number of people. Logistically, I must begin by thanking Professor Emiko Ohnuki-Tierney, who first suggested bringing Professor Amino to the United States. Our institutional collaborators, James George S. Andre at the University of Chicago, Mack Horton and Andrew Barshay at the University of California, Berkeley, and Martin Collcutt at Princeton University, coordinated the schedule and helped create a busy but meaningful trip for Professor Amino. In getting the necessary funding and organizing the event, Lori Coleman of Michigan's Center for Japanese Studies exuded her usual administrative excellence. Leslie Pincus helped by writing a letter of support to the Japan Foundation. Brett Johnson both oversaw the visit and wrote an outstanding article about Professor Amino in *The Journal of the International Institute*.[1]

I must give additional thanks to Martin Collcutt, who took the time to read through the translation. He caught errors and omissions, made suggestions, and argued for switching the order of Amino's Foreword and the Translator's Introduction. His comments were accepted without reservation. This is a much better book because of his efforts.

Of course, no translated book should be published without including the original illustrations, and Professor Amino's books happened to have a rather large number of them. This meant someone had to track down copyright owners, purchase high-resolution electronic scans or glossy prints, obtain permission letters, request credit lines, and secure addresses for deposit copies. Ms. Takei Masako in Tokyo graciously accepted our request to perform this time-consuming and intricate task, an additional responsibility to her work at *Monumenta Nipponica*. It took her months of intensive labor over two years to obtain everything, but the finished product was a remarkably detailed, organized photo album of illustrations with permission letters, captions, and copyright owner information. As a result of her work, this book has wonderful illustrations of Amino's text. There is no way to thank Ms. Takei sufficiently. This book is in large part a product of her efforts.

In making illustrations possible, we also express our appreciation to Azumi Ann Takata. The captions and credit lines of the illustrations and the addresses of the copyright owners were, of course, in Japanese. Ann translated them into English or romanized them. Her work was invaluable for page layout.

Sue TeVrucht handled page design and layout and cover design, and she has been there from the beginning. Her patience over prolonged lapses in work and during rounds and rounds of corrections is greatly appreciated. She is an incredibly talented designer, and I know that Professor Amino would have loved the cover design. We are also indebted to Sue for redrawing all the maps so beautifully and for substituting Japanese place names in

---

1. Brett Johnson, "Yoshihiko Amino's Contentious History: Emperor and Outcastes in Medieval Japan," *The Journal of the International Institute* 4.1 (Fall 1996). Website: http://hdl.handle.net/2027/spo.4750978.0004.109.

kanji with their romanizations or translations. Thanks also go to the indexer, Pamela Herzog.

Last but not least, we all owe a debt of gratitude to Alan S. Christy for his excellent translation. From the start, Professor Amino was very happy to be working with Alan, and the wonderful dynamic between the two was evident during the visit to the United States. Prior to his death, Professor Amino had received comments on how accurate and readable Alan's translation was. I think I am not wrong in saying how much the entire Japanese studies community has looked forward to the publication of this important work of translation. We all thank Alan for bringing this to reality.

In looking back over the decade and a half that have passed since the project's inception, I admit that there were times of doubt and frustration and even a dark sign of possible demise. But Bruce Willoughby, Executive Editor of the Center for Japanese Studies Publications Program, stood with me and just wouldn't let the project die. He has spent hours and hours checking words and paragraphs and pages. He spent more time proofreading text for this volume than any other. He, along with the others, is a part of *Rethinking Japanese History*.

This book is part of the John Whitney Hall Book Imprint series, and we again thank the late Mrs. Robin Hall for her generosity in creating this series in our Publications Program. We are grateful for the financial and institutional help we have received from the Japan Foundation and the University of Michigan Center for Japanese Studies.

Finally, I wish to close with an expression of deep appreciation to Mrs. Amino Machiko, Professor Amino's lifelong companion who traveled with him to the United States in 1996 and in 2004, shortly after Professor Amino's passing, entrusted me with his photo to be placed on the book jacket. Many more years have passed since then, and I am very thankful for her immeasurable patience. I am pleased to present this book to her, at last, and to commemorate the indomitable spirit of Professor Amino and the indelible influence his scholarship has had on all of us.

Hitomi Tonomura
Ann Arbor, 2011

A Map to Amino Yoshihiko's Historical World

Amino Yoshihiko was one of the most distinguished and recognizable names in the study of Japanese history for nearly a quarter century. His area of expertise was medieval history, but since the late 1980s he expanded his work to include the entire span of time from the prehistoric to the early modern eras. What enabled him to make his mark and then sustained him outside his area of specialization was a trenchant critique of the prevailing wisdom and practices of the study of Japanese history in Japan. After he exploded onto the academic stage in 1978 with his groundbreaking *Muen, kugai, raku* (Disconnectedness, Public Space, and Markets), Amino produced an enormous volume of books, essays, and interviews in which he consistently attacked both the narratives and presumptions of mainstream Japanese historiography. By the mid-1990s, Amino's works and stature were so huge that bookstores frequently devoted entire shelves in their history sections to his work. Despite all of that published work and his profound impact on the field, however, very little of his work has been translated into English for audiences outside Japan.

The book that you now hold in your hands is a translation of a work published in two volumes in the mid-1990s in which Amino took his fight for a new vision of Japanese history to the lay reader. When he approached me about translating his work, we both agreed that these two volumes, with their intended audience of nonspecialists, were likely to be easier to translate and would reach a broader audience than a highly specialized book on medieval Japan such as *Muen, kugai, raku*. Ultimately, we hope that a translation would serve a similar purpose to its intent in Japanese: to introduce to a lay audience a radically new vision of how to approach the study of the past in Japan. Ideally, it would also spur its non-Japanese readers to question some of the fundamental premises of their own histories.

The original two volumes were compilations of five lectures. Since each chapter was originally a stand-alone lecture, the present volume is probably best approached as a collection of essays instead of a continuous narrative. Nevertheless, when brought together, it was clear that each volume had an underlying theme that distinguished it from the other. The chapters that compose book one are held together by means of their "maritime view" of the expanse of Japanese history. These chapters emphasize movement, the creation of transport routes and interregional networks, and nonagricultural production. The chapters that compose book two share a concern for historical ethnography of sacred and profane space. These chapters emphasize a reevaluation of the status and functions of people who have been either marginalized or effaced by mainstream historiography.[1] In both books, Amino's goal was to raise a number of commonsense assumptions about the Japanese past, to show that these were untenable in light of the actual historical evidence, and to stimulate his audience to fundamentally rethink their assumptions not only about the past but about what it means to be Japanese today.

If there is any serious obstacle to making this book intelligible to a non-Japanese audience, it is that many may fear that the assumptions (and their implications) that Amino attacks are largely unfamiliar and irrelevant to Western readers. The major task of this introduction, then, is to enumerate those assumptions, make clear the kinds of conclusions they support, and indicate how Amino's criticisms of historiography may also prove suggestive to those whose main interests are in histories other than Japan's. Fortunately, I believe the reader will find that many of those assumptions will prove to be *not* uniquely Japanese. Indeed, they resemble many of our own commonplace assumptions about the process of history. As I see it, Amino's criticisms are basically of two kinds: ideological and procedural. In other words, some of the assumptions Amino attacks have to do with ideas about what the

---

1. Book two (*Nihon no rekishi o yominaosu* [Rethinking Japanese History] [Tokyo: Chikuma shobō]) was in fact the first to be published, in 1991, while book one (*Zoku Nihon no rekishi o yominaosu* [Rethinking Japanese History Again] [Tokyo: Chikuma shobō]) appeared in 1996. I reversed the order in the translation because I felt that book one had more of the character of a survey and book two was more akin to a series of case studies. I anticipate that readers who are unfamiliar with Japanese history will find it easier to understand Amino's work if they enter it through the survey portion.

past was like and how it relates to the present (the ideological assumptions) and others have to do with how one actually studies the past (the procedural assumptions). If the reader keeps these in mind, he or she will find it much easier to follow the train of Amino's narrative and feel the impact of his evidence and conclusions.

THE AGRICULTURAL IDEAL

Let us begin with one of the most central assumptions about Japanese history: the idea that the most important and fundamental activity in Japan prior to the modern period was agriculture. The idea is that Japan has always been an agricultural society in which the vast majority of the people were farmers (usually called peasants and estimated to have constituted about 80 percent of the population) who lived in rural communities and paid taxes to the government in the form of harvested crops. Supporting this idea are such facts as (1) the vast majority of official documents that survive from the past are concerned with land and agriculture, (2) native religious practices (Shinto) are deeply related to agricultural cycles, and (3) the premodern ruling class valorized agriculture as the fundamental moral activity (after governance, of course). In other words, it appears that classic historical (documents) and anthropological (studies of native beliefs) evidence are both nearly overwhelmed with references to agriculture. Moreover, the statements of moralists, philosophers, and petitioners of the past seem to be in near universal agreement as to the ideological centrality of agriculture.

Such evidence is also reinforced by common assumptions as to what constitutes the modern condition: a radical break from the past that produced industry, commerce, urbanization, mass society, and the breakdown of a consensus on morality. If the modern era is marked by the rise of industry, then the premodern era, we are inclined to believe, must have been its opposite: agricultural. If the modern era is defined by a general obsession with commerce and currency, then the premodern age must have been a time when people were largely self-sufficient and bartered to meet their other needs. If the modern era is the age of great cities and rural depopulation, then premodern life must have been overwhelmingly rural, with the majority of people living in small, mutually supporting (or stifling) communities. If the modern era is the heyday of the masses (with universal education, mass communication, and mass travel), then the premodern world must have been composed of relatively isolated communities whose illiterate inhabitants lived in ignorance of the outside world. And if the modern age is a time of relativism and ideological diversity, then the premodern past must have been an era of philosophical absolutism and conformity. Thus, not only does most evidence suggest that the premodern past in Japan was agricultural, but, given our tendency to view modernity and premodernity as opposites, we are inclined to find in the premodern past evidence of the opposite of our present lives.

These assumptions about the difference between the modern present and the premodern past are largely legacies of nineteenth-century European thinking about what made "the West" great, and justified in its colonial conquests. These oppositions were seen as reflecting real differences between the "industrial" West and the "agricultural" East. Married to ideas about the evolution of human societies, the difference could also be phrased as that between the "progressive" West and the "stagnant" East. The "humanitarian" project of the colonial powers was to free their subjects from the bonds of premodern stagnation and raise them on the evolutionary scale to an industrial present. Lest we see this as merely a nineteenth-century conceit, a simple scan of any daily newspaper, popular magazine, or television newscast in the United States today will quickly reveal that this basic view of the world is alive and well.

But how did Amino's Japanese readers, people who would have been classed as members of the "stagnant" East, come to embrace these Euro-American beliefs? The answer is to be found in the ways in which the Japanese made sense of their country's success as the only non-Western nation to successfully industrialize and modernize in the first half of the twentieth century. There are many elements to this story. We might first note that with the creation of Western-style universities in the late nineteenth century the disciplines and methodologies embraced by these institutions were explicitly Western. Studying a discipline such as history meant studying the great texts of Western historiography and historical theory and learning to apply their insights to the study of Japan. From the beginning, therefore, the study of history in modern Japan has been guided by the basic assumptions of modern European historiography that were generated during the age of high imperialism.

Next, we might note that there was a strong inclination on the part of the modern Japanese state, which came into being after the Meiji Restoration toppled the Tokugawa shogunate in 1868, to differentiate itself from the regime that preceded it. As the modern state mobilized its people and strove to inculcate in them a sense of Japan's modern destiny, the basic Western historiographical notion about premodern societies, applied to Japan's recent past and the soon to be colonized Asian present, became a way to measure the progress of modern Japan. An emphasis on Japan's overwhelmingly agricultural past would serve to accentuate just how far the country had come in a short time and thus give modern Japanese a sense of national pride. At the same time as the modern present was valorized at the expense of the premodern past, there were many who switched poles and castigated the present with a vision of a healthy past. Here, too, standard Western ideas about the agricultural character of premodern life prevailed. In this view, the modern present had produced industry, mammoth cities, war, and destruction, and ultimately alienation from one's true cultural identity. For such critics of Japanese modernity, the notion of a premodern agricultural past offered a vision of community, self-sufficiency, and a true cultural identity.

In sum, Amino's Japanese audience was inclined to believe that the modern present and the premodern past are nearly opposites and that the modern present is industrial while the premodern past was agricultural. Many non-Japanese readers will find that this view is also deeply ingrained in themselves. If we recognize the power of this idea we are likely to find it stunning that Amino takes it on as one of the main ideas that must be debunked. How does he do that? Without giving it away (I'll let Amino do that), I want to foreshadow his methods. Amino does not do this with a simpleminded numbers game. He does not claim that agriculture was an unimportant activity and peasants a minority. What he does is draw our attention to the ways in which our assumptions of an agricultural past blind us to the complexities and diversity of that past. He does not tell us that people in rural communities failed to grow crops, but he forcefully argues that agriculture was not the only dimension in their lives. The problem is one of the degree to which we are captured by the terms we use. Amino points out how hard it is for most of us to picture someone we call a peasant also engaging in maritime commerce, proto-industrial production, or financial activities. Large-scale statistics may lead us to believe that most people were engaged in agriculture most of the time, but when we let statistical generalization force from sight all activity not subsumed in that category, we have lost sight of a real and important set of activities from the past. In other words, the agricultural assumption leads to a sterile, homogenized view of the past, with all nonagricultural activity being marked as "exceptional" and "abnormal." This is why, as the reader will discover, Amino repeatedly stresses that not all villagers were farmers.

Amino also undermines the agricultural ideal by homing in on its presumptions of self-sufficiency and immobility, as these are represented by the ideal of the rural community. The idea of an unadulterated rural community has had a central place in most modern imaginings, as it has in Japan. The notion supports two powerful desires: that there be communities in which people create and sustain long-term interpersonal relationships and that, in being self-sufficient, they are free from outside contamination. The outlines of this myth of rural communities become clear when we recognize that the myth was constructed as an explicit opposite of images of the city. Cities are seen as diametrically opposed to rural communities because they are places where people are alienated and there is constant influx of people and goods from the outside (making them places of "contamination"). Therefore, nationalist ideologues almost always place the ideal of pure self-sufficient, rural communities at the heart of their imagery.

Amino destroys this illusion by undermining the notion of a pure, self-sufficient community. Such a community, he insists, never existed. Even the prehistoric Jōmon-era inhabitants of the islands (he tells us in his maritime survey of Japanese history) engaged in constant, wide-ranging trade that both covered the archipelago (see his discussion of obsidian production) and spanned the East Asian oceans. Thus, the reader of this book will find that Amino's attention is consistently drawn to movement—networks, routes, and circulations—and exchange—of goods, peoples, and cultures. In that regard, he draws a distinction between administrative labels and popular presumptions, on the one hand, and actual practices on the other (see chapter one). Early modern government labels, which designated all settlements without samurai as "villages," had more to do with the attempt to realize an ideological system than with a reflection of actual practices. These labels are compounded by contemporary popular assumptions about what constitutes "backwater" places. For Amino, the terms *rural* and *urban* have little to do with scale and everything to do with the character of daily life. An urban settlement is inescapably part of a circulation network. It is a place where exchange is a fundamental activity, where production is premised upon consumption elsewhere, and where equivalences between things are determined. Amino characterizes as urban town after town that most Japanese would think of as hopelessly isolated and miniscule. He highlights the vast networks and constant mobility that he believes animated the Japanese past. With the proliferation of urban nodes in a network covering the islands, even the images of rural communities where agriculture was dominant are unstable, for the "city" is no longer far away.

THE MAINSTREAM AND THE MARGIN

Amino's work has long been focused on those people and classes that have generally been disregarded in the mainstream histories. These include itinerant merchants, miners, gamblers, pirates, wandering entertainers, slaves, servants, prostitutes, and outcasts. From the perspective of mainstream political histories, these were not the people who shaped the major political trends of Japanese history. They were the nameless many who were the object of governance. For others, particularly those on the Left who are concerned with class struggle in Japanese history, these people are easily lumped into the category of the oppressed or else dismissed as residing outside the bounds of the major class conflicts between the ruling warriors and subjected peasants. Many have dismissed Amino as excessively concerned with marginal peoples and experiences. They are willing to grant him some degree of accuracy in his deception of marginal types and even allow that those voices might be legitimately recovered. But they accuse him of exaggeration in his insistence on their importance in Japanese history.

However much Amino argues that their experiences have been effaced by an overemphasis on the majority, his goal is not to simply recover their voices. His argument is much more ambitious. In placing these "marginal" types at the center of his view of Japanese history, Amino wishes to show us how the so-called mainstream is constantly engaged in a struggle with that which it wishes to place on the margins. It is the struggle that places some at the center and some on the margins, and both are equally constituted as such by that struggle.

In this sense, Amino argues, we cannot understand the mainstream simply by the stories it tells itself, stories in which those on the margins are deemed so unimportant as to be invisible. Instead, he urges us to recognize that the story of how the marginal came to be marginalized is absolutely central to the story of how the center became centralized. For Amino, the normal/center/mainstream is not naturally so. It was historically constituted as such out of political and social struggle. As we live today in the society that resulted from the victory of the "now-center," the history of the marginalized, made to confront its opponent once again, offers us a rare opportunity to critically reevaluate what we have become. Amino tells his story in a variety of ways, for example, as a struggle between an "agricultural fundamentalist" and a "mercantilist commercial" ideology, with the latter being the worldview of those who would be marginalized. But while we might find heroic resistance in the stories of the despised outcast Amino refuses to romanticize. At one point, he strikingly indicates that there were serious "despotic" tendencies on the losing side as well.

At a more general level than the battle between the proponents of agriculture and commerce, Amino urges us to pay attention to what he calls "the world of relations" (*yūen*) and "the world of nonrelations" (*muen*). Again, he urges us to recognize that the marginalized people of the nonrelated world were not just passive victims who were excluded by the mainstream. Instead, he insists that they actively rejected the mainstream. A word is surely in order here about this key concept in Amino's work.

When explaining this concept to nonspecialists, Amino refers first to a phenomenon of the early modern period: the "relationship-ending temple" (*enkiri-dera*). These were Buddhist temples to which those seeking to sever a defining relationship in their lives could flee for asylum. Women who wanted to divorce their husbands (a right they did not have under the legal system) could flee to a relation-severing temple and thereby force their husbands to divorce them. Servants who wanted to break a relationship of servitude with their masters could do so as well. In many cases, these places functioned very much like Catholic churches in Europe: criminals who managed to escape to churches could claim asylum. The principle, in both Japan and Europe, was that these were places into which secular power did not extend. They were places through which one cut off one's mainstream relations in the world. When one entered these spaces, one was seen as unrelated, no longer defined by standard social relations.

Amino argues that these were not simply safety valves but emblematic of the social organization of space. In his view, we need to understand societies in which such spaces existed as composed of a patchwork of spaces and peoples, some of which were fully beholden to society and some of which were "free" from social constraints. Resisting such places as free spaces, Amino asks us to reexamine the activities that were linked to them and to rethink the meaning of freedom.

Translator's Introduction

There is, for many, a stunning reversal at work here, for the people populating these free spaces were precisely those who could be labeled "outcast" by the mainstream and often called themselves "slaves of the gods." Ironically, the spaces of freedom are those in which the socially subordinate (such as women, servants, and slaves) and the socially despised (outcasts, wandering entertainers, and prostitutes) moved and lived. In the end, we are left with a dilemma that cannot be resolved in our contemporary imaginative framework, for the people of the free places were both bound and superior. Viewed in this way, these remain social phenomena that we simply cannot understand. Amino's provocative juxtaposition of freedom and servitude in relation to differentiated social functions ultimately calls on us to reject such binary notions and radically reimagine that past.

CONTINUITY AND JAPANESENESS

Amino received his presecondary education prior to 1945 in the years when Japanese were taught (at the insistence of the Ministry of Education) that their country had existed since time immemorial as a unified and homogeneous nation under an unbroken line of divine emperors and distinct from all other peoples. Since the war, the worst excesses of this historical worldview—such as the insistence on the divinity of the emperor—have been removed from the curriculum. But there is still a strong tendency to view Japan as having been culturally and racially homogeneous for thousands of years and to see the distant past of archaic Japan as smoothly continuous with the present. Prime Minister Nakasone Yasuhiro infamously articulated this vision of Japan when he argued that the root of America's economic woes lay in the nation's radical diversity. For Nakasone and many other cultural conservatives, the key to understanding Japanese success in the 1980s was that the country always remained essentially Japanese, unchanged since the dawn of time. The guarantee and proof of that durable national character, for these people, is in the unbroken line of emperors.

Amino's work throws buckets of cold water on this notion. Beginning with the name Nihon (the Japanese word for Japan), Amino insists on its historicity. That is, he insists that the word has not meant the same thing—either conceptually or geographically—at all times. While the name may have been coined in the sixth or seventh century, Japan, as we think of it today, did not come into being until the nineteenth century. To demonstrate the difference, he painstakingly shows us how the borders have shifted over time and how the idea of Japan as a kind of social-political unit also changed dramatically. One of my favorite moments is when Amino inverts the famous legends of the origins of the name Nihon. Since he does not spell this out, assuming the familiarity of his audience, I will do so here.

The word *nihon* literally means the "origin of the sun." Popular lore in Japan portrays this name as the invention of a proud people one-upping the Chinese empire: China may be the central kingdom, but we are the source of the sun! Chinese and Korean scholars, particularly since World War II, have been known to claim that the name was invented in their countries as a gesture of respect that was to be betrayed in subsequent histories of Japanese violence against them. Amino's view is closer to those of the Chinese and Korean scholars, but he focuses on its meaning within the islands. Rather than seeing *origin of the sun* as a term of overweening pride, Amino sees it as the moment when a ruling class in the Japanese islands forthrightly recognized the centrality of China in all things. For Amino, "origin of the sun" is not a claim to priority but simply a statement of direction: Japan is to the east (where the sun rises) of China (the point of reference for all things). There are important, sometimes subtle differences between Amino's story and those told popularly in Japan, China, and Korea. His view is the opposite of those in Japan who see "origin of the sun" as a proud rejection of China's claim to centrality and superiority. Unlike the Chinese and Korean stories, which give agency in the act of naming to the "superior and civilized continentals," Amino sees the origin of the name in the islands as a sign that it was the people of the islands who willingly recognized that superiority themselves; it was not foisted upon them by haughty, self-important people.

Amino's vision of Japan's geopolitical past is one that sees constant fracturing, realignment, conquest, and fragmentation yet again. The only way to accurately convey this geographical instability is to buck convention and give up using the name Japan when talking about the past. As long as people in the present think of Japan as naturally conforming to the present borders with its current number of islands, using the name Japan will simply invite confusion. The careful reader of this translation will notice that I have been at pains to retain Amino's avoidance of the name Japan, especially when he is discussing the time before the name Nihon was invented (at which times he resolutely refers to the place as "the islands").

Some readers will note that while Amino sometimes refers to time in consistently broad strokes (often in terms of two-hundred-year spans), he is always agonizingly specific as to place. At its broadest, Amino's realm is always culturally split between eastern Japan and western Japan.[2] At his more specific moments, location, whether in mountains, on coasts, on plains, near major continental travel routes, or along rivers, is crucial. At points, his list of place names gets so detailed that I felt compelled to reduce them so as to not spin the heads of those who are not Japan specialists.

Perhaps one of the most significant ways in which Amino upsets our commonsense notions of what Japan is geographically is his adoption of "the perspective of the sea," as he calls it. For too long, he argues, we have seen Japan from a land-based perspective, one that views it as naturally isolated—as islands often are—from the rest of the world. From the land-based perspective, the islands naturally cohere among themselves, apart from the Asian mainland and the rest of the world. Of course, the history of Japan would be contained strictly within these bounds, we are told. Japanese were cut off by the ocean from the rest of the world, and that isolation enabled them to create a unique culture. In contrast, Amino argues that the ocean can also be a conduit that links people. In general, water-based travel was always easier and more fully developed in the islands than was land-based travel. People traveled along rivers, across lakes, along the coast and across the ocean to the Asian mainland. In fact, Amino argues that there is no real reason to believe that the ancient "kingdom" of Wa, known to most as the name of Japan before Nihon was invented, was restricted to the islands. In a stunning geographical rereading, Amino argues that Wa was more likely an ocean-centered polity, with settlements in the Japanese islands, on the Korean Peninsula, and on the Chinese coast all linked politically, commercially, and culturally by the ocean. With that claim, Amino sweeps aside decades of stale debate about the location in the Japanese islands of the "kingdom of Wa," which exchanged emissaries with the ancient Chinese emperors. For Amino, the key to understanding Wa is not to know where it was centered but the spaces across which it spread. With this change in perspective, he beckons us to adopt a fluid vision of constant movement of people and goods across the oceans, between the islands, and along rivers. He urges us to replace a static vision with a mobile one.

All in all, Amino forcefully argues that the belief that except for brief periods of exchange the people of the Japanese islands have always been

2. Most non-Japanese might be inclined to call it northern and southern Japan, with the dividing line somewhere around Nagoya or Kyoto. But the Japanese convention is to call this a divide between the east (what we see as north) and west (south).

isolated from the rest of the world must finally be put to rest. He argues that we must instead recognize that the Japanese islands have always been linked to multiple sites on the Asian continent, sites not restricted to China and Korea but also located far to the south and north. For Amino, there is simply no way to understand society in the Japanese islands without recognizing its deep connection with the rest of Asia. He has a favorite illustration of this idea, which has to do with how we draw our maps. Most maps of Japan are framed so as to show the country surrounded only by water. Amino likes to show his audiences a map of Japan turned so that west is at the top. The northern boundary of his map lies far north of Hokkaido far enough to include all of Sakhalin. Likewise, the southern border of the map is located south of Taiwan. In the center of this map lies not the islands, but the Japan Sea, broad in the middle but remarkably narrow at the northern tip of Sakhalin and the southern tip of Korea. Whenever Amino displays this map, he urges his audience to reenvision the relationship between land and water and to see the Japan Sea not as a vast, dividing body of water but as a kind of inland sea, like Lake Superior. For those who recast their vision, the ocean loses its obstacle quality and the land links come to the fore.

But a recasting of the usual geography is not the only way in which Amino disrupts the common notion of the unity, continuity, and homogeneity of Japan. He also pays close attention to real political divisions. For him the continuity of the imperial throne was not meaningless—indeed, it was more meaningful in some ways than otherwise imagined—but this continuity should never be mistaken for political unity. Instead, he is fond of pointing to moments when political units formed that rejected the practical authority of the imperial government in Kyoto. While some of these were short lived—such as the rival kingdoms formed in the tenth century by rebellions east and west of Kyoto—others were quite durable, most notably the Kamakura shogunate. To emphasize the difference between the Kamakura shogunate and the imperial government in Kyoto, Amino chooses the provocative terms *monarchy of the west* (the imperial government) and *monarchy of the east* (the Kamakura shogunate). While specialist scholars may be accustomed to such a debate, this is very shocking language to a lay audience in Japan.

Amino has one further bucket of cold water for those who believe that Japanese culture has been continuous since ancient times: his argument that there are fundamental, radical breaks in sociocultural history. He refers to these major transitions as periods when the relationship of humans to nature undergoes a radical change. This is a gritty, material way of designating a radical change in worldview. According to Amino, in certain periods prevailing worldviews become unsustainable and undergo radical transformations. There are many reasons why a worldview becomes unsustainable. Some refer to gradual changes in culture and society that eventually place earlier ways of understanding in jeopardy. Others refer to such far-reaching changes in human interaction with, and alteration of, the landscape that human beings literally cannot interact with nature in the same ways as before. Whatever the case, these major transformations may not happen overnight (he tends to see them as occurring over a period of a century or two). But once the change has occurred, earlier ways of viewing and living in the world become almost unimaginable because they are so divorced from current physical and social experience.

In his grand scheme of things, Amino locates one such fundamental transformation in the fourteenth century in the Japanese islands. As he sees it, people on either side of such a transformation are almost unintelligible to each other. As he states in his foreword, the world the Japanese live in now began in the fourteenth century. The time before that was not irrelevant, but it cannot be understood within the conceptual framework that had its beginning after the divide. To put it as radically as possible, modern Japanese are far more conceptually and culturally attuned to modern Americans than they are to their pre-fourteenth-century ancestors. The notion that a single, unified Japanese culture made the transition unmolested and fully recognizable across that divide is a fantasy. Moreover, to heighten our sense of what this means he suggests that we may be in the middle of another such long-term transformation at present. One or two hundred years hence, he speculates, our descendants may live such utterly different lives, both physically and imaginatively, that we may be almost inconceivable to them. If they lack historians who are sensitive to the enormity of historical change, we would barely recognize their stories about us.

DOCUMENTS AND HISTORY

History is often seen as having a great deal in common with judicial law. Both are concerned with establishing an objective account of an event (in their search for the "truth"), and both have rules of evidence that tend to privilege documents. Personal testimony, particularly that of eyewitnesses, may have a place in both, but ultimately testimony retains too much potential subjectivity, that is, the possibly idiosyncratic perspective of the individual. Documents, however, are taken to constitute a kind of material and public witness and therefore are far more reliable. Of course, few historians or judges would view all documents as inherently truthful, but the reliance on them is nevertheless very strong.

One of Amino's most important and fruitful methodological attacks on mainstream history in Japan is that it is far too uncritically reliant on documents. His rereading of Japanese history is based upon his materialist approach to documents and his generous embrace of the nondocumentary evidence of the past provided by ethnography. By a materialist approach I mean that Amino reads documents not just for their content but for evidence of how they were produced, circulated, and retained (or discarded). For example, in chapter 6 Amino reminds his readers that Japan has three orthographic systems (*hiragana, katakana,* and *kanji*) and that these systems are not simply transparent renderings of meaning. Instead, the orthography is itself a code that produces another set of meanings that accompany the semantic meaning of the words. Take, for instance, the 1275 *katakana* petition of the villagers of Kami village. The *katakana* is not a sign of the villagers' lack of sophistication, as Amino says he and most people once believed. Instead when one understands the representative function of *katakana* one sees that by writing the petition entirely in it the villagers may have been signaling to their anticipated reader the immediacy of their testimony (*katakana* being used to transcribe it) as well as the truthfulness of their statement (*katakana* being related to speech, particularly that of the deities). Likewise, the skill with which a letter is written in *hiragana* signals to its reader the literary accomplishments of the writer. Beyond orthography, Amino reminds us to pay attention to format as he notes the dizzying range of writing styles that existed in premodern Japan.

In even more materialistic terms, Amino asks us to consider the physical existence of a document. In his discussion of his investigation of the Tokikuni family documents, he highlights for us the distinction between documents that survived to the present because they were meant to be saved (because they had been produced for and exchanged with the domainal lord) and documents that survived accidentally (because they were meant to be destroyed or recycled for other uses). Not surprisingly, Amino finds two very different worlds represented in these sets of documents. And he finds that mainstream historiography relies almost exclusively on documents that were meant to survive and either ignores or discounts as aberrational the accidental survivals. As he is quick to point out, the mainstream historical narrative is unsustainable when one takes "accidents" seriously.

The most serious problem with the accidentally surviving documents is that they are at best mere traces of a world that has vanished. Disposal was either conscious (an attempt to hide something) or incidental (lacking a discernible value in keeping a document). Recovery of the consciously hidden is the dream of every historian and so is familiar territory. But the other kind of lost evidence relates to something far more mundane and yet difficult: everyday life. Many of the documents found stuffed into walls, which Amino discusses in chapter one, were of the most commonplace class: lists, receipts, mundane notes, and such. Much like our grocery lists, laundry receipts, and whatnot, these were items of no enduring value to the people who produced them. After serving their original purpose, they were best used as insulation But, like the innumerable scraps of paper we throw away today, these were items that filled and constituted daily life, the common ground and common sense that formed the context for the remarkable "events" with which historians deal. Although historians value "contextualization," the idea that history is the tale of "great men and great events" still holds true for many. The history of everyday life is a field that is still in its infancy.

Amino's concern with daily life led him to a fruitful engagement with ethnography, a field that specializes in the analysis of everyday life. The clearest example of Amino's use of ethnographic evidence is his use of notions of the sacred and the profane in relation to class and commerce. His rereading of the notion of pollution, a central concept of religious belief in the islands, is at the core of most of book two. It is ethnographic evidence that compels him to rethink the status of the archaic and medieval groups known as nonhumans and divine slaves. It also allows him to show us how that which is now loathed was in fact once feared for its superior power. It is ethnographic evidence related to sacred space that allows him to link marketplaces, monks, and women and thereby reveal hidden circuits of exchange and production. When Amino speaks about changes in "civilization" or "ethnic" history, it is to these dimensions of society and culture that he refers.

THE AUTHOR

The experience of World War II, and especially prewar and wartime education in Japan, was fundamental to Amino's development as a historian, as it was for so many other postwar scholars. Born in 1928, Amino was seventeen and on the verge of being drafted when the war ended. As he described in a recent memoir, in the months after the defeat he immersed himself in books on history and historiography in order to confront the momentous changes of an uncertain future. As with so many, this study of history was critical, one that was at least subconsciously driven by the question, "Why did we lose?" The question could be posed in terms of defeat caused by incomplete modernization (the "Japan was still feudal" argument), or it could be posed in terms of a corrective to prewar Japanese ideology ("the lies my teacher told me"). Whatever the intent of the study, immediate postwar Japan was a time when the study of history was understood to have tremendous import for contemporary political practice. If, as many argued, Japanese modernity was tainted by the perdurance of premodern "feudal" characteristics, which then gave rise to self-destructive militarism, a study of Japanese feudalism would enlighten postwar seekers of true, modern democracy. If prewar Japanese had been brainwashed by an educational system that infused them with self-destructive myths of emperor-centered history and divine nationhood, then a free postwar Japan would need a people-centered, humanist history.

Amino's recollection of this time in his life is encapsulated in the title of the introduction to his memoir of postwar historiography, "My Postwar 'War Crimes.'" He recalled this as a time when, despite the belief that history would reveal a new politics, it was political passion that ruthlessly drove historical research. While in college, Amino became a leading member of the leftist student movement. With the responsibility of a leader and in the midst of political ferment, he spent more time in meetings, giving speeches, and organizing on other campuses than he remembers spending in the classroom or library. He insisted he had no regrets about having fought for "people's history" at the time. "However," he writes, "without ever having put myself into any physical danger, I merely went from meeting to meeting giving lip service to 'revolutionary' things and writing stupid and embarrassing essays about 'feudal revolution' and 'the concept of feudalism.' For the sake of my 'good name' I drove others to sickness and death. I was nothing other than a 'war criminal.'"[3] Regardless of whether he was really responsible for others' lost lives, I believe his self-accusation was primarily a charge against his hav-

---

3. Amino Yoshihiko, *Rekishi to shite no sengo shigaku* (Historicizing Postwar History Writing) (Tokyo: Nihon editā sukūru shuppanbu, 2000), 4.

ing subordinated historical research to political ideology, precisely what the prewar Japanese state did with its militarist indoctrination.

After graduation, Amino got a job at a research center called the Institute for the Study of Japanese Folk Culture, but he continued to be more involved in the student movement and national historical association debates than in his new position.[4] For reasons he did not make clear, he claimed that problems he was having at the institute finally woke him up to the shallowness of his historical studies. With that, he dropped out of the student movement and the historical debates and rededicated himself to a "document by document" study of history. It is likely that the force of his rejection of his pre-1953 self was behind the fact that he was particularly harsh in his critique of mainstream Marxist historiography in Japan. While Americans embraced the labeling of Japan as feudal during and immediately after the war, it was a term that was at the heart of Marxist historiography. And in the postwar struggle to overturn prewar historical narratives, it was Marxist historians who led the way. But as the struggles over a new historiography continued, greater attention was paid to fitting Japan within the preexisting categories of Marxist historiography than was paid to basic research. In other words, the framework superseded the history, reducing the past to the supporting role of mere evidence. Given Amino's attacks on historical categories and ideologies, it is this aspect of Marxist historiography that continued to bother him the most. Yet, when asked in a 1997 interview if he was no longer a Marxist, he adamantly rejected the suggestion.

> I don't think of myself as distanced from Marxism at all. When I came to the conclusion in 1953 that everything I had done was wrong, I struggled to return to the basics. I read all I could of medieval and early modern documents and of the best of modern histories, books by people like the legal historian Nakada Kaoru. I also reread the entire selected works of Marx and Engels. As I did

4. The institute was founded in the early 1930s by Shibusawa Keizō, grandson of the Meiji industrialist Shibusawa Eiichi and the minister of finance in the first postsurrender Japanese cabinet. The prewar institute, known until 1942 as the Attic Museum, had been one of the key organizations in the native ethnology movement, which rejected the "great men, great events" version of historical writing in favor of ethnographic histories of the "common folk." In the postwar years, the institute was attached to the Fisheries Agency, due mostly to the interest in fishing history of Shibusawa and several of its key members. While Amino spoke of "problems" he encountered there, it is clear that he treasured his time at the institute and considered its members, particularly Shibusawa Keizō, to be exemplary historians.

so, I came to see a Marx who was entirely different from the one I thought I had known. You know, Marx himself gradually changed his way of thinking. For example, when you read his Eighteenth Brumaire, you find that he was also a superlative critic of the "present" [in addition to his historical talent]. I believe I still have much to learn from Marx, so I still call myself a Marxist.

Three years after his change of heart, the institute folded, and he spent a year, newly married, taking odd jobs until he finally landed a position teaching Japanese history at a high school in Tokyo. Thus began the second phase of his disenchantment with the mainstream narratives of Japanese history. It was not the grind of teaching unimaginative and unmotivated students that we now commonly imagine high school teaching to be. In fact, Japanese high schools in the late 1950s and early 1960s gave their teachers time off for research.[5] But in several essays and interviews he has credited his students with asking questions that shook him out of a complacent reiteration of the standard narratives. To take one example that is closely related to the content of this book, while he was lecturing on the rise of the new Kamakura era Buddhist sects a student asked him why so many great religious leaders appeared in the thirteenth century. "Because it was a time of transformation," Amino replied, repeating the pat explanation. Unsatisfied, the student kept on. "But there were lots of other times of transformation [which did not produce great religious leaders], so why the thirteenth century?" he asked.[6] With questions such as these, his high school students left him with itches that he scratched for the next thirty years.

In the late 1960s, Amino moved from teaching high school to university (at Nagoya University). His work on *shōen* estates from 1966 to the late 1970s was idiosyncratic, but it did not result in much notoriety. In 1978, however, he published the book that would make him famous and touch off a minor industry in historical studies: *Muen, kugai, raku: Nihon chūsei no jiyū to heiwa* (Disconnectedness, Public Space, and Markets: Freedom and Peace in Medieval Japan). Amino's radical break with the prevailing historiography of medieval Japan was apparent in two words in the title: *disconnectedness* and

5. Amino published one book, a study of the Tara no shō estate, as a result of the research he conducted while teaching high school (*Chūsei shōen no yōsō* [Medieval Estates in Transformation], Hanawa sensho 51 [Tokyo: Hanawa shobō, 1966]).
6. Amino Yoshihiko, "Watakushi no ikikata" [My Lifestyle], in *Rekishi to shite no sengo shigaku*, 291.

freedom. Against the standard characterization of medieval Japan as an agricultural slave society, Amino argued that medieval society had a variety of "unconnected spaces" (*muen no ba*) that allowed for considerable free agency on the part of those whom the mainstream historians lumped together as the oppressed. Most of all, the book argues persuasively that these places and the activities that took place therein were not exceptions to the rule but were constitutive of the very fabric of economic life. Amino's argument was disturbing to historians on both the Left and the Right. To leftist historians, his depiction of the freedom and agency of the "oppressed" seemed to deny their oppression and undermine the progressive narrative of history as a movement from slavery to freedom. Many accused him of having an altogether too rosy vision of medieval society. To right-wing historians, Amino had shunted aside the beloved rural community as the central stage of Japanese history. He even had the audacity to claim that outcasts and degenerates were the closest associates of the emperor. There was little room in his history for heroic tales of loyal, self-sacrificing warriors and cultured, aloof courtiers.

I remember clearly my own amazement at first reading the book. When I met Amino in 1989 in a seminar at the University of Chicago, I visited him one afternoon to clear up some confusion about for whom it was that these "unconnected places" existed. My confusion turned to shock when it became clear that he saw these as places not merely for outcasts and wanderers. "This isn't just the history of a marginal few," I said incredulously. "You're telling me this is the history of the majority!" He smiled and nodded.

In the years since the publication of *Muen, kugai, raku,* Amino became one of the most prolific and sought-after historians in Japan. He also encouraged and trained a host of historians who are pushing his insights even further. But while his "line" is becoming familiar to most readers of Japanese history, it still resides on the margin. I saw a perfect example of his continued marginalization in 1992. Kawai Juku, the national chain of college preparatory schools, approached Amino about producing a series of videotapes on Japanese history for its students. Always eager for an opportunity to take his historical vision to nonspecialists, Amino quickly agreed. The tape, *Japanese History as Viewed from the Sea,* was a fascinating presentation of Amino's recent work. But Kawai Juku never showed it to its students. Why? Amino's critique of mainstream historiography was so trenchant and his rejection so thorough that Kawai Juku feared it would prove counterproductive to its students' scores on the history portion of their college entrance exams. Herein lies the greatest obstacle to Amino's successful overthrow of the historical myths of the mainstream. As long as those myths remain on the college entrance exams (and the textbooks on which they are based), teachers will have no choice but to teach them and students will have no choice but to memorize them.

FOREWORD

THE PROBLEM OF JAPANESE IDENTITY

The questions of who the Japanese are and where they came from became hot subjects of debate in the 1990s. For example, in September 1993 the Australian National University in Canberra sponsored an international conference called Stirrups, Sails and Plows. Scholars from Australia, Canada, Great Britain, Indonesia, South Korea, the United States, and Japan attended. The Japanese delegation contained a good number of members, around forty, with a variety of perspectives—Marxists, liberals, and conservatives—all of whom took part in a lively debate on Japanese identity. I can neither speak nor understand English, so I do not know exactly what kind of argument was carried on at the conference. But the debate crossed a broad spectrum of topics and fields, from reports in anthropology and archaeology to a paper on the Japanese army and "comfort women." The debate about the Japanese army and rape was particularly heated.

The conference organizers gave me the topic "The Emperor, Rice, and Villagers." Apparently the scholars in attendance from the West were interested in identifying the unique substance that made the Japanese so different from them. The Indonesians and Koreans, on the other hand, were severely critical of those characteristics of the Japanese people that could support such cruel acts as mass rape by the Japanese army. As a result, the conference stimulated me to think about a number of things, my incomplete understanding of the proceedings notwithstanding. Two years later, the famous French historical journal *Annale* published its first special issue on Japanese history. No matter how late it came, this special issue was a sign of the great interest in Japan that can be found abroad. With such growing interest abroad, the time has come for the Japanese people to give serious thought to who we are. We are undoubtedly being asked this in a state of unprecedented tension. Unfortunately, I have recently come to feel strongly that most Japanese do not accurately understand their own history and society.

Of course, the way in which Japanese approach their own society and history has undergone some changes. Signs of those changes were clear at the Australian conference. But in general the dominant belief among Japanese is that Japan is an island nation isolated from its surroundings and existing as a closed society. One supposed result of that isolation is that Japan received little influence from others and developed a unique culture. On the flip side of that coin is the belief that this culture is incomprehensible to foreigners. Both arguments are made to support the belief that Japan is a unique society. The next common assumption is that this culture has been supported by agricultural production centered on rice paddies. Building on this, the common notion holds that from the time Yayoi culture reached the Japanese islands (about 300 B.C.) to the Edo period (1600–1867), Japanese society was essentially agricultural. Japan only became industrial after the Meiji period and truly so only during the period of high economic growth in the 1960s.

The dominant view has been that simply by living in this island nation, the Japanese—with their homogeneous and uniform language and rice as the basis of their diet in a society based upon wet paddy agriculture—have developed a unique culture in these islands. This view has been dominant not only among ordinary Japanese but among the elite; since the Meiji period, this view of Japanese society has been the basis of political and economic policy. Over time, the human sciences of history, economics, and political science have failed to break out of the framework of this conventional wisdom.

But is this view of Japanese society really correct? I have had doubts about this for some time and have made a number of statements about it. In this book, I would like to take up a number of problems and use them to reconsider the shape and history of Japanese society.

THE GREAT TRANSFORMATION

In my ten years of teaching at a junior college I have encountered many surprises. During the roughly forty years that separate my students from myself, the basic patterns of our everyday lives have completely changed. For example, for the past several years I have been using Miyamoto Tsuneichi's *The Forgotten Japanese* in my seminar.[1] Reading Miyamoto's book with my students has alerted me to the ways in which the students and I approach even the most basic issues from very different perspectives. This is due, I believe, to fundamental changes in the way we live our lives rather than to superficial differences in generational experience.

Take, as a concrete example, the word *nawashiro* (rice seedling). I thought that all my students would naturally know the word. But in fact no one did. Nor did anyone understand the word *gotoku* (a kind of brazier used in traditional sunken hearths). None of them had ever seen a horse or cow used for work. They at least knew that cows, such as Holsteins, give milk, but none had ever seen a horse used for anything but riding, such as at a race track.

The word *kattai* or *katai* (leper) also appears occasionally in Miyamoto's book, as does *repura* (leper), but none of my students had ever heard of this disease. Even when I tried using a more common term *raibyō* (leprosy), none of them seemed to grasp its meaning. Of course, they knew a variety of things about AIDS, but they knew nothing of either the word *leprosy* or the disease itself. They did not know that people still suffer from it or of the discrimination that accompanies it here in Japan, let alone in the rest of the world.

Confronting these differences has shown me that the relations between Japanese society and its environment are currently undergoing a number of drastic transformations on a variety of levels. The quality of the technology available to much of humanity at present has certainly progressed enormously. The very fact that humanity has extracted from nature the power to exterminate itself possesses tremendous significance. While technological advances raise a number of issues for world history, in the specific context of the history of Japanese society the current changes have had a major impact. What was considered common knowledge from the Edo period through the Meiji, Taishō, and into the early years following World War II is now almost incomprehensible.

---

1. Miyamoto Tsuneichi, *Wasurerareta Nihonjin* (Tokyo: Iwanami shoten, 1984). Translated into English as *The Forgotten Japanese: Encounters with Rural Life and Folklore* by Jeffrey Irish (Berkeley: Stone Bridge Press, 2010).

For example, my students no longer know anything of the stench of a toilet. When I was a child, a trip to the bathroom was a frightening experience. But living in today's houses, where there are no longer any dark places, my students have no concept of the fear of the dark that gripped my generation. Fear has now taken other forms, such as AIDS. Even such small changes have far-reaching implications.

Until now, the flow of Japanese history has usually been analyzed by dividing time into a general framework of primitive, archaic, medieval, early modern, and modern periods. However, this periodization cannot fully account for the fundamental ways in which the relationship between people and nature has been transformed over time. And I believe that we cannot truly comprehend history unless we take such changes into account.

It is my conviction that we must come up with alternatives to the usual periodization. In my own work, I have focused on ethnic or civilizational dimensions rather than "social formations" in order to arrive at working periodizations.[2] Whether or not my formulations stand the test of time, the orthodox periodization of Japanese history must be reevaluated in terms of the immense changes that have taken place in the relationship between human society and nature.

How far back can we trace the society in which the basic experiences of my generation are rooted, a society that is in the process of disappearing and being forgotten? Scholars generally agree that its origins date roughly from the Muromachi period (1338–1573). That is, the fourteenth century served as a turning point, with the immense transformations that took place in the midst of the chaos of the Northern and Southern Courts resulting in huge differences between the thirteenth and fifteenth centuries. The ways of life practiced since the fifteenth century have shaped my generation's common sense, thus constituting a coherent unit of time. However, when it comes to matters before the thirteenth century, we are dealing with something outside our common sense, a world of a radically different nature.

---

2. This distinction is probably just as difficult for the lay reader in Japan as it is for the lay reader in the English-speaking world. In part, it is an oblique reference to a long-running debate Amino carried on with another medieval historian, Araki Moriaki. Araki defined the history of social formations as "the necessary, legal development" of a society. As practiced by Araki, this was a macrolevel form of historiography that attempted to discern the broad movement of history through a predefined set of sociopolitical stages. Amino's reference to "ethnic or civilizational dimensions" is, first of all, a turn to historical specifics over broader generalizations. It is also a gesture toward a history that incorporates insights from the fields of ethnography and anthropology.

The current period of transition can in some ways be seen as akin to the great changes that occurred during the chaos of the fourteenth century. Reexamining the meaning of that transformation in light of the present period of transition is, I believe, a significant undertaking in terms of both the future of humanity and problems specific to Japanese culture and society. My contribution to this project will be to offer a discussion of the concrete forms in which the changes of the fourteenth century appeared.

ARCHAEOLOGICAL EVIDENCE OF THE ESTABLISHMENT OF VILLAGES AND TOWNS

As a concrete illustration of this transition, I would like to make a few prefatory comments about villages and towns, the sites where Japanese live their everyday lives. The great ethnographer Yanagita Kunio estimated that approximately three-quarters of all Japanese villages have their origins in the Muromachi period.[3] Further research needs to be done before we can be confident of this figure. But if we examine the results of recent archaeological surveys it does appear that towns and settlements formed after the fourteenth and fifteenth centuries are significantly different from those that existed prior to that time.

According to a recent study by Hirose Kazuo, archaeologists have not yet located sites dating from the twelfth and thirteenth centuries that bear any resemblance to the type of village that is most familiar to us today. The kind of settlement that we think of as a village today might more specifically be called a "concentrated village" (*shūson*). It is characterized by the dense concentration of many houses into a compact settlement. It is questionable whether we should call the settlements of the thirteenth century villages at all. Rather, they took the shape of what might be better designated "dispersed settlements" (*sanson*). In fact, the documentary evidence supports Hirose's archaeological data. The word *mura* (meaning "village" today) appears in documents from long ago. But from the ancient through the early medieval eras the word *mura* was used to describe newly opened rice paddies and fields or fields not yet officially registered with the government. This

---

3. Yanagita Kunio (1875–1961) is commonly known as the father of modern Japanese folk studies or native ethnology.

is considerably different from the meaning of the word in the Edo period. When we investigate the terminology and form of settlements (*shūraku*) in historical documents, we find "settlements" where there may have been two or three houses in a small valley or settlements where housing compounds were widely scattered. The type of settlement that was a direct precedent for the Edo period, "the encompassing village" (*sōson*), emerged only around the end of the fourteenth century.

The excavations at Shimofurudate in Tochigi Prefecture provide us with evidence for a similar reconsideration of the history of "towns" (*machi*). The area under excavation was apparently a grassy commons during the Edo period. When the commons was excavated, archaeologists found a fairly wide road passing through the middle of the site, with some sort of settlement, surrounded by deep ditches, on both sides of the road. That ruins of this kind were found beneath a commons is itself thought provoking.

It was immediately apparent that the site was not a warrior's home, lacking as it does the earthworks so often associated with a warrior compound. Archaeologists did not recover a large number of artifacts at the site, but what they did find was unusual, for much of it came from quite distant locales. They found green celadon and white porcelain, such as one usually finds in Kamakura, and stone bowls originally made near Sonoki District in Nagasaki, which must have been transported all the way to the northern Kantō region. The site also turned up pottery from Seto and Tokoname and round wooden boxes (*magemono*). In addition, the site contains innumerable small square pits lined up in rows, which appear to be divided by the main road. In the southwest section of the dig, there is a shallow moat surrounding the remains of a small dugout structure—what may have been a Buddhist worship hall. The area nearby is clearly a graveyard. Archaeologists have been able to determine that the site dates from the middle of the Kamakura period because they recovered some wooden tablets that had the date Kōan 8 (1285) written on them. The artifacts uncovered here generally accord with that date.

What kind of remains might these be? Many archaeologists argue that the entire site was a graveyard. I feel, however, that this site may be seen as a kind of urban space. I cannot say definitively whether this was a post town or a marketplace. Whatever the case, I believe these ruins have an urban character.[4] However, by the early modern period the site had disappeared

4. See the translator's introduction for a discussion of what Amino means by "urban character."

from view, having been abandoned for some reason or another, and the area became a village commons. The abandonment of this site suggests that marketplaces (or post towns) of the early medieval period operated under extremely unstable conditions.

Let us turn to another, very similar set of remains, this time in Kasugai City, Aichi Prefecture, near the famous medieval *shōen* estate of Shinoki. Here, in a place called "the lower market" (*shimoichiba*), archaeologists are excavating remains of an elusive character. Apparently once situated on a riverbank, the site contains a number of foundation stones placed in a circle two meters in diameter, with traces that suggest a fire was maintained there. Archaeologists have confirmed that several dugout structures stood to one side of this circle, and from these dugouts they have uncovered the stone bowls from the Sonoki District—bowls that still have not been found at any other site in this region. Archaeologists have also turned up Chinese-made celadon items. Thus, this site has produced the kinds of artifacts one never finds in a normal farming village. What is particularly striking is that even though the site is very close to Seto, there are no Seto pottery shards to be found. Nor is there any pottery from nearby Mino. Instead, there are a number of pottery shards from fairly distant places such as Chita and Tokoname.[5] Although we cannot be absolutely certain, it seems likely that this was also some kind of urban site, perhaps a marketplace. However, this, too, had vanished from sight and memory by the Edo period.

The disappearance of these urban sites suggests that both "villages" and "towns" of the thirteenth century differed considerably from such settlements after the fifteenth century. In Japan, the harbors and inlets that became ports figured prominently in the establishment of towns. But there were also many cases in which a town developed around a marketplace that was set up on a riverbank, or on an island in the middle of a river, populated by the merchants, craftsmen, and performers who gathered there. Since itinerant merchants and craftsmen often based themselves at harbors and anchorages, these sites naturally developed into towns. This trend became most marked in the fourteenth and fifteenth centuries.

Settlement patterns are less clear in the case of eastern Japan, since there are fewer surviving documents. But in most of the archipelago it appears that stable settlements that could clearly be called villages and towns only

---

5. Chita and Tokoname are also in Aichi Prefecture but well to the south of Kasugai. They are on the Chita Peninsula across Ise Bay from Ise.

emerged in the fifteenth century. This coincides with the fairly intuitive assessment of Yanagita Kunio, mentioned above. These towns and villages continued to emerge and grow throughout the Edo period, consistently maintaining a self-governing function and eventually constituting the basic units of Edo period society. Katsumata Shizuo has labeled this development the "town and village system." For our purposes, the main point is that this system emerged in the fifteenth and sixteenth centuries. Furthermore, we should note that it was these settlements that formed the prototype of today's hamlets and cities.

So we might next ask ourselves, why was it in this period that villages and towns began to appear? The standard explanations have focused on a growing social division of labor and a rise in productive capacity. This is no doubt true, but there are a number of issues related to the appearance of towns and villages that cannot be reduced to a matter of productivity. I believe we should see the emergence of towns and villages as the cumulative effect of major transformations on a variety of levels. The significance of each of these changes needs to be individually investigated. Only when we have done that will we be able to understand the true significance of the growth in productivity.

In the chapters that follow, we will explore these transformations in some of their more specific dimensions, namely, religion, commerce, the status of marginal groups, women, and writing. I will also reflect on the relationship these transformations have with the form of the state in Japanese history. With my interest in the cumulative effects, however, the discussion of specific issues will frequently focus on their overlap with other transformations.

BOOK ONE

Circuits of the Sea
and
Nonagricultural
Production

CHAPTER ONE

Was Medieval (Premodern) Japan an Agrarian Society?

WERE "VILLAGERS" FARMERS?

Many Japanese today believe, almost as an article of faith, that at least until the Edo period Japanese society was agricultural. Such beliefs are commonly affirmed by high school textbooks such as the widely used *A Detailed History of Japan* (1991).[1] The section of this book covering the first years of the Edo period reads, "Agriculture was the central form of production of the feudal society, and the farmers (*nōmin*) lived self-sufficient lives." Another textbook, *A Revised History of Japan*,[2] published in the same year, contains the following description of farmers' lives: "Agriculture at the time was mostly a matter of self-sufficient production carried out at the level of the village (*mura*) unit." Even in his fascinating study, *What Was the Edo Period?*[3] Bitō Masahide develops his argument on the assumption that the agricultural population constituted 80 to 90 percent of the total. Since even an excellent historian of the early modern era such as Bitō makes that assumption, it seems reasonable that this would be the view of society held by a wide range of Japanese people today.

1. *Shōsetsu Nihonshi* (A Detailed History of Japan) (Tokyo: Yamakawa shuppansha, 1991).
2. *Shintei Nihonshi* (A Revised History of Japan) (Tokyo: Tōkyō shoseki 1991).
3. Bitō Masahide, *Edo jidai to wa nanika: Nihon shijō no kinsei to kindai* (What Was the Edo Period?) (Tokyo: Iwanami shoten, 1992).

To reiterate, the key assumptions most high school textbooks make about the Edo period is that the society was overwhelmingly agricultural, that agriculture was dominated by rice production, and that villages were self-sufficient (in other words, they provided for their own needs, without significant consumption of outside production). The textbooks mentioned above even refer to the same pie chart to prove this assertion (fig. 1). This particular chart was constructed on the basis of 1849 population figures, divided by occupation, for the Kubota domain in Akita. Of a total population of approximately 372,000 people, the textbooks tell us that farmers constituted 76.4 percent, townsfolk (*chōnin*) 7.5 percent, samurai 9.8 percent, clergy (Buddhist and Shinto) 1.9 percent, and others 4.2 percent. If this chart is correct, then the population of the Kubota domain at the end of the Edo period was clearly and overwhelmingly agricultural.

Of course, the chart does not include categories for coastal people (*kaimin*) or mountain dwellers (*sanmin*), neither of whom lived in areas where rice agriculture predominated. Even if those involved in so-called miscellaneous occupations, such as the people of mountain and coastal villages, were added to the numbers for merchants and artisans, that segment of the population would still only hover around 10 percent. Therefore, if the population of Edo period Japan was composed the way the pie chart suggests, one would

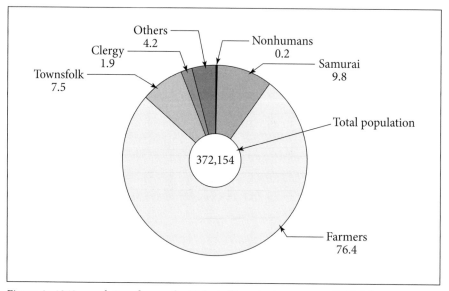

Figure 1. 1849 population figures for Kubota Domain, in percent, divided by occupation. Source: *Shōsetsu Nihonshi* (Tokyo: Yamakawa Shuppansha, 1991).

have to conclude that nonagricultural people were indeed a small minority in the society of the time.

There are very few passages in these textbooks related to such major industries as fishing, salt production, or forestry. Since these textbooks provide the basic knowledge for the college entrance exams, it is difficult to draft exam questions related to fishing, salt, or forestry. In fact, everything that the colleges deem unrelated to the exams has been left out. As a result, all one can do in the classroom is let students know that the occupations of those industries were also important. But from the perspective of the pie chart such short shrift would not be unexpected for such a small minority.

In examining this chart closely, one cannot help but wonder if there were no fishermen, marine merchants (*kaisenjin*), or mountain folk in Akita at all. I began to wonder whether something odd was going on, so I bought Sekiyama Naotarō's *The Population Structure of Early Modern Japan*, on which the chart was based.[4] The percentages in Sekiyama's table and those of the textbooks' chart were the same, but where the chart lists 76.4 percent for farmers (*nōmin*), Sekiyama's table has 76.4 percent for villagers (*hyakushō*). So it is clear that the textbook version of the chart was produced with the understanding that all *hyakushō* were farmers (table 1).

However, careful consideration of whether the Japanese term *hyakushō* originally carried the implication of agriculture reveals that the conflation of *hyakushō* and farmer so common today is groundless. In fact, prior to the modern era the term described many nonagricultural people, that is, people

Table 1   POPULATION OF KUBOTA DOMAIN, 1849, BY OCCUPATION

	Number	%
Warriors	36,453	9.8
Villagers	284,384	76.4
Townsfolk	27,852	7.5
Clergy	7,256	1.9
Miscellaneous	15,720	4.2
Nonhumans	489	0.1
Totals	372,154	

Source: Sekiyama Naotarō, *Kinsei Nihon no jinkō kōzō* (Tokyo: Yoshikawa kōbunkan, 1959).

4. Sekiyama Naotarō, *Kinsei Nihon no jinkō kōzō* (The Population Structure of Early Modern Japan) (Tokyo: Yoshikawa kōbunkan, 1959).

who participated in forms of production other than agriculture. If that is the case, then premodern society in the Japanese islands was probably quite different from the way we have commonly envisioned it. To be honest, I came to understand this only recently.

THE TOKIKUNI FAMILY OF OUTER NOTO

Around 1985, I began to participate in a long-term historical study of an old and prominent family, the Tokikuni of the Noto Peninsula, conducted by the Institute for the Study of Japanese Folk Culture at Kanagawa University. Our readings of the premodern documents in the family's possession provided me with an opportunity to reconsider the common understanding of the term *hyakushō*.

The Tokikuni family is currently divided into two distinct lineages, the "upper" and the "lower." My first visit to the upper Tokikuni family occurred ten years ago [1986] when I went to discuss the return of family documents that had been borrowed by the institute more than thirty years before.[5] The matron of the family at the time told me that there seemed to be more documents in the family's storehouses. She asked whether I might be interested in examining the storehouses for her one more time.

Seizing the opportunity she presented, I entered the storehouses with several young graduate students from Kanagawa University. Delving into every corner, we found nearly ten thousand documents dating from the Edo period; if we include documents from the modern period—the Meiji and Taishō eras—the grand total of documents discovered comes to several tens of thousands. We were also allowed to examine some of the holdings of the lower Tokikuni household, where we also discovered many old documents. Since the institute had failed to return the materials borrowed more than thirty years ago, we decided to repay the Tokikuni family's extraordinary patience by properly cataloging and repairing the newly discovered docu-

5. The institute borrowed several hundred family documents in 1954 and brought them back to Tokyo for transcription and cataloging. At the time, the institute was an adjunct research center at the Fisheries Agency in the Ministry of Agriculture and Forestry. Shortly after borrowing the documents, funding for the institute was cut and its collection of documents, most of which were not returned to their owners, had to be maintained for nearly thirty years at the expense and through the efforts of former members. When the institute was reconstituted as an official research center in 1983 and moved to Kanagawa University, Amino and other members rediscovered the documents.

ments. From that time on, we visited both Tokikuni households twice a year, in summer and autumn, for a period of ten years, to catalog and organize their documents. We also gradually broadened our perspective to include the whole region of Outer Noto (fig. 2). At the same time, we conducted a seminar for graduate students at Kanagawa University focused on the Tokikuni family documents. As we read through them one at a time, we began to see to what extent our previous understanding that all *hyakushō* were farmers was mistaken.[6]

At present, the lower Tokikuni household (fig. 3) is located downstream (along the Machino River) from the upper, but originally both families lived under one roof. In 1634, due to a division of ruling authority between the Tokugawa bakufu and the Maeda clan over the lands possessed by the Tokikuni, the family was divided in two. The upper household was located

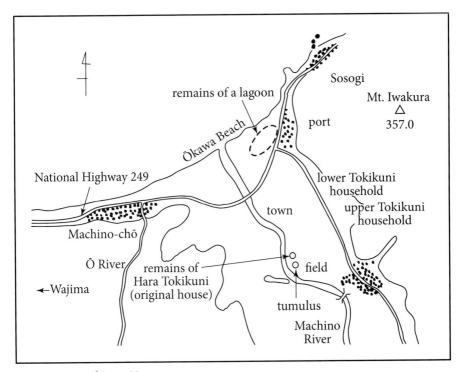

Figure 2. Map of Outer Noto.

6. Amino credits all the members of the Tokikuni seminar at Kanagawa University for the revised concept of *hyakushō* articulated in the rest of the chapter.

in the Tokugawa-governed portion of the valley, and the lower resided in the Maeda-governed portion.[7] The current upper Tokikuni dwelling (fig. 4) was constructed in 1831 and is a good example of the largest class of vernacular housing in Japan. The lower Tokikuni dwelling is smaller in scale, but our investigation confirmed that it was built nearly two hundred years earlier, in 1634, making it one of the oldest examples of Japanese vernacular housing still in existence. If you visit them today, you will find the two houses only a short distance apart, set back from the river along the base of the mountains that form the walls of the valley. Facing the Machino River from the houses, you will see a broad expanse of rice paddies opening up before them, giving the impression that they are two extremely large houses belonging to wealthy farmers.

The family name of the Tokikuni is a remnant of the medieval period. Many paddies in the medieval period were named (*myōden*),[8] that is, they were officially registered with two-character names such as Sadakuni, Sadatoki, or Kunisada. The Tokikuni family undoubtedly took the medieval paddy name of Tokikuni as its family name. For that reason, researchers have viewed the Tokikuni as characteristic of the older families of the Outer

7. The Tokugawa shogunate, in order to check the power of large *daimyō* such as the Maeda, who ruled Noto and surrounding areas, claimed a number of small settlements throughout the domain, inserting itself into the domain like air pockets in Swiss cheese. These settlements were governed by vassals of the Tokugawa family. During the period in which the Tokikuni split, the governors were of the Hijikata family. The shogunate's holdings in the area were recognized by their designation as Tenryō or "heavenly domains." It was the shogunate's decision to claim a portion of the lower Machino Valley in 1634 that led to the Tokikuni family's decision to split. Half of the family (the lower) moved to Maeda-controlled land slightly downstream, while the other half (the upper) remained in the large house the entire family had once occupied, which was now located in the heavenly domain. The split took the form of a retirement. The former head of the household retired from his position and moved into the newly constructed lower house while his son became head of the new upper Tokikuni family. The form of this division has lead to a heated debate between the two families as to which is the "main" lineage and which the "branch." The upper family claims status as main lineage because they stayed in the large house. Family members also cite the retirement of the head of the household as the act that constituted the creation of a branch family. The lower Tokikuni argue that the split was carried out to enable at least a portion of the family to remain under the rule of Lord Maeda and that the creation of the upper lineage was the act that constituted a break from the family's long-standing position. Amino and the Tokikuni Research Group have argued that the concepts of main and branch family are meaningless in the kind of split the Tokikuni undertook. See chapter five for a further discussion of the significance of the Hijikata domain.
8. In the process by which rice paddies, the basic unit of taxation in the Ritsuryō state, were transformed from imperial grant to privately owned lands, paddies were designated by a two-character combination, usually reflecting the name of their legal owner, more often than not an aristocrat in the capital. Thus, paddies with names are among the clearest residues of the Heian and medieval period system of land control. See the account of the dispute over the fields named Suetaka-myō in "The Women of Tara no shō" in chapter nine for an example of a named field.

Figure 3. The lower Tokikune residence. Photograph courtesy of Nobuhiro Tokikuni.

Figure 4. The upper Tokikune residence. Photograph courtesy of Nobuhiro Tokikuni.

Noto region. That is, as Outer Noto still retains many traces of the medieval period, some historians have suggested that the Tokikuni were the managers of a well-known plot of land called Tokikuni.

In fact, at the beginning of the Edo period, before its division, the Tokikuni possessed nearly two hundred indentured servants (*genin*). Most scholarship to date has viewed these indentured servants as slaves, particularly agricultural slaves. So, the Tokikuni family has been seen as a large landowning family that made use of "slaves" to cultivate a broad expanse of fields (some tens of *chō*).[9] The famous ethnographer Miyamoto Tsuneichi, who visited the Tokikuni families shortly after World War II, made a number of astute observations on their condition at the time. But in the end even Miyamoto concluded that the Tokikuni were large-scale farmers who belonged to what scholars call the "patriarchal, large-scale, slave-owning class," a class with strong traces of the medieval era. However, a careful reading of every document in the *Outer Noto Tokikuni Family Documents*,[10] one character at a time from beginning to end, suggests that this characterization is mistaken.

The Tokikuni were of *hyakushō* rather than warrior status and possessed land valued at about 300 *koku* of grain.[11] After they split, the upper Tokikuni possessed 200 *koku* while the lower had 100, so even after the division both families were involved with large-scale agriculture. But apart from their agricultural activities the family had owned large ships since before the early Edo period. We were able to confirm, from a document dated 1619, that with these ships the family engaged in trade over an area ranging from Matsumae (southern Hokkaido) in the north to Sado Island, Tsuruga, and even across Lake Biwa to Ōmi, Ōtsu, Kyoto, and Osaka.

From quite early on, their ships carried such things as *konbu* (a kind of seaweed), which they acquired from Matsumae and sold in Kyoto and Osaka. But what did these ships carry to Matsumae from Noto? First of all, the Tokikuni family had a number of salt fields on the coast. We have documents from the early Edo period showing that they produced salt, which they carried to ports on the northern Japan Sea coast such as Noshiro in Dewa and Niigata in Echigo. So salt appears to have been shipped to the north. In addition, the mountains behind the Tokikuni lands were rich in wood,

---

9. One *chō* equals approximately 2.45 acres.
10. *Oku Noto Tokikunike monjo* (Outer Noto Tokikuni Family Documents), 4 vols. (Tokyo: Jōmin bunka kenkyūjo, 1956).
11. A *koku* was a cubic unit of measure that was supposed to equal the amount of rice necessary to feed one man for one year, approximately 45 U.S. gallons or 180 liters.

from which they produced a great deal of charcoal. There is thus substantial evidence to conclude that salt and charcoal were produced for trade (and not just for subsistence).

Around the same time, the Tokikuni family bought a residence in the town of Ushitsu, a quiet harbor on the inner bay side of the Noto Peninsula, which was provided with docking facilities (fig. 5). Before its division, the family had a huge house of 990 square meters near the banks of the Machino River, and the large lagoon at the mouth of the river served as its harbor. Even today, that area, now dry land, is known by locals as "the harbor." Thus, we are certain that the Tokikuni worked out of this harbor and

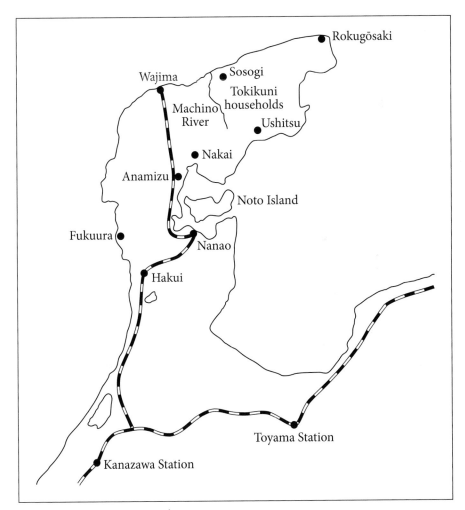

Figure 5. Map of Noto Peninsula.

Ushitsu, engaging in marine trade on a grand scale. We also know that the family received a variety of permits from the Maeda lords, which means that the Tokikunis' trading had official recognition. Therefore, one cannot simply call the Tokikuni "wealthy landowners" and hope to capture the full extent of their activities.

In 1618, the Tokikuni found deposits of lead in the mountains behind the nearby village of Najimi, and they petitioned the Maeda for permission to mine the deposit (fig. 6). We do not know how this mining venture turned out, but it is significant that the family extended itself to the operation of a mine. Moreover, from the late medieval period, the Tokikuni owned storehouses near the Machino *shōen* estate harbor, through which they administered the transportation and storage of such items as the annual tax of rice and salt. The Tokikuni served as the domainal lord's local managers (*daikan*) for these storehouses. The lord issued orders to release appropriate amounts of rice and salt as necessary, and on that authority the Tokikuni made their own decisions as to when items in storage should be released and at what volume. So, from the early Edo period on, the Tokikuni performed administrative functions as storehouse managers. It is also likely that they provided financial services with the silver equivalent of the goods they stored.

Thus, we can see how misguided it is to define the Tokikuni family as a large-scale agricultural producer using slave labor in the fields. It is not completely mistaken, but it only captures one aspect of their activities. There is no accurate terminology at the current level of academic knowledge to describe members of this class, so we may provisionally call them multiventure entrepreneurs. As awkward as this sounds, it most accurately describes the two houses of the Tokikuni family (fig. 7).

Figure 6. Petition for lead mining submitted by Tokikuni Tōzaemon to the Maeda House. From the collection of Kentarō Tokikuni. Photograph courtesy of the Institute for the Study of Japanese Folk Culture, Kanagawa University.

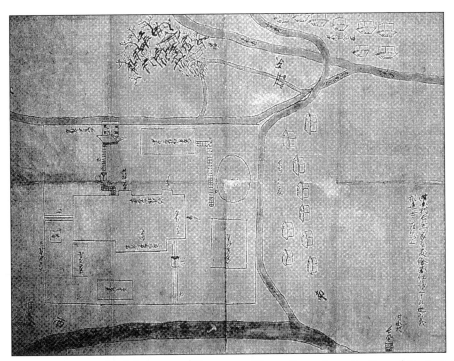

Figure 7. Layout of Tokikuni-mura Chōzaemon House. From the collection of Kentarō Tokikuni. Photograph courtesy of Institute for the Study of Japanese Folk Culture, Kanagawa University.

LANDED AND LANDLESS VILLAGERS
IN THE SHIPPING INDUSTRY

In the early Edo period, a shipper named Shibakusaya, who was closely associated with the Tokikuni, plied his trade from the harbor at the mouth of the Machino River. We know that one Shibakusaya lived in the residence the Tokikuni owned in Ushitsu in the late sixteenth century, so members of the Machino Shibakusaya family are probably his descendants. We believe the Shibakusaya employed two or three large ships for their trade in the Japan Sea. Documents show that the Tokikuni borrowed one hundred *ryō* of gold from the Shibakusaya in the early Edo period, so it is clear that the Shibakusaya were wealthy enough to handle that volume of money.

However, when we read the Tokikuni documents of the early Edo period, we noticed that the Shibakusaya family was designated a member of the *atamafuri* (literally, head shaking) class. In the Maeda domains of Kaga, Noto, and Etchū, villagers who did not produce taxable crops were called

atamafuri. In the Tokugawa lands on the Noto Peninsula, *atamafuri* were
called *mizunomi* (literally, water drinkers), which was the term most commonly used in the Japanese archipelago to describe people who had no land.
Mizunomi had different names in different regions, for example, *mōto* (gate
men), *mawaki* (at the side), *muen* (unconnected), and *zakke* (various houses).
Today's history textbooks explain that these were poor, small-scale farmers.
That is what I also believed until I read these documents.

When we confirmed that there were people like the Shibakusaya, who,
although their status was technically *mizunomi*, were actually maritime
merchants able to lend large sums of money to such powerful families as the
Tokikuni, the members of our study group could hardly believe their eyes. At
the same time, it was something of an epiphany. Without a doubt, the Shibakusaya were called *mizunomi* because they did not own land, but it would be
wrong to think that they were poor farmers. Rather, they *did not need* to own
land, since they were extremely wealthy people who specialized in shipping
and commerce. However, we also saw that under the system that prevailed in
the Edo period even these people were officially placed in the landless class.

To give another example, two or three years ago we discovered a document hidden in the insulated sliding doors (*fusuma*) of the upper Tokikuni
house. It contained an appeal from a villager named Enjirō. Enjirō lived in
a small hamlet called Sosogi, which was located on the right bank of the
mouth of the Machino River. According to this document, Enjirō's father
was a maritime merchant who had gone to Matsumae with his sailors. Having failed to return home for several years, Enjirō believed that they had
been shipwrecked. As a result, the family members he left behind, including
Enjirō, his mother, and several small children, were having trouble supporting themselves. In particular, they were unable to pay back money that their
father had borrowed from a number of people.

Of particular interest to us were Enjirō's father's creditors. They included
merchants such as Echigoya Chōjirō in Dewa Shōnai, Kamiya Chōzaemon in
Wakasa Obama, and Itaya Chōbei in Noto Wajima.[12] Meanwhile, in their
home village of Sosogi, their father had borrowed large sums from a man
named Saburōbei. We know that he traded throughout the Japan Sea with
this capital, visiting merchants in every port. But when the loans were called
in Enjirō fell into dire straits. After a time, he was able to scrape together a

---

12. Dewa Shōnai is present-day coastal Yamagata. Wakasa Obama refers to the town of Obama in
    present-day Fukui Prefecture. Amino's point is that these sites are quite distant from the Machino
    River in Noto.

living by selling sundries such as wax and oil, so in the document he appealed to the domainal managers (the Tokikuni) to allow him to reschedule the loans over a fifty-year period.

Until recently, Sosogi had been considered an impoverished village with few resources other than salt production. So we were intrigued to learn through this document that one of its villagers sailed a relatively large boat (not the largest in the area—the Kitamaebune class—but large enough) trading in ports all along the Japan Sea and even going as far north as Matsumae.

It happened that during that summer a number of newspaper reporters visited Sosogi. I showed them this particular document during an interview. The first question they asked was, What was a "farmer" doing going all the way up to Matsumae? That is, they were wondering why a *hyakushō*—in their minds a farmer—would travel to Matsumae. I replied that this *hyakushō* was not a farmer but a maritime merchant, as indicated by the document. Still, the reporters did not seem to understand. They wondered why someone engaged in shipping would be called a *hyakushō*. I spent nearly two hours trying to explain.

Among the journalists was a very enthusiastic reporter from the local newspaper, the *Hokkoku Shinbun*. This man followed up on our meeting with several phone calls, during which he asked many detailed questions. Afterward he showed me his article so I could check it for accuracy; I thought he wrote a fine piece. So, expecting an interesting article in the following day's paper, I arose to find it topped by the headline "Farmers (*nōmin*) Also Engaged in Shipping." Two hours of explanation and several phone calls had all been in vain. The article itself was precisely written, but the copy editors, apparently deciding that this was not clear enough, inserted the word farmers. But of course the headline was clearly in error. I could not help wishing that they had at least written "*Hyakushō* Also Engaged in Shipping." But I was also surprised to discover that the Japanese mass media refused to use the word *hyakushō* (villager) since it was viewed as discriminatory.[13]

13. *Hyakushō*, as a term that was used during the Edo period, has connotations of feudal submission today. As happens frequently elsewhere, a movement to raise the social status of farmers in post-war Japan insisted on the use of a new term, one with the appearance of greater neutrality: *nōmin* (literally, agricultural people). The problem Amino encountered with the newspaper has to do with the fact that since *hyakushō* had come to be identified with discrimination (much the way *Negro* is no longer used in the United States), the editors felt they had to choose a word that was more objective. But their choice of *nōmin* was precisely counter to what Amino had spent hours telling the reporters, that is, that these people were not farmers but maritime merchants whose Edo period class status happened to be within the category of *hyakushō*. That is why, in part, I have chosen to translate *hyakushō* as "villagers" rather than use the standard translation of "peasants." The following section explains this decision further.

The other newspapers had headlines such as, "Noto Villagers Were Active on the Seas" and "A Farm Family in Outer Noto Participated in Ocean Trade during the Edo Period." Never was it more clear to us how deeply entrenched was the idea that *hyakushō* means "farmer." The prime example was a veteran reporter who kept agreeing with me but, after listening to me talk for thirty minutes, went back to his office and wrote, "A starving peasant in Sosogi named Enjirō migrated to Matsumae for work." There was nothing for us to do but laugh. It showed us how the deeply rooted belief that villagers were invariably farmers can lead to grave misunderstandings.

CITIES DESIGNATED AS VILLAGES

After the misunderstandings with the newspapers, Izumi Masahiro, a member of our study group and a historian at Atomi Women's College, began to pursue the problem of wealthy nonagricultural villagers. Using some interesting materials listing the number of *hyakushō* and *atamafuri* households in the Maeda-controlled counties of Fugeshi and Suzu in 1735, including village productivity and tax rates, Izumi was able to draw some important conclusions about the percentage of *atamafuri* households (table 2).

Izumi found that in 1735 Outer Noto's largest city, Wajima, had a total of 621 households with a probable population of several thousand people. Interestingly, a full 71 percent of those households were considered to be *atamafuri*. The remaining 29 percent were households with average production of only 4.5 *koku* (from about 4.5 *tan* of land).[14] Ushitsu, on the other side of the peninsula, where the Tokikuni family also had a boathouse and a residence, was also a large city. Its population of *atamafuri* reached the extremely high figure of 76 percent.

From this we were able to confirm that in addition to such coastal cities as Wajima and Ushitsu inland urban-type settlements such as Iida, Kabuto, and Hanami also had a high percentage of *atamafuri*. If the common notion that *hyakushō* were invariably farmers and *atamafuri* were poor farmers were true, then Wajima would have been an extremely poor town since farmers holding a mere 4.5 *tan* of land comprised 29 percent of the town while the remaining 71 percent were landless. Ushitsu would have been even

14. One *tan* equals 0.25 acres.

Table 2   VILLAGE STATISTICS FOR FUGESHI AND
SUZU COUNTIES, 1735

Village	Number of Households	Hyakushō	Atamafuri	Atamafuri (%)	Village Tax (koku)	Tax Rate (%)	Tax per Household (koku)
Kawai/ Fugeshi	621 (59 unnamed)	183	438	71	823	88	1.210
Ushitsu	433	104	329	76	540	83	1.247
Minatsuki	263	144	119	45	141	81	9.536
Iida	223	157	66	30	383	70	1.717
Nakai	190	110	80	42	342	79	1.800
Matsunami	184	120	64	35	901	58	4.897
Nakai-minami	174	90	84	48	255	70	1.466
Ogi	157	106	51	32	142	74	0.904
Kenchi	138	67	71	51	122	80	0.884
Ushitsu-sanbun	124	82	42	34	400	46	3.226
Michishita	121	70	51	42	382	65	3.157
Ugai	117	76	41	35	460	55	3.932
Kabuto	114	36	78	68	552	50	4.842
Nabune	108	57	51	47	222	70	2.056
Hanami	108	33	75	69	280	65	2.593
Kaiso	105	38	67	64	31	72	0.295

more impoverished. We were able to prove that this conclusion is mistaken. Wajima's *atamafuri* undoubtedly included many lacquer craftsmen, noodle makers, large-scale merchants dealing in these items, and traders owning ships of the Kitamaebune class. There were also a number of powerful merchants in the *hyakushō* class.

When we first went to Outer Noto, we thought of it as a poor region with little farmland. A glance at the famous Senmaida—many extremely small and terraced paddies one above the other on a hillside—clearly conveys this image (fig. 8). Even the people of Outer Noto characterize their region as mountainous, with little room in which to establish rice paddies. Moreover, Outer Noto was known as a place of exile. For example, Tokikuni family legend has it that they are the descendants of Taira Tokitada, who fled to Noto after the fall of the Taira clan of 1185. However, our preconceptions of

Figure 8. Thousand-layered rice paddies (Senmaida). Photographed by Shibata Akisuke.
Source: *Karā Kaga Noto no miryoku* (The Appeal of Kaga Noto in Color) (Kyoto: Tankōsha, 1978).

Noto as an extremely backward and undeveloped region—where one could find until relatively recently many remnants of medieval "named paddies" and where there were families who utilized two hundred or more indentured servants and/or slaves in archaic farm management—were overturned once we began to investigate conditions among members of the *atamafuri* class.

Until the Edo period, Outer Noto boasted many port towns and cities where shippers were at the forefront of the Japan Sea trade. In fact, it was one of the few regions that could be considered quite wealthy in monetary terms (as opposed to landed wealth). But the consequences of our findings are not limited to the Noto region alone. Rather, I believe they extend to society in the entire Japanese archipelago. When I talk to early modern historians about Outer Noto, they often claim that the area must be an anomaly. However, even an amateur in early modern history can find similar conditions in many other regions once he or she begins to dig.

For example, Kaminoseki on the Inland Sea side of Yamaguchi Prefecture has been a port town since the medieval period. Here as well we have accurate figures for the number of villager households. Kaminoseki was divided into two parts, the inland and the port-side sections. According to the late Edo period *Bōchō Land Development Plan,* only nineteen of the thirty-six *hyakushō* households in the inland section were engaged in farming. Of the remaining households, ten were merchants, five were shippers/wholesalers, one was a blacksmith, and one was a fisherman. Of the eighty-eight *hyakushō* households in the port-side section, only twelve (13.6 percent) were engaged in farming, while fifty-four were merchants and others were boat owners, sailors, ship's carpenters, fabric dyers, or tofu makers.

Landless villagers were called *mōto* in this region. In the inland section, 98 of 135 *mōto* were engaged in farming while the rest included twenty merchants, ships carpenters, bucket makers, and wall painters. Of the 178 *mōto* in the port-side section, none was a farmer, sixty-eight were merchants, and eighteen owned boats. Others were carpenters, blacksmiths, bucket makers, fabric dyers, tatami makers, and so on—all urban occupations.

We can see that in the population structure of Kaminoseki, even among the *hyakushō*, farmers were in the minority while merchants, boat owners, and various craftsmen constituted the overwhelming majority. The *mōto* of this region were fundamentally the same as the *atamafuri* of Outer Noto; the majority were nonagricultural, and it appears safe to say that many of them were well off. Of course, we still must consider why there were so many farming *mōto* in the inland section. But taken as a whole it is certain that the many ports and inlets along the Inland Sea, from Shikoku to the San'yō region, had the same population structure as Kaminoseki. Thus, we cannot dismiss the Noto region as an exception.

To give another example, the city of Izumisano in Osaka has been well known as a fishing port since ancient times. There was a family in this city named Meshino, commonly known as Izumiya or Tachibanaya, that engaged in large-scale shipping, trading as far away as Akita and Matsumae. In the foreword to Ihara Saikaku's *The Eternal Storehouse of Japan*, this family is described as "quieting the waves in their ship, the *Shintsū-maru*." Saikaku describes another family, the Karakaneya, from the port of Sanoura in Waizumi, as "running swiftly with even 3,700 *koku* throughout the northern seas." Both of these families were of the *hyakushō* class. Thus, we can say that there were likely a great number of *hyakushō* and *mizunomi* in the coastal towns of Edo period Japan who were engaged in large-scale shipping.

The Japanese archipelago is composed of over 3,700 islands with 28,000 kilometers of coastline. Only 25 percent of the land is level enough for agriculture. Thus, the landscape of the Noto Peninsula can be found in other peninsulas and islands throughout the archipelago. Moreover, the landscape has changed significantly since the medieval period. For example, the small lagoon at the mouth of the Machino River has almost completely disappeared, although it appears to have been much larger long ago. We also know that the coastline along the Japan Sea was full of such inlets. Meanwhile, on the Pacific side of Honshu, Gifu Prefecture is now a landlocked prefecture. But in ancient times the ocean was close to the town of Ōgaki. Those sections along Ise Bay that are often submerged in water after a typhoon were also originally under water. Osaka Bay was similarly expansive, while southern Kanto was an alluvial plain. So, when we take into account the landscape as it was before the medieval period, my argument for the Noto Peninsula becomes applicable to the entire archipelago, since much of the land that is now agricultural was in fact covered in water. Thus, the common belief that Japanese society was overwhelmingly agricultural—and that by extension society was fundamentally based on agricultural production—is also overturned.

This is not only an issue for coastal towns; one can make a similar case for the mountains. My home prefecture of Yamanashi is a mountainous area with few rice paddies, truly a nonagricultural region. For that reason, the people of Yamanashi also consider themselves poor. Yet Yamanashi is famous for its Kōshū merchants and conglomerates (*zaibatsu*).[15] One can resolve this apparent contradiction with the same kind of approach we took with the coastal areas. For example, the population of the village of Ichibe in Isawa, an area known for its hot springs and a market town from ancient times, was 51 percent *mizunomi*. Likewise, the village of Yamaoku became quite wealthy due to its lumber industry. There are also many *mizunomi* in the village of Kamiyoshida, at the entrance to the Mount Fuji trail, which was clearly a city during medieval times. Just as was the case with coastal villages, mountain villages cannot be considered poor just because they were remote and had little farmland.

Yet until recently most historians, including myself, did not take this into consideration. In a book I wrote twenty years ago, *A Portrait of the Medieval Japanese People*, I was well aware that not all *hyakushō* were farmers in the medieval age.[16] I knew that taxes paid in rice by *hyakushō* were in the minority, with most being paid in silk, cloth, salt, iron, paper, and oil, so I knew that medieval villagers could not strictly be called farmers. But by the Edo period Japanese agriculture had made great strides, so I concluded that, "Just as we use the term '*o-hyakushō-san*' today for farmers, we may conclude that villagers were farmers." As a result, I have had to add endnotes to subsequent printings of that book in which I clearly state that I was mistaken and that this was the result of my incomplete understanding nearly twenty years ago.

Since most historians read historical documents assuming that *hyakushō* were farmers, the images they have produced are greatly distorted. This is not limited to the Edo period but is true for medieval and ancient Japan as well. Once we recognize that villagers included many people engaged in other industries—including many nonagricultural peoples—we find that we must reconsider our image of Japanese society.

I will eventually discuss how this misunderstanding arose and spread throughout Japan, but first I would like to touch on one more area of confusion. We tend to think of a village (*mura*) as a farming village. This belief has an extremely strong hold in Japan. In general, coastal and mountain villages are considered poor places with very little farmland and hence with very little social standing. In fact, the terms *fishing village* (*kaison*) and *mountain*

---

15. Kōshū is the older name for the Yamanashi region.
16. Amino Yoshihiko, *Nihon chūsei no minshūzō* (A Portrait of the Medieval Japanese People) (Tokyo: Iwanami shoten, 1980).

village (*sanson*) have barely made their way into common usage, even though a harbor settlement was admittedly considered different from a village in the Edo period land system.

I have found it difficult to understand why places like Wajima and Ushitsu in Noto, Kaminoseki in Suō, and Sano in Izumi, all of which were clearly cities in medieval times, were legally registered as villages in the Edo period. During the Edo period, the only places recognized as towns were castle towns and such venerable large-scale cities as Sakai and Hakata. Places that were cities in fact but unrelated to the governing power of the *daimyō* were all designated as villages. Places designated as villages were allowed to conduct their own land surveys, and people who owned and worked the fields were designated *hyakushō*, while the rest were given the status of *mizunomi*. So, when one assumes that a place that was known as a village was in fact a farming community, one ends up committing all kinds of ridiculous mistakes.

In fact, in medieval times the designation village was reserved for non-agricultural communities and was considered outside such administrative designations as a district (*gun*), hamlet (*gō*), and estate (*shō*). *Village* referred to communities that remained outside the category of aristocrat-owned lands or to communities where farmland was developed late.

For that reason, many of the settlements known as villages in the medieval period were on the coast or in the mountains. An examination of an early-thirteenth-century document called the *Ōtabumi*, a medieval land register for Noto, shows that many of the communities designated as villages were later known as port towns during the Edo period. Therefore, we need to do away with the assumption that villages were farming communities and take a fresh look at Japanese society.

TAXES LEVIED ON PADDY LAND

Why have Japanese held these mistaken convictions for so long? When we consider the literal meaning of the Chinese characters Japanese have used for *hyakushō*, we see that the term originally meant nothing more nor less than the common people, who have "many ('one hundred') names." This original meaning does not imply "farmer." I believe the archaic Japanese reading of the character was *ōmitakara*, which contains no reference to farming.

In present-day China and Korea, the characters for the term *hyakushō* are used in their literal sense. When I asked a student from China how he would translate the meaning of *hyakushō*, as it is used in his country, into Japanese, he replied, after brief reflection, "a common person." In other words, anyone who was not an official was usually called a *hyakushō*. The term is often used that way today as well. The exchange student said that he found it strange that in Japan everyone thought of *hyakushō* as farmers.

The same argument can be made for the term village. The term is derived from the word for a "gathering" or "group" (*mure*), so its original meaning had nothing specifically to do with farm villages. So why is it that many historians who otherwise strive to be strictly empirical—historians who emphasize scientific history—forget about empirical principles and scientific rules when it comes to interpreting words in documents? Rather than interpreting words by way of the meanings they had at the time the document was written, these historians make the basic mistake of assuming from the start that *hyakushō* means farmers. I made the same mistake, so I am not speaking from arrogance. Rather, this is a serious problem with no easy answer. However, I believe I can suggest several reasons.

Perhaps the most important is that the first true state in the Japanese archipelago—the archaic Ritsuryō state—designated the rice paddy as the foundation of the state system in the islands, excepting Okinawa, Hokkaido, and the northern parts of Tohoku. That is, the Ritsuryō state created a system whereby its support would be drawn from taxes levied on land. This state listed everyone under its control in family registers, everyone age six and up, discriminating, however, between men and women. Each was allotted a specific amount of land, and on that basis the state collected taxes in rice (*so*), labor (*yō*), crafts (*chō*), and other forms. This system was an attempt to bring a state into being in a place that had not yet formed a centralized government, characterized by an overpowering will to treat all subjects as farmers, as producers of rice. For example, even though nearly all of the villagers of Shima Province were fishermen, each was allotted paddy land by the state. Since there were no rice paddies in Shima Province, they were given paddies in Owari. Naturally, the people of Shima were unable to till their assigned land.

To give another example, the head of the early-eighth-century government, Prince Nagaya, planned to establish one million *chō* of new rice paddies. This is an astonishing figure. Even by the medieval period, the entire country's paddy acreage probably did not reach this total. Since Japanese society in the eighth century had a high proportion of coastal and mountain dwellers, with many long involved in trade and handicraft production, it is fair to say that no communities were strictly self-sufficient. Nevertheless, the government attempted to carry out this policy for one year, although in the end it was found to be impractical.

So why is it that the Ritsuryō state chose a system based on the taxation of rice paddies and tried so desperately to implement it, despite the fact that so many communities lacked the material means? Granted, rice paddies and rice itself supported religious rituals in the state's center of power in the Kinai region as well as in regions as far west as northern Kyushu. But the fact that this impossible task was even *conceived* reveals the importance placed on the rice paddy by this state. As mentioned earlier, the decision of the Ritsuryō state to employ this system was to have great and long-lasting repercussions in Japanese history. Even though this taxation system subsequently underwent significant change, its traces could still be found in the medieval estate system (*shōen-kōryōsei*).

The estate system, which was clearly in effect by the early thirteenth century, used rice paddies as the fundamental unit of taxation, with new tax categories of annual tribute (*nengu*) and public service (*kūji*) added. Payment of annual tribute was not restricted to rice but frequently included items such as silk, cloth, iron, and salt. However, the latter items were collected in conversion equivalents to rice paddies, such as two bolts of silk per *chō* or five *ryō* of iron per *tan* of paddy. This system proceeded from the assumption that rice, silk, and iron would be exchanged, but the principle of taxation was still based on the unit of the rice paddy.

The next state system to come into being was the *bakuhan* system, which was formed in the late sixteenth and early seventeenth centuries.[17] It designated the *kokudaka*—a volume of estimated rice production—as the basic unit for payment of annual taxes on the assumption that income from fields, homes, mountains, the ocean, and salt fields and even profits made in commerce could be converted to a standard measure of value expressed in terms of rice. In effect, fields, homes, mountains, coastal water, and salt fields were all made equivalent to rice paddies. The domainal lord's income was expressed in the standard price of rice, with taxes levied on that basis. Production was measured in *kokudaka,* and a rate, called a *men*, was estab-

---

17. The term *bakuhan* system derives from the fact that the Japanese islands were ruled under a dual policy system during the Tokugawa era. On the one hand, the shogunate (bakufu) had many of the functions of a national government, at least in terms of its legal control of the warrior class and across national borders. On the other hand, the realm was divided into more than 250 domains (*han*) ruled by warlords (*daimyō*) who were principally semiautonomous rulers of their domains. The political system in which a national *bakufu* coexisted with regional *han*, with slightly overlapping yet significantly different jurisdiction, is described by historians as the *bakuhan* system.

lished for tax collection; five *men*, for example, would constitute a tax rate of 50 percent. Therefore, the early modern *bakuhan* system of taxation used the productivity of rice paddies as the basic measure of the value of land.

From the archaic Ritsuryō state through the governments of the medieval and early modern periods, the ruling class consistently took the stance that "agriculture is the foundation of the country," aggressively promoting an ideology of "agrarian fundamentalism." As a result, the ruling class also consistently claimed that subjects should be farmers. It was the will of the state that taxes be levied on land production, and it was the state's decision that the people would be tied to the land as farmers, all in its own interest.

For this reason, administrative terminology was largely focused on agricultural matters. For example, our Edo period seaman-villager Enjirō possessed land that produced only a minuscule amount of *kokudaka*. He spent most of the year engaged in shipping and trade, farming only occasionally when home from the sea. However, his primary occupation of shipping was represented as "agricultural idle time income" or harvest interval income." In other words, according to administrative terminology, it was by-employment, a side job.

Yet properly speaking, for Enjirō farming was "shipping idle time income," not the other way around. Even today, if a company employee has a small bit of land that he farms in his spare time, he is designated a "secondary, part-time farmer" by the government, a carryover from the Edo period notion of "agricultural idle time income." Official agrarian fundamentalist terminology thus persists to this day and for this reason the idea that *hyakushō* are farmers gradually spread among people in general.

THE WORLD OF THE *FUSUMA* DOCUMENT

Around the sixteenth and seventeenth centuries, this understanding of the term *hyakushō* began to spread throughout Japanese society, so that by the end of the Edo period a farmer "was commonly called a *hyakushō*." The idea is so widespread that scholars like myself must go out of their way to say that "farmer" is not what *hyakushō* originally meant. Nevertheless, public education in the modern era has entrenched this idea even more thoroughly.

If historians were strict about the meaning of words and upheld the iron principles of empirical research, this kind of mistake would have been cleared up long ago. But there is one other trap into which many have fallen.

Historians basically rely on written documents, many of which are produced in the course of the administration of the state. In light of this, it is not surprising that the agrarian fundamentalist state mostly produced documents about farming and fields. Moreover, the documents that have come down to us today were selectively saved, so only a small portion of the many documents produced in the past survive in the present. The state system has had a decisive influence on this process of selection.

Since taxes were based on land holdings, nearly every household from medieval to early modern times kept careful documents related to its fields. Under these circumstances, it is natural that such documents as land registers, land sale transactions, and materials related to the levy of land taxes would be the ones most likely to survive into the present.

An examination of the documents in the Tokikuni family storehouse shows that these kinds of documents constitute an extremely large proportion of the whole. The same holds true going back to the medieval period. The vast majority of documents remaining in temples or in the possession of aristocratic families are those related to the fields of estates or noble lands. Moreover, many still extant appeals of the villagers relate to taxes levied on fields. Generally, when villagers wanted their taxes lowered, they claimed that the rice crop had been blighted by insects or that the harvest would be reduced due to cold weather. In other words, they based their appeals for lowered rates by claiming agricultural losses. It is natural that these appeals were framed in this way since annual taxes were levied on fields.

If one only reads the tax appeals submitted by villagers, one would think that they were all farmers, even though many spent the majority of their time and effort engaged in nonagricultural production. For that reason, we historians believed that the villagers we see in historical documents were unquestionably farmers.

However, we have recently begun to examine other documents—whose numbers are admittedly smaller—which were once meant to be disposed of but were reused and, through their recycling, survived. The best examples are the wooden tablets (*mokkan*) found at the excavation of Heijō Palace.[18]

---

18. See chapters six and seven for more detailed discussions of these wooden strips. See also William Wayne Farris, *Sacred Texts and Buried Treasures: Issues in the Historical Archaeology of Ancient Japan* (Honolulu: University of Hawai'i Press, 1998), chapter 4, "Wooden Tablets." As Farris reports (201), as late as 1978 only 30,000 such tablets were known to exist. In the twenty years since, approximately 140,000 more have been discovered. The discovery of the Heijō Palace tablets was made in the winter of 1961.

Many of these served as a kind of label; once used, they were thrown away. However, since the Heijō Palace is situated on marshy land, the tablets were unearthed in nearly pristine condition. Many were labels for marine products. Under the Ritsuryō system, marine products were carried to the capital from various regions, and it is only with the discovery of these tablets that we have begun to realize how significant they were.

In another famous example, a number of family registries discarded in the Nara period have survived because the paper on which they were written was reused by the great Nara temple Tōdaiji to keep records of the treasures in its possession. From the late Heian period as well, there are any number of documents that were reused as scrap paper for diaries and other records. Paper was a precious item, so many documents that might otherwise have been thrown away were turned over and the backs used for diaries or records. Japanese historians call these "backside documents," *shihai monjo*. In general, people who participated in nonagricultural industries appear more frequently in these backside documents than in the documents preserved by the usual routes. Another characteristic particular to these "backside documents" is that many are related to movable goods. As a result, these documents give us a picture of a world quite different from that preserved in the mainstream documents.

Documents have also been discovered inside screens and sliding, insulated, lattice-frame doors (*fusuma*) dating from the Momoyama to the Edo periods. We call these *fusuma* insulation documents, *fusuma shitabari monjo*. They are documents that would ordinarily have been thrown away but were recycled as a lining or insulation inside *fusuma*, and in this way they were unintentionally preserved for us today. Both households of the Tokikuni, upper and lower, preserved their *fusuma*, so we were able to remove the insulation documents from some of the older doors and examine them one by one.

After we completed our investigation of the documents kept in the storehouse, we turned to the *fusuma* documents. So far we have come across some surprising facts. We had heard that both households operated Kitamaebune ships in the late Edo period, and we have the ships' storage chests themselves. But none of the nearly ten thousand documents preserved in the upper Tokikuni storehouse directly substantiated the existence of these ships. When we examined the *fusuma* documents, however, we found many shipping receipts and product lists. Without a doubt, these were documents that the upper Tokikuni family no longer had any need for, so the papers were turned over to a crafts-man, who mounted them inside the *fusuma* for use as insulation.

Thanks to Izumi Masahiro's research of these documents, we were able to confirm for the first time that the Tokikuni family owned and operated four Kitamaebune ships. That is, they had at least four ships large enough to carry eight hundred to one thousand *koku* of goods, which they sailed from Osaka to Hokkaido, trading in goods worth more than a thousand *ryō* and making a profit of three hundred *ryō*. Moreover, we were able to ascertain, through Izumi Masahiro's and Kitsukawa Toshitada's investigation of the *fusuma* documents of the Inoike Mitsuo family of Outer Noto, that these ships sailed as far north as Sakhalin.[19] These documents also showed us that the upper Tokikuni family acted as financiers, using the money earned by the ships they owned. In other words, throughout the Edo period the upper Tokikuni were large-scale entrepreneurs.

Research by Sekiguchi Hiroo turned up other surprises. A sailor on one of these boats, one Tomonosuke, appears in the documents kept in the Tokikuni storehouse as an indentured servant (*genin*) who rented a small portion of Tokikuni land for farming. In other words, if we go only by the documents in the storehouse, we see Tomonosuke as a poor indentured ser-vant of the Tokikuni and a small subsistence farmer. But in the world of the *fusuma* documents Tomonosuke was a great sailor who was entrusted by the Tokikuni to make transactions of up to one thousand *ryō*. This illustrates how big a difference there is between the worlds represented in the docu-

---

19. The *fusuma* documents of the Inoike family provide a great tale of historical accidents. The Inoike family is located in the hills well inland from the coast, but the *fusuma* in the house were brought there from the coastal village of Sosogi as part of a bride's dowry. Some years later her natal home burned to the ground. The only thing that survived of the family's history were the *fusuma* that she had taken with her to her new home in the hills, the very same *fusuma* that were filled with her family's decades of scrap paper. By the early 1990s, Inoike Mitsuo, grandson of the *fusuma*-bearing bride, had replaced his grandmother's doors, but in the process he had the foresight to remove and store the thousands of scraps of paper that had filled them before he disposed of the frames.

These *fusuma* documents also revealed the tremendous amount of work facing historians of early modern Japan. In placing the documents inside the *fusuma*, little concern was given to preserving them whole. Since they were turned into scrap, they were frequently cut into several pieces to fit the door. When Amino's group was given access to the documents, the first task was attempting to reconstruct some of the documents out of the thousands of scraps jumbled together. It was literally like trying to piece together a jigsaw puzzle. Thanks to hard work, several of the longer documents were reconstructed, but the task was so time consuming that little more study has been done. Multiply the situation at the Inoike household by the tens of thousands of other households in Japan that possibly (and unwittingly) possess *fusuma* documents, and you have an idea of just how much more work remains to be done.

ments purposefully preserved in storehouses and those unintentionally preserved inside the *fusuma*.

Up to now, very few historians have carefully examined these *fusuma* documents. Of course, the number of early modern documents is staggering, and for the most part historians have not had a chance to examine the *fusuma* materials. Yet because of that everyone fell into a trap. Much of the world of sailors and mountain folk can be found in these latter documents, which were meant to be thrown away. This was an alternative world that must be brought to light or our image of Japanese society will remain distorted.

Academia was unable to avoid this agrarianist distortion for other reasons as well. Confucianists in the early modern period were for the most part agrarian fundamentalists. The European scholarship that was introduced in the modern era was also largely economic history that centered on agriculture. Of course, there were also some Europeans who looked at commerce, but in general economic history has been focused on agriculture. The medieval period in Japan has been characterized as a feudal system based on agricultural slavery, and it is commonly assumed that the feudal lords who ruled the farmers were in a position of absolute control. Marxist historians were in agreement on this point.

So Japanese economic historical terminology is dominated by words rooted in this agricultural mind-set, such as *wealthy farmer, middle farmer, poor farmer, wealthy landowner, subsistence farmer, agricultural slaves,* and so on. Sea and mountain folk have been completely ignored. There are almost no terms in academia to describe these people. Likewise, we possess no academic terms to accurately express the multiple activities of a family like the Tokikuni. Even if you coin terms for seamen who seem solidly characterized by terms of indenture, such as sea slave (*kainu*) or fishing slave (*gyonu*), no one in academia will understand. Nevertheless, since these people did not possess land, there is no way to use terms based on farming to convey an accurate sense of their lives. Thus, we are forced to conclude that academic terminology is imbued with agrarian fundamentalist ideology. Even analysis of the ruling class employs terms such as *feudal lord, private domain holder, local lord,* and so on, all of which are linked to agriculture.

In my research, I have focused on the lives of those who did not participate in agriculture. My work has often been seen as focused on an insignificant minority from which little could be concluded about Japanese society as a whole. Others have argued that it is ridiculous to theorize about the emperor in terms of a connection to nonagricultural people. But if *hyakushō* were not farmers, then nonagricultural people cannot be said to have been a minority. Of this I am certain, so I have attempted to present a vision of Japanese society that includes nonagricultural peoples along with farmers and thereby set in motion a thorough reconsideration of Japanese history.

CHAPTER TWO

The Maritime View
of the Japanese Archipelago

WAS JAPAN AN ISOLATED ISLAND COUNTRY?

In the previous chapter, I demonstrated how the deeply held conviction among Japanese that *hyakushō* were farmers was mistaken. As I suggested, a very high percentage of those classed within a category of *hyakushō* were engaged in industries other than agriculture. The task of this chapter is to indicate the significance of this new insight in macrohistorical terms. When we reexamine the history of the society of the Japanese archipelago in light of this new understanding, all of our commonsensical images become subject to revision.

According to the prevailing view, rice cultivation was introduced into the Japanese islands at some point between the late Jōmon (14,000 B.C.E.–300 B.C.E.) and early Yayoi (300 B.C.E.–300 C.E.). From that time on, society became essentially agricultural, with rice production at its core. Believed to be isolated from the Asian continent by the ocean, this rice-cultivating society was held to have been self-sufficient. But I argue that this view is biased and presents a false image of early society in the islands.

First of all, the idea that the islands were separated from the Asian continent is strictly one-sided. Without a doubt, the ocean can function as an obstacle that can separate people. But that is only one way of looking at it. The ocean can also have the opposite, and extremely important, function of being a pliable transportation route that links peoples.

The Japanese archipelago is composed of more than 3,700 islands, each of which is linked by the ocean. We know that from early on people and things circulated across the waters between the islands, the Asian continent, the islands of Southeast Asia, and even islands further south. Within the archipelago itself, lakes, rivers, and even mountains had important roles as transportation routes. Each of these features also generated a wealth of commodities. Thus, these environmental features all possessed great meaning for peoples' lives. Our inquiry into how society in the archipelago has changed over time must examine not just the paddies and fields of the plains but the functions of the ocean, lakes, rivers, and mountains.

We have recently obtained clear evidence that people were living throughout the archipelago during the period when the islands were connected to the continent in the early Stone Age. Until this information came to light, the culture of the people of the Jōmon period was considered to be unique to the Japanese islands. It is true that the culture of the Jōmon period constituted the most basic level of "Japanese Island culture." But we are often presented with maps that depict the Jōmon cultural sphere as restricted to the territory of the present-day Japanese nation. As a result of these assumptions, we find lines drawn on the maps (or, more commonly, shading) separating the island of Tsushima from the Korean Peninsula or Hokkaido from Sakhalin. Okinawa, particularly the outer islands of Miyako and Yaeyama, is also placed in a different cultural sphere. But this does not make sense.

Some time ago I had the opportunity to travel to Tsushima by boat. The trip from Kyushu to Tsushima was particularly difficult for me. I did not get seasick, but I had to endure several hours of the boat rolling from side to side before we reached the island. In contrast, the Korean Peninsula is close enough to be visible from Tsushima on a clear day. According to the maps we commonly see today, Jōmon culture is supposed to have crossed the rough channel between Kyushu and Tsushima, but the same maps would have us believe that Jōmon culture was unable to cross the far shorter distance between Tsushima and Korea. How is it possible that the Jōmon people could not cross the short distance between Tsushima and Korea but could cross the rough waters of the Genkai Sea? Is it not unnatural to think that the Jōmon was an isolated "island" culture restricted solely to the Japanese islands? This was the commonsense notion of archaeologists until quite recently.

Research conducted by Watanabe Makoto of Nagoya University has swept this "common sense" away. Watanabe has shown conclusively that a common culture characterized a region that included the east and south coast of Korea, the islands of Tsushima and Iki, and northern Kyushu, a fishermen's culture that used conjoined fishhooks, stone anchors, and Sobata-style earthenware.[1] According to Watanabe, the culture of this region was also related to the cultures whose remains are found from Okinawa to the San'in region of Honshu and the Inland Sea. With this evidence, we know that people have traveled across to the Korean Peninsula and among the Japanese islands since the Jōmon period. In no sense was Jōmon culture limited to the territory of present-day "Japan," nor was it limited to the Japanese islands. In fact, it is clear that it had deep ties to the Asian continent.

Similar discoveries have been made time and again since Watanabe's work first appeared in the early 1970s. According to Mori Kōichi, for example, obsidian from Oki Island has been recovered in archaeological digs at sites all along the Sea of Japan, and obsidian from Kōzu Island near Izu has been found all over the eastern part of Honshu. Thus, obsidian was transported across a wide area, which can only be attributed to the sea borne trade. Likewise, stone tools closely resembling those of the early Jōmon period have recently been discovered in sites along the Japan sea coast. Thus, it appears certain that culture from northeastern Asia crossed the northern seas into the Japanese archipelago early on.

In the field of linguistics, Ono Susumu has argued along similar lines, claiming that Japanese has its origins in Polynesian languages. He has also recently noted a relation to Tamil. I do not have the expertise to argue on the merits of his theories, but we must give due consideration to the movements from the south as well.

JŌMON CULTURE

As mentioned earlier, the ocean was an important means of transport within the archipelago, as can be demonstrated by countless examples. During the expansion of the Chitose airport in Hokkaido, a large amount of jade was discovered at a Jōmon period site that has come to be known as the Bibi remains. This jade came from the Itoigawa area of Niigata, on the Japan Sea coast; over time, a huge volume of goods was carried over the ocean from Niigata to Hokkaido. Moreover, the remains of what appears to have been

---

1. See Watanabe Makoto, *Jōmon jidai no gyogyō* (The Jōmon Period and Fishing) (Tokyo: Yūzankaku shuppan, 1973).

an obsidian mine have been found in Nagano. There was a very active trade in obsidian in the Japanese islands, the widespread distribution of obsidian being not at all incidental in nature. Thus, even in the Jōmon period, obsidian was produced on the presumption that it would be traded. The standard line has it that the beginnings of commerce dated from a later period, but it is clear from the case of obsidian that commerce was already taking place in the Jōmon period.

Obsidian was not the only commercial product of the time; salt presents us with a similar case. Since there is no rock salt in the Japanese islands, it had to be processed from seawater. The excavation of large vats on the coast near Kasumigaura suggests that salt was produced in large stoneware vessels in the late Jōmon period. Salt was manufactured by extracting salty water from boiled seaweed. When salt is produced in such stonewater vats, it can be made in substantial quantities. I believe it is likely that this salt was produced for trade. This salt also made it possible to preserve, and thus trade, fish and shellfish. Therefore, trade in salt and preserved seafood was probably one of the earliest forms of commerce in the Japanese islands and salt traders and fishmongers the earliest merchants.

Our prevailing image of the Jōmon period has been one of nearly naked people—lightly covered with furs and skins and running about barefoot—hunting animals with bows and arrows or stones. However, this image must be revised. For clothing, they had textiles woven from the fibers of plants like wisteria and vines as well as woven bags for carrying nuts (fig. 9). Jōmon people also wore shoes. Their tools were not limited to bows, arrows, and stones; they also used fairly highly developed wooden tools. A neatly lacquered woman's hairpin was discovered at the famous Jōmon period Torihama remains at Lake Sanpōgo in Wakasa. The Sannai Maruyama remains in Aomori City also yielded a large number of magnificent lacquerware items, along with a surprising number of stoneware artifacts. The Sannai Maruyama site also contains the remains of a number of huge, evenly spaced pillars, suggesting that the people of this era had some type of measuring tools.

Thus, life and culture in the Jōmon period was rich and complex. Although primarily a fishing and hunting society, it also exhibited some sophistication in the gathering and processing of nuts, and archaeologists have recovered some evidence of the cultivation of plants and trees. Gourds have been discovered at the Torihama site along with sesame and bitter cucumber seeds. Gourds, in particular, are not native to the Japanese islands, so one can

Figure 9. A Jōmon-era purse found at the Sannai Maruyama site. Photograph courtesy of *Bunkazai Hogo-ka, Aomori-ken Kyōiku-chō.*

only conclude that they were imported and cultivated. Millet has also been discovered at Jōmon sites, leading to the hypothesis that dry field agriculture began in the late Jōmon period. Thus, while we tend to think of Jōmon people as strictly hunter-gatherers, I believe that planting and cultivation technologies were established in the Japanese archipelago at least by the latter part of the Jōmon period. Since rice cultivation was also introduced at this time, it is clear that Jōmon people had a diverse culture.

As mentioned earlier, we have found pillars constructed from huge trees at sites all along the Japan Sea coastline—from the Mawaki remains in Noto to the Sannai Maruyama remains. So archaeologists also call this a "gigantic pillar culture." We are not sure whether these pillars were parts of buildings or sites of worship. Either way, these enormous pillars could not have been raised without a fairly high level of social organization. Thus, it appears that, along with a series of wide-ranging trade relationships, each local society was considerably complex in and of itself. Of course, this does not necessarily imply a hierarchical structure of power with rulers and ruled, but one must consider the possibility that there existed leaders of some kind.

I began my discussion with the Jōmon period because we have had a tendency to view the Yayoi period as the era when rice cultivation began. Fixation on this idea has led to an obsession with rice cultivation. As a result, we have long believed that society in the Japanese archipelago was uniformly centered around rice. This leads us to ignore the development throughout the Jōmon period of a variety of industries with their consequent technologies and cultures. If we do not recognize the fact that the people of the Jōmon period engaged in a variety of forms of production and were linked across a wide area, then we cannot fully understand the cultures and societies that came afterward.

YAYOI CULTURE

Rice cultivation in the Japanese islands is usually believed to have begun in the Yayoi period. However, because rice cultivation actually began earlier, in parts of the Inland Sea region and northern Kyushu, prior to the Yayoi era, rice cultivation and Yayoi tools do not always come as a set. Nevertheless, by and large the technology needed for rice cultivation arrived as part of a technological system brought in by a group that emigrated to the islands.

Rice cultivation was not the only new technology. A variety of cultural elements began to enter the western portion of the archipelago from China and the Korean Peninsula around 300 B.C. We believe that new dry field crops, bronze and iron tools, sericulture, and new weaving technologies, as well as improvements in salt vat production, were introduced at that time. Cormorant fishing also entered the western portion of the islands around this time, spreading to the entire archipelago by the medieval period. In other words, as a fishing method it was sufficient to support a lifestyle.

There are various debates over the sources of Yayoi culture, but it seems likely that for the most part it came from southern China and the Korean Peninsula. On the one hand, the know-how to make metal tools and gigantic stone dolmens spread from the Korean Peninsula into northern Kyushu. On the other, cormorant fishing and the recently excavated remains at Yoshinogari have drawn attention to connections with southern China.

Around 300 B.C. Yayoi-style rice cultivation quickly spread throughout western Japan, affecting the territory west of a line from Ise Bay to Wakasa Bay. It is true that remains of rice paddies have recently been uncovered in the northern prefecture of Aomori, so we know that rice spread even that far north. But this appears to have been a temporary phenomenon; rice cultivation became permanently established in the north much later.

Yayoi culture originally crossed the ocean and spread along the coasts and up the rivers; therefore, the people who brought it must have had a strong connection with the ocean and would have possessed advanced sailing technologies. There are many shell mounds from the Yayoi period, so we know that fishing, salt production, and hunting and gathering continued as before. Thus, I believe that Yayoi culture cannot be understood solely with reference to rice, as is so common today. Instead we must also take into consideration its relation to the ocean.

Exchanges with the Asian continent and the Korean Peninsula were more frequent and intimate than we have supposed. Yayoi stoneware produced in Japan has been unearthed in the southern portion of the Korean Peninsula. Although this is a topic of some debate, I believe that a group known as the *wajin* with a strong connection to the sea came into being through trade within the western portion of Japan, the southern portion of Korea, and the Chinese continent. Under no circumstances should the *wajin* be considered the "ancient Japanese." They were the bearers of Yayoi culture in the western portion of the Japanese islands, but they were also a people whose lives centered on the sea, moving among the regions of southern Korea and parts of the Chinese continent.

This is well documented in *Wei zhi wei ren chuan*, a Chinese text produced in the latter part of the Yayoi period. The text states that there was no agriculture in Tsushima and that its people lived by trading to the north and south. The text records a similar situation for Iki, another island located between the Korean Peninsula and the Japanese islands, where the few fields that did exist were insufficient to support the population. On Iki as well, trade was an important element of local life. In this regard, the text records a similar state at a place called Matsura—now known as the Matsuura region. As these observations all refer to islands, they can be applied to the Japanese archipelago as a whole.

Since Yayoi society initially developed through trade, it is hard to believe that there ever was a "self-sufficient" society in the archipelago, as the history textbooks mentioned in chapter one assert. The assumption that a certain level of population in a given area requires a commensurate amount of paddy and dry field cultivation is based on the premise that a sustainable lifestyle must depend primarily on agriculture. It ignores other forms of production such as fishing, hunting, and gathering and is thus misleading.

The *Wei zhi wei ren chuan* also states, "There are markets where exchange is conducted in every province." The province referred to in the text was approximately the size of a present-day county or perhaps even a little smaller. Nevertheless, the importance of exchange in this society is demonstrated by the fact that each province had a market. Society could not have developed without these marketplaces.

The people of the plains produced grains as well as such crops as mulberries, sumac (for lacquer), hemp (for flax), and ramie, not to mention the various products processed from these materials. Horses and cows were raised in pasture lands at higher altitudes. Coastal peoples brought in foodstuffs from the sea, while mountain peoples gathered fruits and nuts and lumber to produce charcoal, wooden tools, lacquerware, and, with wood as fuel, pottery. Iron and copper, mined and refined in the mountains, were processed into iron and bronze implements. Once we take all of this into consideration, we can see that this society was founded on the basis of a wide variety of products that were exchanged over a broad area.

While a division of labor between mountain and coastal peoples emerged during the Jōmon period, it appears that specialization on the part of the plains people emerged in the Yayoi. Thus, the primitive commercial activity of the Jōmon period— in which such materials as salt, seafood, and stone tools were exchanged—became even more widespread in the Yayoi. Specialized merchants probably did not exist; instead the producers themselves traveled widely to conduct their trade.

We can tell from the distribution of remains and artifacts from this period—which are generally located along waterways—that rivers and the ocean served as the primary means of transportation supporting this trade.

It seems likely that these waterways were more active than previously imagined and that a number of transportation routes were established very early on across the entire archipelago. For example, it appears that there was at the time a heavily traveled route from the Inland Sea into Osaka Bay, up the Yodo River, and further up the Uji River, where, after a brief journey by land, Lake Biwa could be crossed. After another short trip across land, the Japan Sea and points north were fully accessible. Moreover, curved jewels called *magatama* from the Hokuriku region on the Japan Sea have been uncovered in large amounts in Chiba Prefecture on the Pacific coast. This suggests that there were well-traveled river and land routes spanning the central mountains and the Kanto plains, linking the Japan Sea and the Pacific Ocean coasts of Honshu. River travel in particular was carried out on a scale unimaginable today.

CULTURAL DIFFERENCES BETWEEN
WESTERN AND EASTERN JAPAN

Nevertheless, despite the connecting trade routes, there remained stark differences between the eastern and western portions of the archipelago in this period. Although this disparity had existed since the Stone Age and Jōmon periods, a major contributing factor to it was the rapid spread of Yayoi culture across the west as far as Ise and Wakasa. However, for two hundred years thereafter the Yayoi cultural sphere did not expand further because it encountered the stiff resistance of Jōmon culture. As a result, a clear distinction between the Jōmon culture of the east and the Yayoi culture of the west continued for a relatively long time. When considering later social developments, we must keep this division between the eastern and western regions of Japan in mind.

For example, Aoba Takashi's 1981 study, *Vegetables*, draws on research in turnip genes to show that turnips of the Siberian/European type were found in Kanto, Tohoku, and Hokuriku while the Chinese/Korean type was distributed throughout the western portion of the islands.[2] Drawing on precise research of botanists such as Aoba, we can conclude that a number of cultural attributes entered eastern Japan from the north. There was probably a route from Hokkaido to northern Honshu, and goods also crossed the northern

---

2. Aoba Takashi, *Yasai* (Vegetables) (Tokyo: Hōsei daigaku shuppankyoku, 1981).

Japan Sea. In any case, this shows that the routes from China and Korea to the western portion of the archipelago were not the only routes into the Japanese islands. Therefore, the difference between western Yayoi and eastern Jōmon cultures cannot be understood in reference to the Japanese islands alone.

Most theories of Japanese culture and society have operated on the following premise: advanced culture and technology from China and the Korean Peninsula first entered northern Kyushu and from there moved into the Inland Sea and the Kinki region. In other words, advanced culture moved from the west into the backward regions of the east. This cultural migration was believed to have had a definitive influence on later social development in the Japanese islands.

However, I believe this view must be thoroughly revised. We must also look at the influx of a different culture from northeastern Asia, which entered through Sakhalin and Hokkaido into northern Honshu and the Kanto Plain or across the Japan Sea into Hokuriku and the San'in coast. We must construct a more synthetic and comprehensive understanding of the state of culture and society at the time in light of such exchanges between the cultures of east and west.

The same thing can be said for rice cultivation. Traces of Yayoi culture appear in the eastern portion of the islands from around 100 B.C., with rice cultivation spreading to the southern portion of Tohoku. But we must remember that equating rice cultivation with social progress reflects the perspective of western Japan. The culture of the east cannot be accurately grasped from that perspective.

Even as the peoples of the eastern portion of the archipelago absorbed and adopted the technologies of rice cultivation, they continued to develop an independent culture. Recognition of independent eastern cultural development reminds us that one cannot simply say that the west was advanced and the east backward. There were many progressive elements in the east, as is clearly reflected in the history of the islands after the establishment of a state in the sixth and seventh centuries. Mulberries, for example, were widely grown in the eastern portion of the islands, and sericulture was widely practiced there from the Yayoi period on. Moreover, the modes of rice cultivation in the west and east were quite different. Rice cultivation in the east was developed alongside dry field production of hemp, ramie, and mulberries. The significance of this will become clear when we consider what happened after the establishment of the first state.

THE TOMB PERIOD

The third to fifth centuries A.D. are usually called the early Tomb period. This period was marked by early political activities around the Inland Sea, from the Kinki region of Osaka, Kyoto, and Nara to northern Kyushu and the Izumo and Kibi areas to the west. Among the various "kings" of these regions, one, known as the Great King (ōkimi), came to occupy a position of primacy within the group. Another well-known sovereign, Himiko of the kingdom of Yamatai, was known as "Wao" (The Queen of Wa). As mentioned earlier, there is a great deal of debate among historians today over whether Yamatai was in the Kinki region (Osaka-Nara) or northern Kyushu.

The movement of people and goods between the archipelago and China and Korea became even more pronounced during this period, with a variety of technologies entering Kyushu, the Inland Sea, and Kinki region from the west. Horses and iron were among the most significant items to be introduced at this time, raising the hotly debated issue of the arrival of a "horse-riding people."[3] While I am not a specialist in this area, even if we do not think of their arrival as an "invasion" of a different race, it is clear that riding technology came as a discrete culture in a series of waves. Moreover, the number of people who moved into the western portion of the archipelago from the continent during the Yayoi and Tomb periods was not on the scale of ten or twenty thousand but approached several hundred thousand to a million over the course of about a thousand years. Hanihara Kazurō insists that there are too many puzzles that cannot be solved unless the migration of this period is recognized as having been on such a large scale.[4] I will not go into the details of his genetic research here, but according to Hanihara there is a very close physical resemblance between the peoples of western Japan and Korea. In fact, the differences between the people of western and eastern Japan are far greater than those between the people of western Japan and

---

3. Amino is referring to a debate begun by Egami Namio in 1948. For a good English-language overview of the debate, see William Wayne Farris, *Sacred Texts and Buried Treasures: Issues in the Historical Archaeology of Japan* (Honolulu: University of Hawai'i Press, 1998), 62–63. In brief, Egami postulated that the Japanese islands were invaded by a horse-riding people from the continent who went on to establish the archaic Japanese state.

4. See, for example, Hanihara Kazurō, "The Origin of the Japanese in Relation to Other Ethnic Groups in East Asia," in *Windows on the Japanese Past: Studies in Archaeology and Prehistory*, ed. Richard J. Pearson, Gina Lee Barnes, and Karl L. Hutterer (Ann Arbor: Center for Japanese Studies, University of Michigan, 1986); and "Estimation of the Number of Early Immigrants to Japan: A Simulative Study," *Journal of the Anthropological Society of Nippon* 95.3 (July 1987): 391–403.

Korea. The people of eastern Japan, on the other hand, are closer to the Ainu, who themselves are similar to the Okinawans. Hanihara argues that these latter groups represent remnants of an old Mongoloid strain. People of a new Mongoloid type came into the islands from the west during the Yayoi period. While the issue of migration into the archipelago continues to be debated, there is no question that a relatively large number of people moved into the western portion of the Japanese islands from the Asian continent. Attendant upon this long-term migration was the introduction of a variety of cultures and technologies. However, we must also remember that the influx of overseas cultures during this period did not come only from the west.

The conventional wisdom is that the spread of large tombs was itself equivalent to the spread of the influence of the Yamato clans. As the Yamato federation of clans with its Queen of Wa/Great King enlarged its sphere of influence, leaders of other regions adopted the keyhole-shaped tombs of the Yamato.[5] There were, of course, relations between Yamato and other regions, but even in the case of ancient tombs we must recognize that there were cultural differences between Yamato, the northern Kyushu regions, and other regions in the archipelago. Each region, in other words, had its own tomb style.

For example, on Noto Island in Ishikawa Prefecture there is a peculiarly shaped tomb called the Ezoana Tomb (fig. 10). This tomb has drawn a great deal of attention for the ways in which it differs from the keyhole-shaped tombs with which most Japanese are familiar. One theory suggests that it was constructed under the influence of the ancient Korean state Koguryŏ, which controlled the northern portion of the Korean Peninsula and parts of northeastern China. At a recent international symposium hosted by the Japanese archaeologist Mori Kōichi, there was a great deal of debate over the question of whether the person buried in this tomb had come directly from Koguryŏ. While there was no resolution of this particular point, there was a general consensus regarding the distinctive character of the tomb. The participants also agreed that the possibility of culture being carried across the Japan Sea from the north required greater attention, since in the eighth century emissaries crossed the Japan Sea from the Bohai Sea region near present-day Tianjin.

Variation in tomb shape is not the only indication of regional differences. Recent studies have suggested that horses and "horse culture" did

5. For a nice visual illustration of this process, see the outline of regional tomb development in Joan R. Piggott's *The Emergence of Japanese Kingship* (Stanford: Stanford University Press, 1997), 32–33.

Figure 10. Suso Ezoana Tomb. Photograph courtesy of Board of Education, Nanao City, Ishikawa Prefecture.

not enter the islands solely from the west. This has not yet been proven irrefutably; nevertheless, riding gear recovered from fifth- and sixth-century tombs in Northern Honshu and the Kanto Plain has provided supporting evidence. In addition, Kanto and the Kōshin region just to its west, as well as the Emishi region of northern Honshu, were known as horse-breeding areas in the eighth and ninth centuries. So it appears likely that the introduction of horses could not have been only from the west. We must also give thought to the likelihood of the diffusion of a number of cultural elements from the north.

The same goes for iron technologies. The conventional wisdom has held that materials necessary for iron production entered the islands from Korea, passing through northern Kyushu, disseminating throughout the islands, and eventually gravitating toward the western Honshu Mountains and the Ōmi Plain. The technology for minting is also said to have been transmitted from west to east. But lately there has been growing interest in the suggestion that there was another, independent route from the north by which these technologies entered. Early kilns of a structure different from those in the west have been found in northern Honshu and Kanto. Moreover, the raw material for iron production in the west was "iron sand," while in the east it was probably produced from mined ore. In the case of minting, the remains of a ninth-century mint have been discovered in southern Tohoku. We also know that there was a mint in Noto during the Heian period. It has been suggested that both of these were developed with northern technology. Thus, the influx of culture into the archipelago was not only from the west.

The same is true for the south. A tribe known as the Hayato in southern Kyushu clearly shared a common culture with Amami and Okinawa to the south. Likewise, the tombs of the Hayato are of a different character from the keyhole tombs associated with the Yamato clans. For these reasons, I believe that the attempt to examine Japanese culture as solely deriving from a cultural influx from the west—based on the spread of Yamato rice paddy culture—must be revised.

TRADE RELATIONS WITH SURROUNDING REGIONS

With the advent of the Tomb period, the flow of goods and peoples along the seas and rivers became even more active, and the federation of leaders in the Kinki region known as "the Yamato court" came to have an increasingly close-knit relationship with the leaders of the eastern portion of the islands. These relations were maintained in the form of tribute. Tribute would be offered to the Yamato court, which would provide return gifts in acknowledgment. The movement of goods and peoples as well as the transmission of information that went along with a tribute economy picked up pace again during the transition from the Yayoi to the Tomb period. This was true not only in the case of relations between the Yamato court and other regions, for these regions engaged in independent and wide-ranging trade among themselves as well. A particularly well-traveled route cut across the archipelago from northern Kyushu through the Inland Sea and into Osaka Bay, over Lake Biwa, and up the northern Japan Sea coast (Hokuriku).

At the beginning of the sixth century, the royal line that ruled in Yamato produced no heir. In place of a direct heir, a man known as Keitai (r. 507?–31) moved south from the Echizen region into Yamato to become the new ōkimi. The traces of Keitai's movements can be found in Echizen,

Ōmi, Owari, Mino, Kawachi, and Settsu. After traveling across a wide area, visiting consorts in several places—including a consort in Owari named Menoko-hime—he finally settled in Yamato. It is also recorded that at one time all of the consorts gathered together in the place where the new *ōkimi* resided.[6]

In any case, it is clear that the routes from Echizen into Lake Biwa, passing through Ōmi to Kawachi—or again going upstream along the rivers from Echizen, crossing the mountains into Mino, and exiting into Owari—were important arteries for the circulation of goods and people. Thus, pan-archipelago routes for the exchange of people, goods, and information had become firmly established by the Tomb period. Only on this basis could a royal succession spanning several regions—such as that of Keitai—take place. Furthermore, given the existence of water routes through the Inland Sea and along the Japan sea coast, which connected Yamato and the Echizen region to the Korean Peninsula and the Asian continent, it does not make sense for historians to restrict Keitai's sphere of activity to the islands alone.

In fact, a war that historians call the Iwai Rebellion took place shortly after Keitai's succession. Although it is generally called a rebellion, the concept of a revolt presumes a single center (against which the rebellion is launched), which in this case was presumed to be Yamato. But Yamato was not the only center of power during this period. Therefore, this disturbance should not be considered a rebellion but a war between the Yamato kingdom and the Iwai kingdom of northern Kyushu. At the same time, we cannot limit our view of the war to a struggle confined to the Iwai and Yamato kingdoms, for the Yamato had allied itself with the Kaya principality of the Korean Peninsula, while the Iwai joined with the kingdom of Silla, also of Korea. Therefore, the Iwai war was not limited to the Japanese islands alone. Rather, these alliances linked the struggle between two kingdoms in Japan to the struggle between two kingdoms on the Korean Peninsula. We cannot understand this kind of war unless we recognize the existence of tightly knit transportation routes along the Inland Sea, northern Kyushu, and across the Japan Sea to the peninsula and the continent.

Shifting our focus to the Japan Sea, we note that there was at this time an extremely active route running along the coast from San'in north to Hokkaido. Jewelry produced by craftsmen in Sado and Echigo was exported in huge quantities to Yamato, and many pieces have also been found along

6. See Mawaki Teiji, Mori Kōichi, and Amino Yoshihiko, eds., *Keitai ōkimi to Owari no Menoko-hime* (Emperor Keitai and Princess Menoko of Owari) (Tokyo: Shōgakkan, 1994).

the San'in coast all the way to Izumo. This, too, would be inexplicable without reference to the Japan Sea routes.

Until quite recently, the waters in the Enshū Sea (off the coast of present-day Shizuoka Prefecture) were very rough, and crossing them was quite difficult. It was thus commonly believed that the Pacific coast route was not fully functional until the Edo period. However, ocean trade routes were surprisingly active even in those seas from early times. For example, we have accurate evidence that pieces of Sue stoneware, produced on the shores of Lake Hamana,[7] were imported into the Kanto region in great numbers as early as the Tomb period. When editing the town history of Miwa in Ibaraki Prefecture a few years ago, the editorial collective took all the pottery fragments unearthed from tombs and other sites in the town and carefully analyzed them. We found that the majority were from the Sue kiln. This pottery had to cross the rough Enshū Sea to reach Miwa. Transportation of large quantities of pottery along land routes was impossible, so it was usually carried by water. Therefore, the discovery of Sue fragments in Miwa reveals that the Pacific routes were already relatively stable by the Tomb period.

I also believe that there was considerable movement of people and goods between the Okinawan islands and the Japanese archipelago. Gohoura shells, used for making bracelets in the southern islands, were transported into northern Kyushu during the Yayoi period (fig. 11). The custom of wearing such bracelets even reached as far as Yamato. Thus, we must always think of the Japanese islands as open on four sides (rather than closed in) by the ocean.

I mentioned earlier that trade had been conducted since the Jōmon period and that by the Yayoi there were marketplaces in every region. By the Tomb period, a certain critical mass had been reached that made possible what might be called a cash economy. We find clear examples of primitive currency in archaeological digs dating to this era. A wide variety of commodity currencies were used as means of payment and measures of value. Thus, it is not unreasonable to call this a cash economy. Although there are a number of debates concerning the origins of currency, in this period it appears that the main commodity serving as a means of exchange in the western portion of the islands was rice. In the east, it was cloth or silk. Rice was a sacred grain—offered to the gods and received from the gods in return. The same perspective applied to textiles. They became a kind of currency by

7. Lake Hamana is on the western edge of Shizuoka Prefecture and drains into the Enshū Sea. Amino is stating that the pottery produced there would have to be carried across the rough Enshū Sea and around the Izu Peninsula to be distributed in the Kanto region.

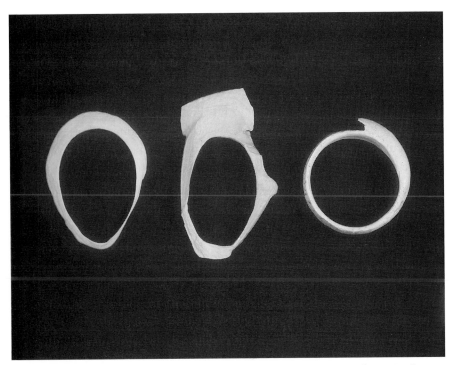

Figure 11. Seashell rings from Matsunoo site, Makurazaki City, Kagoshima Prefecture. Photograph courtesy of Board of Education, Makurazaki City, Kagoshima Prefecture.

being offered to the gods and then received in turn.[8] When similar exchanges were conducted in the profane world between human beings in the form of tribute and reward, cloth served to make the relationship particularly close. I believe that rice and silk became general means of exchange, taking on the function of currency through their role as offerings to the gods. In addition, salt, iron, and livestock functioned as currency.

By the Tomb period a primitive form of finance known as *suiko*—a process in which the first harvest, once offered to the gods, was used as capital, loaned out as seed, and recovered with interest as rice at the next harvest—was being practiced. Management of the storehouses containing this first-harvest rice was probably originally the task of local leaders, and through this practice "wealthy" people first began to appear. I believe it is reasonable to surmise that this primitive form of finance was conducted with capital in the form of rice and sake in the west and silk and cloth in the east.

8. See chapter seven.

Again, as mentioned above, the topography of the Japanese islands was quite different during the Tomb period from the way it is now. The ocean penetrated far into what is now dry land. Miwa is now an inland town with little water. But in ancient times it was on a large river and swamp, and during the Warring States period of the fifteenth and sixteenth centuries a naval battle was even fought there. Only those places where we have unearthed Yayoi remains were not underwater. Along the Japan Sea coast, there was a large inlet wherever a river flowed into the ocean. This is hard to imagine given today's landscape. The Noto Peninsula, for example, was almost cut in half by the Ouchi Inlets. If we do not acknowledge the importance of the natural features of the Japanese archipelago—the scarcity of plains and the preponderance of mountains, rivers, and coasts—there is no way to understand the development of its societies.

THE BIRTH OF JAPAN

The first true government to rule Honshu, Shikoku, and Kyushu—excepting northern Honshu and southern Kyushu—was established with its center in the Yamato/Kinai region around the end of the seventh century and the beginning of the eighth. It was with the emergence of this state that the name of the country changed from Wa to Nihon (Japan). This state also changed the name of its ruler from ōkimi to tennō (emperor). Thus, as I stated earlier, it is anachronistic to use the name Japan or the title emperor to refer to any period or ruler before the founding of this state. Such phrases as "Stone Age Japan" or "Yayoi period Japanese" are misleading.

In fact, once the state of Japan was established, society in the islands underwent a dramatic transformation. The ruling class systematically introduced the first genuine "civilization" into the Japanese archipelago through exchanges with the Asian continent during the sixth century. At the core of this civilizational influx was the Chinese Tang dynasty's system of governance. Society in the Japanese islands at the time was still comparatively undeveloped; one might say it was an "elastic" society. Onto this society the sixth-century ruling class grafted the rigid civilization of the Chinese mainland.

First, a family registration system was established in which all people living in territory controlled by the state were given uji (clan) and family names to be recorded, along with their ages, into registries. Then everyone over six years of age, including slaves, was allotted a certain amount of paddy land.

This land formed the basis of the new taxation system in which taxes were collected in rice (*so*), labor (*yō*), crafts (*chō*), and sundries (*zōyō*). A system of land administration—from the basic unit, a settlement composed of fifty registered households (*gō*), to a county (*gun*) and province (*kuni*)—was then established to extend imperial rule. All official business was to be conducted in writing, making the administration of the state thoroughly grounded in the principle of documents (*monjoshugi*). It was by means of this system that Chinese characters spread throughout the Japanese islands.

The primitive financial system of *suiko* was incorporated into the paddy-based taxation system. At the same time, the prior development of transportation routes made possible the collection of craft and labor taxes in the form of tribute (*mitsugi*). In other words, the new state drew upon developments prior to its establishment, but it also pulled products from every region toward its capital in the Kinai region. Artisans and performers, as those who possessed the accumulated technological knowledge of that society, were attached to general government agencies as well as regional administrative centers.

One other area in which the new state made a significant departure from prior conditions was in its emphasis on a land-based transportation system; paved roads, ten or more meters wide and as straight as possible, radiated out from the capital. The Tōkai, Tōsan, and Hokuriku roads ran to the east (and north), the San'in and San'yō roads to the west, and the Nankai road to the south, forming the axes of a broad regional system. The lone exception to the capital-centered roads was the Seikai road, which ran south from the city of Dazaifu. Since the reader will recall that most transportation prior to this had been on the ocean or along rivers, the state's determination to create a transportation system based on land is a clear departure from the past. Post stations were established along the government roads at ten-mile intervals (despite the predominance of rivers in the islands, we find almost no evidence of river stations). Only on the Mogami River, in the distant and isolated Dewa Province, do we find evidence of a river post. Thus, we must conclude that, at least at the administrative level, no consideration was given to river travel.

There are a number of reasons why such an odd system was established. Recent defeats at the hands of Tang (Chinese) and Silla (Korean) forces presented this early state with pressing military concerns. At a more fundamental level, it also appears that despite its small size this state had imperial ambitions common to archaic dynasties. A common characteristic of archaic states was the desire to expand their power in all directions, and road building was a principle physical expression of that desire. The roads of the Roman, Persian, and Incan empires, for example, were all built as straight as possible. On the basis of such common characteristics, we can see that the Ritsuryō state also aspired to the status of an imperial civilization.

Furthermore, as I stated in chapter one, the Ritsuryō state's governing system was based on an ideology of agrarian fundamentalism. Along with the important step of designating the rice paddy as the basis of its taxation system, the state's agrarian fundamentalism, supported by Confucianism, came to have a strong impact on the entire archipelago, well beyond its main base areas.

Only at this point did the Tsushima Strait come to be seen as a national border, and the island of Tsushima was fortified for defense against kingdoms on the Korean Peninsula. However, the Tsugaru Strait in northern Japan did not constitute a national border. The rulers of the Ritsuryō state saw the Eastern Country, stretching from the center of Honshu to the Kanto Plain, as a distinctly different region. This area was brought under control only through a dual policy of invasion and confederation. Although the Yamato state was concerned with the Eastern Country from the beginning, its control extended only to the Kanto Plain.

THE TERRITORY OF JAPAN

From the perspective of the ruling class of the Ritsuryō state (centered as it was in Yamato), all of northern Honshu and the northern part of Niigata—then known as Koshi—was an area known as Emishi. It was inhabited by a people the Ritsuryō rulers considered different. The same is true, of course, for Hokkaido. Southern Kyushu, home of the Hayato, was also outside the territory of Ritsuryō Japan. For nearly one hundred years after its founding, the Ritsuryō state fought to bring these territories under its control. In the strictest sense, then, the history of "Japanese" invasions is not limited to Toyotomi Hideyoshi's sixteenth-century invasion of Korea or the modern invasions of Korea and China. The ancient Japanese state invaded the lands of northern Honshu and southern Kyushu as well.

This clearly reveals the archaic imperial will of the first state of Japan. In order to extend its own power, the Japanese state invaded surrounding areas and attempted to bring them under its control. The people of northern Honshu resisted the invasion so stubbornly that the northernmost areas remained outside the state's control for centuries to come.

The province/county/hamlet administrative system was implemented throughout the state's territories. But the two northernmost peninsulas on Honshu—the Tsugaru and Shimokita Peninsulas—were not subject to this system until the eleventh and twelfth centuries. Until that time, these areas were composed of territorial units, or "villages," deemed to be outside the official sphere. Therefore, northernmost Honshu could not be considered part of the Japanese state in the strictest sense. This is why Tsugaru Strait did not constitute a national boundary.

Jōmon culture survived in Hokkaido even after most of Honshu had come under the sway of Yayoi culture. To be more precise, northern Jōmon culture was transformed into what has been called Satsumon culture in response to developments in the south.[9] Satsumon culture possessed its own kinds of stoneware and iron tools, and while it showed some signs of agricultural development, it brought fishing to an extremely advanced level. Most archaeologists believe that the Satsumon was not yet Ainu culture. It appears that Satsumon culture extended as far south as the northernmost sections of Honshu.

At about the same time, it appears that a branch of the Amur River–based Tungus people, either the Joshin or the Gilyak, had settled in eastern Hokkaido, bringing with them Ohkutsk culture. This culture was completely different from previous societies in the Japanese archipelago. Its people were so skilled at sailing and ocean hunting (of whales and so on) that they have been called the Northeast Asian Vikings. The bear worship of the Ainu, who came later, is also said to have been influenced by this culture. In any case, the Satsumon people were active traders, frequently traveling across Northeast Asia. Through their movements, northern culture influenced the peoples living in northern Honshu and on the Kanto Plain.

For example, recent excavations have uncovered the remains of a large-scale foundry in southern Tohoku. As I mentioned earlier, it was assumed that casting technology moved from west to east. Of course, if one only examines documentary evidence, then it would appear that it was with the

9. The term *Satsumon culture* derives from the particular scraping patterns found on the pottery it produced.

movement of blacksmiths from the west to the east in the twelfth and thirteenth centuries that the technology was transmitted.[10] But when the Tohoku foundry remains are compared to those found in the west, the Tohoku are found to be much bigger. Traces of ironworks have also been discovered in northern Tohoku. In addition, the "inner ear" pots of the Northeast Asian hunting peoples can be found in Tohoku, Kanto, and the central Alps region. Ritsuryō aristocrats and officials who were stationed in the Kanto area also engaged in trade with the Emishi people. From about the eighth or ninth century on, the frequency with which they bought horses from the Emishi became a problem for the central government, since horses were a major military resource. This means that horses were being raised in large numbers in the Tohoku region, with a culture of horse breeding and training already well developed. There is a strong possibility that this culture came from the north.

We also have clear evidence in Okinawa of exchanges with the Asian continent around the same time. There is still much archaeological work to be done, but so far we have found no evidence of agriculture practiced in Okinawa around the time the Yamato state was established. Rather, Okinawan remains from that time are characterized by a Shell Mound culture,[11] which was centered around fishing. With the recovery of pottery from the eighth and ninth centuries, we now have evidence of exchanges with the Asian mainland as well. Subsequent scholarship in this area promises many new discoveries.

The various administrative systems implemented by the Ritsuryō state in the areas under its control began to deteriorate in the early eighth century. Given that the Ritsuryō system was governed by a land-based principle, all official transportation had to take place on land. At first, commoners had to transport their taxes—even craft and labor tax equivalents—overland to the capital at their own expense, and officials such as regional governors had to use land routes when traveling to and from the capital. But rather quickly the land-based transportation system proved to be impractical, so permission was granted in the first half of the eighth century to transport heavy items on the seas and rivers. Archaeological excavation shows that by the end of the eighth century the main highways had begun to deteriorate, with

10. This corresponds with the movement of the center of power from Kyoto to Kamakura with the founding of the Kamakura shogunate.
11. *Shell Mound culture* refers to a characteristic of many Jōmon period finds in which evidence of a hunter-gatherer lifestyle is found in large deposits of sea shells.

roads becoming more narrow and even unused in some places. By the ninth century, ocean and river routes once again served as the main axes of the transportation system.

At the time of the Ritsuryō state's founding, there was a lively official trade with the Asian continent. However, these exchanges became less frequent in the ninth century, and extraofficial exchanges between the islands and the continent took the lead once again. For example, in the ninth century Silla and Hizen (present-day Nagasaki Prefecture) aristocrats cooperated in the production of weaponry in an attempt to bring Tsushima Island under their joint control. The Korean Peninsula and northern Kyushu had long been closely linked as the territory of the *wajin*, and it appears that the relationship continued outside the framework of the state, resurfacing again in the ninth century.

The Ritsuryō state also tried to bring commerce and distribution under its control, officially licensing markets in the eastern and western sections of the capital and in each of the regional administrative centers. Yet the commercial and financial activity that had emerged before the founding of the state continued to grow and exceed state control. What is perhaps most interesting about this official trade is that many of its practitioners were women and monks. It is difficult to say for certain why this was the case. One reason might be that the state held adult men over the age of twenty responsible for the various official taxes. In other words, while adult males were officially recognized as members of the state, women and monks were essentially outside the state's purview.

This became one of the enduring characteristics of commerce and finance in the Japanese archipelago according to documentary evidence from this time. However, I believe that women, particularly those from coastal and mountainous areas, were centrally involved in commerce even in the Yayoi and Tomb periods. Therefore, this role may not have originated with the state's taxation system, as it reflects a particular construction of women's sexual identity and its relation to commercial activity.[12] Whatever the case may be, there is no doubt that women and monks were responsible for much of the movement of people and goods along rivers and ocean routes during this period. Moreover, this was not simply a radial movement between region and capital but a complex web of transactions between the

---

12. See chapter nine for a more detailed discussion of this issue.

various regions themselves. Indeed, demand from the capital did not lead to a drain on the periphery; rather, commerce in every region prospered due to the demands of the capital.

When we examine the products brought to the capital as payment of "craft" taxes in this period, we see that the technological level of regional handicrafts was very high. As I shall discuss later, craft items such as salt, silk, textiles, and iron, as well as horses, served as a means of exchange. Ocean products such as bonito, abalone, seaweed, and salmon were also frequently used to pay craft taxes. These products were considered divine offerings (*shinsen*) and were often given as gifts. Even today attaching dried abalone (*noshiawabi*) to a package signifies that it is a gift, while seaweed (*nori*) and dried bonito are often given as gifts. The gifts we still give today have ancient origins (fig. 12).

OCEAN TRANSPORT AND TAX CONTRACTS

Things changed even more dramatically from the ninth to the tenth century when the state system became a mere shell of its former self. During the first half of the tenth century, it underwent a complete transformation. First, there was the birth of the short-lived kingdom of Taira no Masakado in the early tenth century, which contained the eight provinces of Kanto and the Izu Peninsula and was based on naval power along the Pacific coast. At the same time, Fujiwara no Sumitomo asserted his independence in the western

Figure 12. Tributes to the domain lord. From *The Illustrated History of Kokawa Temple.* Source: *Kokawadera engi emaki,* owned by *Kokawadera.*

Inland Sea in conjunction with the increasing activity of local coastal leaders whom the Yamato court labeled pirates (*kaizoku*).[13] Pirates were also active in the area of Silla, and it is believed that Sumitomo's grasp at power was based on an alliance with these groups. In other words, a serious political challenge to the Ritsuryō state arose on the basis of ocean transport that linked the Inland Sea, northern Kyushu, and the Korean Peninsula.

As I mentioned earlier, maritime routes along the Pacific coast had become stable and active early on. Therefore, it is possible to conclude that there was communication between Masakado and Sumitomo. Sumitomo extended his control to the Yodo River, making his threat felt in the capital, while Masakado attempted to conquer the Tohoku region. With these two challenges, the imperial court found itself in unprecedented danger. Had Masakado not prematurely provoked war and died young, the imperial court in Kyoto might have been wiped out. However, since Masakado's kingdom lasted a mere two or three months, the Yamato state managed to maintain itself as an imperial entity.

These two events marked major transformations in the state's tax and regional systems. The first was the emergence of the tax contract system whereby governors and local officials contracted with local leaders to collect taxes in their territories, taxes that had previously been submitted directly to the state. With this, the former bureaucratic system of regional governance lost all practical effect, although provincial governors were still sent to their assigned territories. Meanwhile, storehouses for taxes were established in strategic places around the capital—in places like Yodo and Ōtsu on Lake Biwa—to which the products collected in each province were brought independently along river and ocean transport routes. Products from each province were brought to the storehouses near the capital via independent waterways, carried by transporters—rowers (*kandori*) and pullers (*gōtei*)— who had contracts with local officials. The products brought to the official storehouses were commodities that could be exchanged at the markets surrounding the capital for a wide variety of goods—in other words, storehouse commodities were those such as rice, silk, textiles, salt, iron, and horses, which functioned as currency. The difficulties faced by commoners when

13. Amino used the term *umi no ryōshu* instead of the more common *kaizoku* (pirates) in order to avoid blindly adopting the perspective of the Yamato government of the time. The term *ryōshu* itself means "ruler of a territory" and is most often associated with control of land. As the discussion in chapter four will show, however, the restricted use of *ryōshu* to designate only the ruler of agricultural land tends to reduce the historical importance of political control of the sea and mountains.

bringing payment of their craft and labor taxes to the capital via land routes had undermined the imperial system. Hence, there was a reversion to a mode of transportation more suited to the natural features of the archipelago. Provincial governors entrusted the actual management of these tax storehouses to specialized financiers and merchants possessed of the requisite expertise. In this way, the provincial governors provided for the needs of the imperial court by trading at the marketplace.

Second, the artisans and performers who had formerly been attached to the central bureaucracy began to form independent "professional" organizations. This was due in part to the fact that the central bureaucracies had fallen into arrears, so that artisans and performers were forced to pay their own costs. For example, iron casters had been attached to the Ironworking Agency and Bureau of Crafts. By the eleventh century, while they were still attached to the Office of Storehouses for the provision of lanterns to the palace, they had formed their own independent organization. Known as Lantern Purveyors, they possessed a special grant to travel freely throughout the provinces. With this special dispensation, they roamed the islands casting and trading in the ironworks they produced. The same was true for others, such as cypress craftsmen and blacksmiths. The activities of such groups were again only possible after the development of an archipelago-wide system of transport. In turn, offices of the central bureaucracy were created on the premise of these artisanal groups' existence.

Therefore, after the tenth century the state system came to rely upon the independent development of industry, commerce, distribution, and water routes, despite the land-centered principles of the ruling class. The same held for trade with the Asian continent and the Korean Peninsula. By this time, there were no official delegations exchanged between states in Asia; however, exchanges among common people became more frequent than ever.

China at the time was ruled by the Song dynasty, while Korea was unified under the Koryŏ dynasty. Trading ships from both kingdoms arrived continuously in the Japanese islands during this period. Ships also traveled from the islands to the continent, and through this trade a huge amount of Chinese goods entered the archipelago. It was only through such unofficial trade that Chinese goods eventually came into the hands of the rulers.

The layout of Kyoto also changed drastically in accordance with these changes in the governing system. Until then, Kyoto had been crisscrossed with straight roads, like a chessboard, administratively divided into left and right quarters, a city of aristocrats and officials. However, the original plans for the construction of the city were only partially completed. The eastern half was largely left as open fields. After the tenth century, the rivers bordering the city came to be indispensable. It was only through trade conducted on these rivers—the Kamo, Yodo, Ōi, Katsura, and Uji as well as Lake Biwa just across the mountains to the east—that the capital began to function as a true city. That is, Kyoto was transformed into a "water capital" built upon a marine transportation system (fig. 13).

FINANCIER NETWORKS

As I discussed earlier, the management and operation of provincial storehouses were contracted out to specialists, many of whom were active in financial enterprises. We have a relatively clear picture of their activities when we reach the twelfth century. In 1136, a group of legal scholars attested in a signed document that a group of people attached to Hie Shrine and known as Ōtsu Shrine purveyors (*Ōtsu jinin*) were officially recognized as financial lenders. The document records a system in which local officials borrowed rice from these purveyors, who are also believed to have managed tax storehouses for the local officials. Local officials were thereby able to gather and submit the required goods when so ordered by the imperial court. The tax contract was issued in the name of provincial officials and governors; however, the financiers who managed the storehouses were responsible for the release. In this way, a multilayered network supported the state.

The Hie Ōtsu Shrine purveyors used the shrine's "first-harvest rice" as capital for their financial enterprises. In other words, they used the rice that had been offered to the gods worshipped at the shrine for loans they made to provincial governors and bureaucrats. As security for such loans, provincial governors would offer an official promissory note called a *kirifu*, provincial tax collection orders called *kokufu*, or imperial tax collection orders called *kirikudashibumi*. The Hie Ōtsu Shrine purveyors had an extremely wide-ranging network, which extended from the provinces of Hokuriku through the Inland Sea to northern Kyushu. Their ability to collect taxes on their own authority was backed by their relationship to the Hie Ōtsu deities. But it was with the provincial administration's tax collection orders in hand that the shrine purveyors went from province to province withdrawing goods from local storehouses. Moreover, the provincial officials' tax collection orders—and this was true for the provincial governor's contracts and

Figure 13. Going upriver on the Hori River in Kyoto with rafts made of logs. From *The Picture Scroll of the Holy Man Ippen*. Source: *Ippen hijirie*, from the collection of the Tokyo National Museum.

receipts as well—were exchanged among the financiers themselves, with these documents functioning as primitive bills of exchange (*tegata*). It was this network of financiers that guaranteed the payment of these bills. That much is made quite clear in the document from 1136.

The prior development of water transport made possible the financial and commercial networks that collected the state's taxes. The system also depended on the exchange of primitive bills. These conditions suggest that the economy of that time had already developed a high degree of sophistication. I believe that a system of regular ocean shipping was also established around this time. Its first appearance in historical documents is in the twelfth century, but I believe that regular ocean routes and sailors' organizations were formed throughout the archipelago in the eleventh century. Ocean transport on the Japan Sea was particularly active. After entering the harbor at Tsuruga (to the north of Kyoto), merchants from the north would make the short land crossing to Lake Biwa and sail across to the town of Ōtsu, after which there would be just another short trip on land to Kyoto. Likewise, boats from the San'in region would put into shore at Obama in Wakasa, from which point their cargo would be carried across Lake Biwa to Ōtsu and Kyoto. These routes then connected up with the main arteries intersecting the archipelago from the Inland Sea to northern Kyushu.

The harbors of northern Kyushu in those days welcomed many Chinese boats, known as *karabune*. These boats were also sailing into Hokuriku harbors at Tsuruga and Obama and on the Noto Peninsula. The pottery and other Chinese goods shipped into the harbors of Noto were also conveyed across the Lake Biwa route to the capital. While there is little doubt that the route from northern Kyushu through the Inland Sea was the most heavily traveled of these ocean arteries, we must remember that there were a variety of ocean routes from China.

Recent excavations have shown that the settlement at Tosa Harbor on the far northern Tsugaru Peninsula functioned as a city quite early on. Archaeologists in the area have unearthed Chinese porcelains as well as pottery from every region of the Japanese Islands. The remains near Tosa Harbor contain an especially large amount of pottery from the twelfth century, so it appears that Chinese porcelains were transported there from the end of the Heian period. In the thirteenth century, Suzu stoneware from the Noto Peninsula was also transported to Tosa Harbor, as well as to Kaminokuni and Yoichi in Hokkaido. Thus, Tosa Harbor functioned as one of the major bases of the early Japan Sea trade routes. Recent excavations at the Yanagi no gosho Palace remains in Hiraizumi (in present-day Iwate Prefecture) show that the Pacific coast routes were also established far earlier than previously thought. The Yanagi Palace was the base of Fujiwara no Hidehira and Fujiwara no Yasuhira at a time when the influence of the Fujiwara in the capital was on the wane. Excavation of this site has turned up a great many Chinese porcelains. Since the nearby town of Hiraizumi fell into decline from the end of the twelfth century, it appears that the porcelains made their way from China along the Pacific coast to Hiraizumi before the twelfth century. A huge amount of pottery from the ancient Japanese pottery towns of Tokoname and Atsumi has also been unearthed at the Yanagi Palace. Some of the pieces recovered are enormous Atsumi jars, which must have arrived via the Pacific coast and the Kitakami River. Regular shipping routes on the Pacific had to be well established for this amount of pottery, manufactured on the distant Chita and Atsumi Peninsula, to be transported to Hiraizumi. In particular, boats had to be able to safely pass the dangerous seas of the Izu Peninsula, the Bōsō Peninsula, and Cape Inubō.

Tokoname pottery was transported around the Kii Peninsula and into the Inland Sea, as well as passing around the Tosa Sea and the island of Shikoku, for delivery to Kyushu. We are certain that the ocean route around the Kii Peninsula west toward Kyushu was already in operation in the eleventh and twelfth centuries, but it is likely that it was opened even earlier. The shippers probably did not make the entire trip in one boat. Instead, it appears that shorter routes from port to port around the entire archipelago were established by the eleventh century.

Okinawa also imported a great deal of Chinese porcelain in the twelfth century. In fact, Okinawa probably had the largest amount of Chinese pottery in the entire Japanese archipelago, going back to the Tang dynasty. However, the intensity of this trade seems to have increased in the eleventh and twelfth centuries. During the same period, people from Honshu and Kyushu also exerted a great deal of cultural influence on Okinawa. For example, we see at this time the beginnings of agriculture and the construction of fortresses (*gusuku*) at all the sacred sites that functioned as the religious, political, and military centers of the Okinawan islands. In this way, Okinawa took its own steps toward becoming an independent state.

THE ESTABLISHMENT OF REGIONAL CITIES

Around this time, various cities began to form at regional centers and important points in the transportation network.[14] That Kyoto was among these

---

14. The non-Japanese reader faced with the following list of unfamiliar place-names should remember that the significance of Amino's claim is that these places were not villages, a concept that his

goes without saying. However, undoubtedly Hiraizumi in the Tohoku region was also one such city, as were Tosa Harbor, Akita, Tagashiro, and the administrative centers of the Mutsu region. Kamakura, the capital of the Eastern Country, was a city even before Minamoto no Yoritomo established his base there. Mutsuranotsu, closely linked to Kamakura, became an important port town. Likewise, many of the inlets in the Kasumigaura and Kitaura areas, such as Ofunatsu in Kashima, had settlements that were urban in character. Mikuni Harbor, Tsuruga, and Obama in Hokuriku, and Ōtsu, Sakamoto, Umitsu, Katada, and Funaki on the shores of Lake Biwa were all cities. The Uji and Yodo Rivers had urban settlements in Uji, Yamazaki, Yodo, Suita, Eguchi, and Kanzaki. Countless other regional cities existed everywhere, including such towns as Kurashiki, Onomichi, and Komado; Hakata and Munakata in northern Kyushu; Kanzaki on the Ariake Bay; and Bonotsu in southern Kyushu.

The ruling class during this period naturally took the true state of commerce and distribution into consideration when constructing their governing system. In the latter half of the eleventh century, leading families, such as the imperial family and the Fujiwara imperial regents, as well as large temples and shrines—such as Tōdaiji, Kōfukuji, Enryakuji, Shimogamō and Kamigamō, Ise, Hie, Kasuga and Iwashimizu Hachiman shrines—each possessed *shōen* estates and fiefs in every province. Taxes were collected by each estate owner's independent administrative organization from specially designated fields, estates, and public lands to pay for the costs of the Buddhist services and festivals that had become regularized ceremonies.

In the course of these developments, the difference between a *shōen* estate and state lands (*kokugaryō*) gradually became more distinct. The estate and public land system was firmly grounded by the first half of the thirteenth century, and on this basis aristocrats and religious organizations constructed independent economic orders. An examination of the process by which aristocrats and religious orders established estates and public lands shows that in fact the system was quite well thought out. Consider, for example, the case of the family of the Fujiwara imperial regents (the Sekkan family). In Fujiwara no Yorimichi's day (990–1074), they had a villa in Uji, the famous Byōdōin, but they also had two mansions at Lake Ogura. The Uji River and Lake Ogura were strategic points on the water routes to Kyoto. Having laid

---

Japanese audience is likely to associate strictly with agriculture. By stressing their urban character, he is calling attention, among other things, to the centrality of commerce to these settlements.

claim to these points of access, the regents established further bases along the Yodo River in Yamazaki, Kuzuha, and Yodo, as well as at several important points along the Inland Sea.

The imperial family's bases during the Insei period[15] included the east bank of the Kamo River and Shirakawa. The latter was a key point in the Lake Biwa transport route, situated at the intersection of the mountain roads crossing into the Kyoto plain and an entry to the lake. Here the imperial family built Shirakawa Palace as well as two temples, Hōshōji and Rokushōji. In the twelfth century, the imperial family built another villa, the Toba Palace, at the confluence of the Kamo and Katsura Rivers. Meanwhile, they not only built a palace on the floodplain between the Uji and Yodo Rivers, but they had a number of craftsmen assigned to the palace. Thanks to the presence of these craftsmen, the imperial family was able to establish Toba Palace as a vital political and economic base. Thus, we see that the imperial family accurately read the state of river transport around Kyoto. The Office of the Retired Emperor (insei) further claimed land in northern Kyushu at Munakata and Kanzaki, important sites for trade with the Asian continent.

The same was true for temples and shrines. The temple of Shingoji held the estate of Nishizunoshō in Wakasa Province while also claiming the harbors of Tagarasu and Tsurube some distance from Nishizu. While Shinhie Shrine's Kuraminoshō estate was an inland territory, the shrine also claimed the harbor of Mikao at the tip of Tsunekami Peninsula. One thus occasionally finds examples of estate owners possessing harbors geographically separated from their estates. This fact shows how much consideration the ruling class of the time put into obtaining possessions related to ocean shipping.

Similar considerations are evident in the rise of power of the Taira uji in the latter half of the Heian period. First, the Taira became managers of the imperial stables at Toba Palace. With that position, they were in control of the oxen and horses in the stable as well as the people who worked there—the cattle herders, cart drivers, stable hands, trainers, and horsemen (fig. 14). Many of the retired emperor's stables were allotted pasture land along riverbanks. One such stable, called Mizunomaki, near Lake Ogura to the south of Kyoto, was both a pasture and a port. There were many such pasture/port lands along the Yodo River, and once the Taira obtained control of the stables, the lands attached to them also came under their control. The Taira also pos-

---

15. In the Insei period, ruling power was divided between the Office of the Regent and the Office of the Retired Emperor (insei). The period lasted roughly from 1087 to 1221.

Figure 14. Horse and cart transporters. From *The Picture Scroll of the Holy Man Ippen.*
Source: *Ippen hijirie,* from the collection of the Tokyo National Museum.

sessed a number of strategic estates along the Inland Sea, including one at
Itsukushima (near Hiroshima). In Kyushu, they controlled Munakata Shrine
and, by monopolizing the office of governor of Dazaifu, they brought that
city, together with the major port of Hakata, under their control. Furthermore, by becoming the managers of the retired emperor's estate in Kanzaki
in the Ariake Bay on Kyushu, the Taira gained control of trade with Song
China.

Until recently, historians have spoken of *shōen* estates and state lands
only in agricultural terms. But members of the ruling class of the time,
who struggled desperately to preserve their positions, did not think of their
holdings solely in terms of fields. Although there was concern for the annual
tribute taxes that were levied on estate fields, as well as for the unique products of various estates, this was not their own preoccupation. They also took
account of the wealth generated in ports, through water-borne traffic, and
in the mountains into their calculations. That is, they took a comprehensive
approach to the establishment of their *shōen* estates.

As I discuss briefly in chapter seven, shrines, temples, the imperial family, and the Fujiwara regents independently organized the shipping, mercantile, and artisanal groups in their domains, designating them shrine purveyors (*jinin*), imperial purveyors (*kugonin*), or temple purveyors (*yoriudo*). Thus, the rulers of this period sought to control both land and the largely water-based transportation system. By these means, the medieval governments (both the imperial government and the shogunate in Kamakura) came into being around the end of the Heian period.

Most historians have described medieval society as a feudal society based entirely on agriculture. But the society I have just described cannot be understood in terms of that limited notion. Moreover, the standard view of the *shōen* estate as representing a self-sufficient economic order is clearly mistaken. Rice, silk, and textiles—the products of these estates—fulfilled the functions of currency, that is, a means of exchange, a means of payment, and a measure of value. Though still linked to the divinities as offerings, these goods also became irrevocably linked to trade. This economic order emerged in the twelfth century and represented the transformation of the state from the disintegrated Ritsuryō model to the new medieval model.

CHAPTER THREE

The World of the *Shōen* Estate and Government Lands

THE *SHŌEN* ESTATE/GOVERNMENT LANDS SYSTEM

The medieval land system—which I call the *shōen* estate/government lands system—developed between the latter half of the eleventh century to the first half of the thirteenth century. Government lands were divided into administrative districts (*gun*), hamlets (*gō*), neighborhoods (*hō*), and fields (*myō*), while *shōen* estates were simply described as (*shō*) estates. *Shōen* estates and government lands were in fact subcontracting units for the collection of taxes—yearly tribute and public fees—with the district, hamlet, neighborhood, and field units submitting their taxes to the provincial governor through the provincial office (*kokuga*). *Shōen* paid their taxes directly to the imperial family, the Fujiwara regents, or large temples and shrines—in other words, to their proprietors. Each of these administrative units were assigned a governing officer (*tsukasa*) who contracted to gather taxes from a fixed amount of agricultural land in the unit and sent them on to the provincial governor or the proprietor of *shōen* estate. This, simply put, was the *shōen* estate/government lands system.

The establishment and distribution of districts, hamlets, neighborhoods, fields, and *shō* administrative units were particular to each province. Differences existed between eastern and western Japan and between Kyushu and all other areas. In the east and Kyushu, the units tended to be larger; in some cases, districts became *shōen* estates themselves. In the Kinai region, *shōen* could be composed of widely scattered paddy fields. Despite such variations, the *shōen*/government lands system covered all of the three main islands of Honshu, Shikoku, and Kyushu.

Scholars have tended to see *shōen* as self-sufficient economic units primarily composed of paddy fields whose cultivators paid annual rice tribute (*nengu*) and public service fees as land rent. But *shōen* were not actually agricultural units. First of all, the payments of annual tribute owed by the villagers farming *shōen* and government lands were not made strictly in rice. A wide variety of items could be submitted as annual tribute. For example, estates in provinces in the east, such as Ise, Owari, and Mino, tended to pay their annual tribute in silk or cotton cloth. Iron was sent from the mountains of the Chūgoku region, and paper was submitted from Tajima. In Mutsu, payments were made in gold and horses, and the islands of the Inland Sea sent salt. Rice did not even constitute the majority of the taxes submitted from estates. All of these products could be exchanged and could even function as currency, as rice did.

So why is it that we tend to assume that annual tribute meant rice? We do so because annual tribute was levied, in principle, on rice paddy land. In other words, for each unit of paddy land—usually one *tan* (about .25 acres)— five *ryō* of iron might be paid; or for one *chō* (about 2.5 acres) of paddy land two bolts of silk might be submitted. That is, the value of products other than rice would be calculated for tax purposes in terms of equivalent units of paddy land. Submission of iron or silk as annual tribute thus presumed an exchange. For example, if five *ryō* of iron were levied as a tax on one *tan* of wet paddy land then the rice from one *tan* of land had to be exchanged by some method with five *ryō* of iron. There were many possible means of carrying out such exchanges, but the main point is that the tax system itself presumed exchanges of goods. Therefore, this system had nothing whatsoever to do with self-sufficient economies.

YUGESHIMA: THE ESTATE OF SALT

In the Inland Sea, in the province of Iyo, there was a *shōen* called Yugeshima estate (fig. 15). Since this *shōen* was on a small island, there were very few rice paddies, and the villagers all fished or produced salt. Accordingly, annual tribute from this *shōen* was paid in salt, and public fees (*kūji*) were paid in sea products. On paper, it appeared as if the official on this island took from

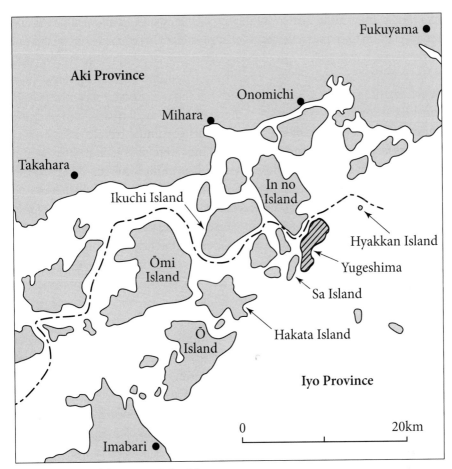

Figure 15. Map of the Eastern Inland Sea.

the villagers wheat in the summer and rice in autumn as annual tribute, and then loaned it back to the villagers as "wheat for salt" (*shiotenomugi*) and "rice for salt" (*shiotenoyone*). In actuality, wheat and rice were probably never gathered from the villagers. The official formally received a document from the villagers acknowledging the loan, which they vowed to pay off in salt. The villagers themselves termed this an exchange of wheat or rice for salt, but in effect, the island paid its annual tribute in salt, becoming famous as an "estate of salt."[1]

1. Just as some estates had a system of "rice for salt," other *shōen* paid their annual tribute in iron, which was collected by granting the villagers loans of rice for iron. There were probably also rice for silk, rice for gold, and rice for paper contracts.

Since Yugeshima estate was on an island on which there was little paddy land, scholars have assumed that it was an extremely poor *shōen*. This is one of those cases in which we need to overturn our mode of thinking. We tend to leap to the conclusion that wherever agriculture was poorly developed, or where there were no paddy fields from which to produce rice, the people must have been extremely poor. Scholars have long assumed that, lacking paddy land and being isolated by virtue of living on an island, the islanders were cruelly forced to take up the hard labor of making salt on the beaches.

But, when we investigate the real situation of the villagers of Yugeshima estate, we find this evaluation to be completely off the mark. To give but one example, around the end of the Kamakura period the property of a villager named Kiyosakin was confiscated by the estate's official. Kiyosakin was a "small villager," with just the tiniest amount of paddy land. But his confiscated property included ten head of cattle, five indentured servants, silk, and a limited number of household items, including *kosode* kimonos.[2] In other words, he turns out to have been very wealthy. The cattle were probably used to carry the "salt wood" that was used as fuel to boil the water in salt production at the beach. The salt wood itself probably came at a fairly high price. Since this small villager possessed ten head of cattle, we can easily discern how well off these islanders were and how ridiculous it is to call them poor.

Yugeshima was not an island isolated by the sea. Just the opposite, it was an island connected to places in all directions by the sea. This was not an island impoverished by its lack of rice paddies. It was an island on which there were many other items that could be produced and exchanged. The salt of Yugeshima estate passed through the Inland Sea and traveled up the Yodogawa River from Yodo to Toba, where it was transferred to rented carts and carried to Kyoto. The boats that carried this salt were owned by the islanders themselves. The annual salt tribute was handed over to the temple of Tōji in Kyoto, but we can confirm that the islanders also sold their salt at Yodo.

In the fifteenth century, the salt of Yugeshima was shipped in large quantities to the harbor of Hyōgo so that even at the end of the medieval period the island was famous as a salt production site. The harbor at tiny

---

2. *Kosode*-style kimonos are formal wear and are not normally associated with the clothing of poor, starving islanders.

Yugeshima was so lively that it was said there were courtesans there even in the Edo period. Imagining this kind of *shōen* estate as a self-sufficient economy is clearly nothing more than an illusion.

NIIMI: THE ESTATE OF IRON, PAPER, AND LACQUER

Niimi in Bitchū Province (present-day Okayama) is another example of a wealthy nonagricultural estate (fig. 16). Niimi estate was located in the mountainous interior near the border with Izumo and Kōki, at the headwater of the Takahashi River, which flows into the Inland Sea near Kurashiki. Many of its land registers from the Kamakura period have survived and show that a fair number of rice paddies were developed along the valley in Niimi estate. Because so many of these registers have survived, it is famous among historians for providing us with detailed information on the system of villager-contracted fields (*hyakushō-myō*). Like Yugeshima estate, Niimi came to be possessed by the Kyoto-based temple of Tōji around the end of the Heian period (most of the surviving documents are kept at Tōji even today). Many studies of the surviving documents have tended to portray Niimi as a landlocked estate located deep in the mountains and not easily accessible.

In fact, it *is* far up in the mountains, far upstream on the Takahashi River. There is far more mountain terrain than rice paddies, and until recently those mountains have been the site of slash and burn agriculture. So, it is not surprising that many scholars have seen Niimi as a remote, backwater estate. But if we approach this estate without assuming that *hyakushō* were strictly farmers, a rereading of the documents of this estate will produce a decisively different picture.

First, the part of the estate closest to the deepest mountains of the Chūgoku region is called Yoshino (present-day Takase village). Until the latter half of the thirteenth century, the villagers of that area submitted their annual tribute in iron. As mentioned above, the tax burden was expressed in the proportion of five *ryō* of iron for every *tan* of paddy field. If you visit this area today, you will find a good deal of slag dating from the medieval era. There is so much slag left over that during World War II a company was formed to try to refine iron from it one more time.

The Yoshino area has a shrine where those involved in the metallurgical trades came to worship—the Kanayako Shrine—and there the

Thick white lines: Ancient roads
Thin white lines: Cross-archipelago roads, connecting the San'in and San'yō
Highways
■ Ancient post stations

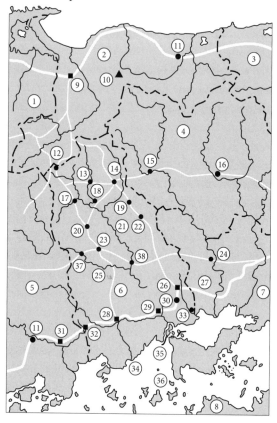

1. Izumo Province
2. Hōki Province
3. Inaba Province
4. Mimasaka Province
5. Bingo Province
6. Bitchū Province
7. Bizen Province
8. Sanuki Province
9. Aimi
10. Mt. Daisen
11. *kokufu* (provincial
    capital)
12. Yoshino
13. Niimi estate
14. *kokuga* (govern-
    ment administrative
    headquarters)

15. Takata
16. *kokufu* (provincial
    capital)
17. *kōshiro* (tribute land)
18. *ichiba* (market)
19. Aga County houses
20. Tetsuta County
    houses
21. Takahashi River
22. Ukan
23. Uji
24. Kana River
25. Nariwa River
26. Kino Castle
27. San'yō Highway
28. Oda
29. Kawabe

30. *kokufu* (provincial
    capital)
31. Kannabe
32. Shitsuki
33. Kibitsu Shrine
34. Minami Bay
35. Tsura Island
36. O Island
37. Kasakami rock steele,
    carved with writing
38. Takahashi (possibly
    the Bitchū Province
    headquarters)

Figure 16. Map of Niimi estate and the surrounding area.

metalworkers maintained an association. Members of the association also had a small amount of paddy land, but it appears that these people essentially made their living in the metalworking trades. Should archaeologists undertake a dig up there, they are likely to find any number of furnaces.

With these ironworkers serving as its base, Niimi estate also had an officially recognized organization of blacksmiths; there were even some metal casters among the villagers. These metal casters were not organized as imperial or shrine purveyors—professionals, in other words—but as *hyakushō* who were metal casters. Although blacksmiths in those days also made swords, they were more closely related to the construction trades, making nails and clamps in particular. We know from the Tōji documents that this estate had set aside fields to pay the wages of blacksmiths, as well as the carpenters who were associated with them, and that both groups had organizational headquarters in the area.

Niimi estate in the medieval era also produced paper, as the area still does today. Manufactured in hamlets throughout the estate, a certain amount of paper was assessed as a public fees tax per field owned by the villagers. In addition to the paper produced by average villagers, the estate also contained paper-making "artisans" who produced the high-quality paper known as *danshi*. Nevertheless, despite the presence of professionals, we should not lose sight of the fact that the technological skills needed to manufacture paper were widely disseminated among the villagers.

Niimi estate also had many lacquer trees, and again it was the villagers who cultivated them. For each lacquer tree, the villagers were responsible for more than one *shaku* (.02 liters) of lacquer as a public fees tax, which they sent to Kyoto. With this sap production, the estate also developed an organization of woodworking lathe turners who worked with the lacquerers who applied the sap to the wood. Thus, finished lacquerware was manufactured in Niimi. The lathe turners were officially recognized as artisans and received wage fields as compensation.[3]

To sum up, the villagers in Niimi estate mined iron ore and manufactured ironware. They also made paper, drew lacquer sap, and manufactured lacquerware. These industries were not restricted to "professional" groups alone; villagers throughout the estate also participated. Moreover, Niimi

3. Wage fields were fields whose taxable produce was granted to officials, craftsmen, and such in "payment" for services rendered. The very idea that these people would need a source of rice as compensation should suggest to the reader just how important rice was as the standard measure of value. This in no way contradicts Amino's argument, however. His point is that we should not let the use of rice as a standard measure of value blind us to the myriad other forms of production that also existed and for which rice served as a kind of universal equivalent.

villagers hunted, gathered, and processed a wide variety of mountain goods such as quail, firewood, charcoal, deerskins, and mushrooms.

There is simply no way to encompass the various forms of production and lifestyles in this estate with the term *farm village* (*nōson*) that is so popular among historians. We must give further thought to the way in which villages with multiple characteristics might be defined, but Niimi estate consisted of farm villages, settlements with typical mountain village characteristics, and manufacturing villages that were home to many craftsmen. To borrow a term from Shibusawa Keizō, we might call the settlements of Niimi "manufacturing villages" (*kōson*). The term *manufacturing village* has not gained currency in academic circles, yet there were undoubtedly many places that could be called blacksmith villages or metalworking villages. The term has solid grounds for adoption.

Rice, wheat, and soybeans grown in the fields of the estate were sent to the capital as annual tribute along with the iron, paper, and lacquer. In addition, these products were sent to markets and exchanged as commodities. We know for a fact that they were traded for coins in the thirteenth century. There were at least two markets on an island in the middle of the Takahashi River where it flowed through Niimi estate (markets were generally located on islands and sandbars in rivers, as noted in chapter seven). One was the estate proprietor's market, and the other was the military steward's (*jitō*) market. The goods exchanged at these markets were loaded onto boats and carried down the Takahashi River to Kurashiki. From Kurashiki, they passed through the Inland Sea to the capital and many other ports.

In fact, this estate had a rather large number of professional boatmen, all of whom received more wage fields than such lower level estate officials as clerks (*kumon*) and field overseers (*tadokoro*). Furthermore, oarsmen in these boats received their rations through a levy on the villagers of the entire estate, a tax known as oarsman's rice. There are many cases in other parts of Japan of coastal villagers having to pay oarsman's rice to support the shippers who passed through their areas, but Niimi is a rare case of villagers in an interior, mountain-bound estate paying such taxes. This gives us a good indication of how active these boatmen were and how lively was the trade in commodities at the Niimi markets. We may also assume that these markets had merchants who brought in a variety of goods for exchange from a wide range of locations outside the estate.

Neither the Yugeshima nor the Niimi estates were exceptional; they are simply well-studied estates that provide excellent examples of the state of

Japanese society from the thirteenth to the sixteenth centuries. In fact, no matter which estate we examine from this period, we find villagers engaged in a variety of production processes and a number of professional groups also working on that basis. Seeing *shōen* as self-sufficient entities composed simply of farmers plowing the fields is mistaken.

Likewise, to consider a place to be remote because it is deep in the mountains or on a small island is a completely modern notion. From the pre-modern perspective, a remote island was open to the world by virtue of the surrounding ocean—in many cases making the island an important point on transportation routes. The deep mountains had more travelers traversing its roads and running its rivers than might otherwise be expected. To say that areas were poor because millet and deccan were consumed instead of rice is simply prejudicial. In fact, those regions were often quite well off.

THE TASKS OF A CONTRACTOR OFFICIAL

Niimi was divided in the middle of the Kamakura period into a military steward's portion and a proprietor's portion. In 1334, the first year of the Kenmu Restoration, the manager of the steward's portion, a man named Sonji, issued a report on the previous year's submission of annual tribute and other miscellaneous goods. Sonji's document, with the final calculations, survives at the temple of Tōji today. What does that document show us about the responsibilities of an estate manager over the course of a year?

Emperor Go-Daigo established the short-lived, revolutionary Kenmu government in 1333, so it was an unusual year in many ways. Since the proprietor, Tōji, had requested an advance on that year's tribute, Sonji borrowed ten *kanmon* from local merchants in the third, fifth, and seventh months of that year. He forwarded those sums to Kyoto in the form of bills of exchange (*kawase tegata*). Purchase of these bills also incurred transaction fees; the cost of sending the notes from Niimi to Kyoto was essentially fixed at fifty *mon*. Since the cost of sending a bill of exchange from Yano estate in Harima Province (present day Hyōgo Prefecture) to the capital at the beginning of the Northern and Southern Courts period was 30 *mon*, it seems that these transaction fees were based on distance. Moreover, we can sense just how established the sending of such bills was by the fact that the fee was fixed. We can also get a glimpse of the stability of the network that bound merchants in Niimi estate and Kyoto. The same was true, of course, for the route between Kamakura and

Kyoto. In fact, bills of exchange were used throughout the country, with these ten-*kanmon* bills of exchange circulating much like negotiable securities.[4]

By the tenth month, rice, millet, soybeans, and buckwheat had generally been harvested from the fields of Niimi. According to the 1334 document, the manager had these grains placed in storehouses and then, in celebration of the harvest, the villagers held a banquet. A similar banquet was held on the second day of the new year, with participants consuming sake, tofu, and fish. The costs of these banquets were met through the sale of a portion of the rice and soybeans.

In addition to storing grains, the estate manager closely watched the setting of prices at the market before putting the rice and soybeans up for sale. Rice and other grains were brought to the market on the third, thirteenth and twenty-third days of the month and sold at the market price determined on that day. The market price would be set for a certain area, and the manager would keep a close eye on fluctuations in order to sell the grain at as high a price as possible. If the grain were sold cheaply, or sold at high price but reported as having been sold cheaply, the manager might be accused of laxity in his duties and be subject to an inspection and dismissal by the estate proprietor. In addition, while small amounts of lacquer and paper were sent directly to Kyoto, the villagers of Takase also sold iron at the local market. The manager collected a portion of these proceeds as the cash tax levied on iron expressed in terms of paddy fields.

The important point is that by the beginning of the fourteenth century the steward's portion on Niimi estate had already taken on the character of an urban system. First and foremost, there was the market on the island in the middle of the Takahashi River where much of the commercial business of the estate was carried out. The houses on the island were officially inspected, and thirty-one were granted authorization to engage in trade. These houses were most likely lined up on both sides of a main thoroughfare. It is likely that there were also unregistered rental houses in the market area. In fact, historians believe that there were quite a large number of buildings at this market.

My characterization of Niimi as urban is based on more than an assessment of its layout and function. Evidence suggests that it was also officially recognized as such. The term *hō* was used to designate the territorial unit of a neighborhood in *shōen* estates and public lands. Originally *hō* was an administrative unit in the city of Kyoto. The city of Kamakura also came to use *hō*

---

4. See Sakurai Eiji, "Saifu ni kansuru kosatsu" (Observations concerning Bills of Exchange), *Shigaku zasshi* (History Journal) 104, no. 7 (1995).

to designate its neighborhoods, and *hō* have been identified in Bungo Province and the Yamazaki District of Yamashiro Province. In sum, *hō* became the term used to describe territorial administrative units for urban-type settlements. The market in Niimi estate at the beginning of the fourteenth century was also designated a *hō* and was under the jurisdiction of two overseers known as *hōtō*. One of these overseers was ordered by the estate's proprietor to specifically oversee matters of the market. Thus, the market of Niimi estate was administratively treated as urban by the beginning of the fourteenth century.

Urban land in the medieval era was recorded in official registries with the character *ji* (land), upon which was levied a tax known as *jishi* (land interest).[5] This was true in Kyoto and Kamakura, but we should also note that the thirty-one authorized houses at the market in Niimi also paid *jishi* on their land. This constitutes further evidence that this market was officially treated as a city.

In 1333, the manager, Sonji, pooled the coins paid for the market land tax and the money earned from the sale of grain to purchase two bills of exchange (worth twenty *kanmon* in cash) in the ninth month and five bills of exchange (worth fifty *kanmon* in cash) in the twelfth month and sent them on to Kyoto. The transaction fees were sixty *mon* in the ninth month and fifty in the twelfth. Final settling of the estate's account books usually took place at the end of the year, but since 1333 was a year of civil strife, it took place the following year. Under accounts receivable, Sonji recorded the cash earned on the sale of grain and iron for the annual tribute tax. He also made entries for the public fees on the marketplace, money earned from the sale of mulberries, and fifty *mon* for an excise tax of five *shō* of rice per *tan* of paddy land under the heading "extra cash." The money earned from the sale of grain was less than the money paid in cash for the annual tribute for iron; grain constituted no more than 41 percent of the total. At that percentage, could this estate really be characterized as agricultural?

Under accounts payable, Sonji recorded the ten *kanmon* loans taken out by the estate proprietor, Tōji, in the third, fifth, and seventh months. The payment period fell in the tenth month, with a monthly rate of interest of 6 percent added to the principal. The total was calculated by adding the transaction fees for sending the bills of exchange to Kyoto, but Sonji kept this sum a secret by recording it on a separate piece of paper.

---

5. What is significant about this is that while land was customarily taxed via the rice tax, based on an assessment of agricultural productivity, such was not the case for this urban land tax.

In addition, he recorded the total of the two bills of exchange (and their transaction fees) that he had sent to Kyoto in the ninth and twelfth months. Paid accounts included offerings to the Suwa Shrine within the estate, costs of other religious services, New Year's celebration costs, and the costs of a banquet for the villagers when the annual tribute was collected. All of these were listed as authorized expenses. Furthermore, under the heading of reception and entertainment expenses, Sonji recorded expenses related to the visit of a messenger from the new provincial governor who had been sent to the estate on an inspection tour by the new Kemmu government in the twelfth month of 1333. Sonji probably held a three-day banquet (*mikka kuriya*) for the official; we know for certain that he had rice prepared for the visitors and provided soybeans for their horses, and that he bought refined and unrefined sake at the market as well as dried squid, radishes, fish, eels, and fowl (probably quail) for the banquet.

The cost of this entertainment and gifts for the provincial governor were officially recognized as necessary expenses, just as they would be today. Sonji recorded all of the details on a separate sheet of paper. After making these calculations, he was to take whatever funds were left over and send them with the bills of exchange to Kyoto. Sonji made some slight mistakes in his calculations, but his accounts payable were supposed to be equal to his accounts receivable.

An account book in which expenditures and receipts would match exactly—in effect a balance sheet—required a rather precise set of records. And in the fourteenth century we find a manager who was able to carry out such a complex task. We do not know much about what kind of monk this Sonji was, but in this period many of the people who were capable of carrying out these kinds of managerial tasks were monks of the Zen, Ritsu, or Pure Land sects or mountain ascetics (*yamabushi*). It is to these latter characters that we now turn.

THE MOUNTAIN ASCETIC AS OFFICIAL

As we saw above, the person contracted to be the manager of a *shōen* estate had to understand market prices, be able to keep an account book, and possess a considerable managerial ability. In addition to these economic skills, a *shōen* manager had to have the personal skills needed to receive important visitors and conduct negotiations.

In the particular year covered by our document, Sonji only had to concern himself with entertainment for the messenger of a provincial governor. However, we also have access to rare documents that show the daily expenditures of the manager of Niimi estate for the entire year 1401. The person who kept these records was one Ozaki, who had been sent by a mountain ascetic named Senshin, who himself had been contracted by the proprietor to manage the estate. Ozaki recorded the following under the heading of expenditures: the costs of food and daily necessities purchased at the market, transportation costs for various messengers, and alms given to itinerants who passed through the estate—picture preachers (*etoki*) and felicitators (*senshu manzai*).[6] We also find extraordinarily high entertainment costs for banquets held for local leaders and the governors and officials of nearby areas. For example, Ozaki would buy badger at the market for stew which he supplemented with tofu and small fish to go along with the sake. Since the market was an urban space, it is also possible that these expenses were incurred at a restaurant, bar, or outdoor stand. In the end, Ozaki's entertainment expenses for that year amounted to quite a sum! Since the more entertainment costs rose, the more the proprietor's profits fell, Tōji tried to keep these expenses as low as possible. In response, the manager argued that these were necessary expenditures. Thus, the manager not only had to be something of an entrepreneur, but he had to have good negotiating skills.

In the fourteenth century, one could also find people with this kind of ability among the leaders of the villager class. The Miyata estate in the province of Tanba was also a mountain *shōen* with its own lively trade in commodities and currency. We have evidence of a wealthy villager in Miyata who was able to quickly pull together one hundred *koku* of rice and two hundred *kanmon* in coins. In the neighboring Oyama estate, the villagers contracted with the proprietor to undertake all of these complicated tasks themselves. Undoubtedly, there were villagers of this caliber in Niimi estate as well. It was these kinds of people who acted as the lieutenants of the estate manager.

The manager's account books also reveal that, despite its location deep in the mountains, not only could one buy such marine products as dried squid and large fish at the fourteenth-century Niimi marketplace, but in the fifteenth century one could buy sea bream, small fish, and *wakame* and *konbu* seaweeds as well. *Konbu* is a seaweed that grows in the northern seas;

---

6. These were people who preached Buddhist sermons using picture scrolls and painting and itinerant performers who went from house to house offering prayers and dances for good fortune on important holidays such as New Year's Day.

it had to be carried by ship down from the waters around Hokkaido and northernmost Honshu, then either across the mountains of western Honshu from the Japan coast or all the way around to the Inland Sea and up the Takahashi River to the mountains of Niimi. In the fifteenth century, fish roe from the Kinai region was also available. The availability of all these products in a mountain estate reveals that a shipping route around the entire archipelago was in place by the fifteenth century. The duties of the *shōen* managers functioned as a precondition for the development of such a shipping route.

One other point of importance is that among the owners of houses in the market at Niimi there were many people who, as far as we can tell from the documents, resembled monks. For example, we find in the registers people who incorporated the names of Buddhist deities in such names as Gyō Amidabutsu or Hō Amidabutsu. In terms of class status, these people were villagers not monks. They were also different from people who had left their homes to take the tonsure. They may well have been lay monks of the Pure Land or Ji sects. But even among the villagers and landowners there were some who held the ranks of full-time monks (such as the Hōkyō or Hōgen ranks). Whatever their particular situation, it is noteworthy that a significant portion of those who lived in marketplaces and urban areas, and those merchants and financiers who became estate managers, were either monks or had the appearance of monks. This connection to religion cannot be overlooked when we consider commerce and finance in this period.

For example, in the early fourteenth century there was a shipper named Hon'a in the port of Hōshōtsu, Etchū Province, who owned one of the largest of the twenty ships registered by the Kamakura shogunate. His name suggests that he was a member of the Ji sect. In the port of Obama, Wakasa Province, there were a number of moneylenders, warehousers, and other financiers who had names just like Hon'a's, with the *a* suffix demonstrating a devotion to Amida Buddha. These people were engaged in moneylending and other financial operations while identified as mountain ascetics, some even eventually reaching the rank of priest. Thus, from ancient times many people involved in commercial and financial enterprises in Japan were monks. By the medieval era, examples of monks from the new Kamakura Buddhist sects who were involved in commerce, finance, and shipping are particularly prominent. The commercial aspects of *shōen* and the central roles of monks and their ilk are therefore the keys to a reworking of our understanding of *shōen* estates.

CHAPTER FOUR

Bandits, Pirates, Merchants, and Financiers

BANDITS AND PIRATES

Tosa Harbor was the base of the powerful Andō *uji* on the Tsugaru Peninsula (fig. 17). As I discussed briefly in my "maritime" survey of Japanese history, the city reached the height of its prosperity in the fourteenth century, rivaling the prosperity of Hakata in northern Kyushu. Tosa Harbor's once lively downtown district has yielded to archaeologists large numbers of Chinese coins and porcelain as well as Koryŏ (Korean) celadon. Indeed, from the fourteenth to the fifteenth centuries Tosa Harbor may well have been *the* international hub of the north.

To the far south, the city of Bōnotsu on the southernmost tip of Kyushu welcomed many ships from the Asian continent from the twelfth century on, and excavations in Kanzaki on the Ariake Bay have uncovered large numbers of Chinese porcelains. But coastal towns are not the only places where Chinese porcelains have turned up. They have also been found in Niimi, high up in the mountains of Okayama, demonstrating its close links to the continent.

But lurking beneath all these traces of trade lies a major problem for historians: what kind of political power guaranteed the flow of goods and bills of exchange? When "checks bounced," exchanges were deemed invalid, or there was a disagreement over bills, who could offer the guarantees that would resolve the disputes?

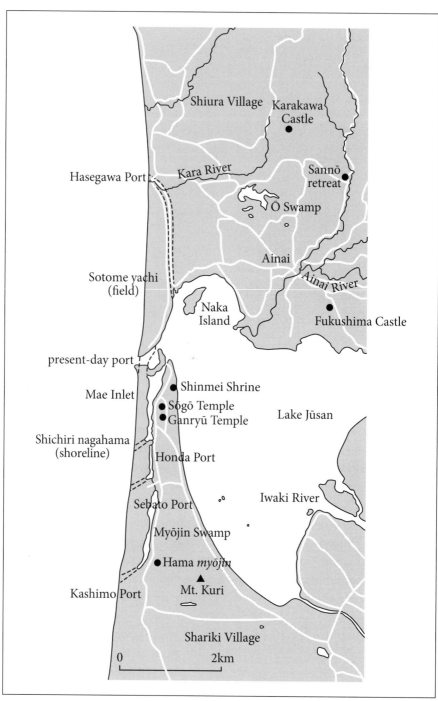

Figure 17. Map of Tosa Harbor, Lake Jūsan, and Fukushima Castle in Tsugaru.

The government did not fulfill this function. The imperial government in Kyoto, the military government in Kamakura, and the managers of *shōen* and government lands focused their attentions on the resolution of land disputes, establishing procedures for handling such problems. Without a doubt, disputes over land and fiefs were among the most serious social problems of the time. In particular, the Kamakura shogunate's power was dependent upon its vassals' well-being, and the vassals' livelihoods, in turn, were dependent on their fiefs. So, the shogunate was extremely meticulous when it came to litigation over titles to fiefs. In contrast to lawsuits relating to land disputes, which the shogunate called its property affairs (*shomu sata*), litigation relating to loans, commerce, or distribution were designated "miscellaneous."[1] As the category implies, these lawsuits were not taken seriously. This had been true since the archaic Ritsuryō state, once again revealing the state's agrarian fundamentalist ideology.

However, the imperial and shrine purveyors who were outside the state land system had organized their own financial and distribution networks by the eleventh century. These groups held their own trials in matters related to commerce and had the power to enforce their decisions. Of course, the imperial government did not find this alternative authority acceptable. In the twelfth and thirteenth centuries, the government strove to strengthen its control over the activities of imperial and shrine purveyors, designing an official system that could incorporate them. However, as the cash economy continued to grow from the thirteenth to the fourteenth centuries, commercial and financial organizations and shipping networks also expanded and grew more complex. At the same time, the organizations for imperial and shrine purveyors continued to expand beyond the framework previously provided by the state, becoming more independent. In particular, new groups that managed the traffic and transportation routes became more active during this period.

As far as the government was concerned, these people were bandits (*akutō*) and pirates (*kaizoku*). For example, a picture scroll depicting the travels of Ippen, the founder of the Buddhist Ji sect, relates the famous story of his service at the temple of Jimokuji in Owari.[2] In the story, Ippen's followers ran out of food during an especially long ceremony. Just as they began to show signs of fatigue, two wealthy "virtuous men" (*tokujin*) in nearby Kayatsu had

---

1. The Kamakura shogunate recognized three classes of lawsuits: land, criminal, and miscellaneous.
2. See chapter eight for a more complete discussion of this scene.

a dream in which the Buddhist deity Bishamon ordered them to give alms to Ippen and his monks. In the scroll, these men are shown in unusual attire, with long, loose hair, wearing tall *geta*, and holding fans. According to the text accompanying this scene, the bandits of Owari and Mino had erected an edict board warning that anyone who attempted to interfere with Ippen's evangelical work would be executed.[3] As a result, Ippen's group was able to preach in that region for three years without interference from bandits in the mountains or pirates on the seas.

In Ippen's time, the ocean reached far inland at Owari and Mino, quite different from the way it is today, and the "outlaws" of that area included groups of "pirates" who worked the oceans and rivers. Even though these groups had no relation to the public authorities, they were able to raise their own edict boards and guarantee the safety of Ippen's passage themselves. In fact, it might be more accurate to call these armed groups masters of the sea (*umi no ryōshu*) or lords of the mountains (*yama no ryōshu*) rather than pirates and bandits. Their power derived from their relation to roads and waterways. Many of them were also mountain ascetics or monks from the Tendai monastery on Mount Hiei who engaged in commercial and financial enterprises. Thus, the circulation of bills of exchange from the thirteenth to fourteenth centuries that the network of merchants and financiers guaranteed was in turn secured by the control of transportation routes by these bandits and pirates.

These people were originally known as wanderers (*yūshu fushoku no tomogara*), and many of them had once been gamblers. By the thirteenth century, however, bandits and pirates possessed an organization covering a wide area. Whenever there was trouble of some kind within their territory, they would take bribes and gratuities, hear lawsuits, and resolve the problems by their own authority. Since they would take up lawsuits refused by the authorities, the disputants would actively seek them out and pay tribute in the hopes of a speedy resolution. A bribe paid before the fact was called a mountain toll (*yamagoshi*),[4] while a gratuity paid afterward was called a contract (*keiyaku*).

3. Edict boards were the standard means of proclaiming new laws and ordinances. That the bandits would erect such a board suggests that they had arrogated to themselves the practices of official government.
4. *Yamagoshi* means "crossing the mountain" and may originally have referred to a payment of a kind of toll to the local powers to guarantee safe passage across a pass.

In a well-known incident at the beginning of the fourteenth century, a large group of bandits broke into the border post at Hyōgo. It was reported that a number of women were seen among their number. Thus, we know for a fact that women were active in these groups and that many of the merchants and financiers who depended on the bandits' organization were women. Some among them, in fact, were probably known as courtesans.

WHAT WAS "EVIL"?

Of course, the state could not ignore their activities. Since its power was based on the real estate holdings of its military estate, stewards, and vassals, the Kamakura shogunate in particular often found its local authorities entangled with the activities of bandits and pirates. The authorities could not look on quietly when order in their domains was thus disrupted. The shogunate issued order after order calling for the suppression of bandits and pirates throughout the thirteenth and fourteenth centuries. Such domestic disturbances were particularly disadvantageous to the shogunate when the Mongols were threatening to invade from the Asian mainland. Having labeled the "rulers" of the sea, mountains, and roads "bandits" and "pirates," the shogunate used military means to suppress and pacify these independent organizations.

Within the shogunate, the harshest opponents of the bandits were those who advocated what was called "beneficent government" based on the principles of "agrarian fundamentalism," the ideology of military landed power. From the perspective of agrarian fundamentalists, "evil" was represented by people who were attracted by the "magical" powers of coinage and currency—the merchants and financiers who pursued profit and interest—and those who inhabited the roadways of the mountains and rivers, who enjoyed the taking of life in hunting and fishing and engaged in gambling.

The word *evil* in those days was applied to phenomena that disrupted everyday peace, to that which exceeded the power of ordinary people. The taking of profits or interest in and of itself, and by extension commerce and finance, were seen as evil in this sense. Such activities as gambling—which decided matters by means of a roll of the dice—and sex, as well as the condition of pollution (*kegare*), were all seen as related to evil powers that exceeded the power of ordinary humans. Many of those who were seen as possessing such extraordinary power were officially called evil, being referred to in documents as Evil Shichibei, Evil Genta, or Evil Safu. It was this view of evil that labeled organizations of financiers, merchants, and rulers of the ocean and mountains "evil bands."

But while the Kamakura shogunate's attacks on evil bands were part of an attempt to suppress the nonofficial networks of merchants, financiers, and distributors, we may also discern an aggressive attempt within the shogunate not to suppress but to acquire control of these groups' activities. Based as it was on lord and vassal relations in which fiefs were divided among one's own family vassals, the shogunate approached the task of controlling the bandits in an essentially "agrarian fundamentalist" mode. But the private vassals (*miuchibito*) of the Hōjō regents (the Tokusō line), who controlled the office of the shogun, took a different approach. The *miuchibito* actively attempted to establish links with merchants and financiers and bring rivers and roadways under their control. They appointed the heads of financial groups to the position of domainal manager and placed them under contract for the collection of land taxes. The case of Niimi estate is one such example where monks and mountain ascetics, otherwise deemed evil bandits, became land managers. However, in addition to the standard contracts for land taxes, they were encouraged to engage in the currency transactions necessary for the development of a prosperous consumer economy.

The Tokusō Hōjō also acquired specific harbors and ports that were important to maritime shipping and issued special licenses for their use. Thus, the Tokusō Hōjō derived a significant income from maritime trade. The existence of approximately twenty huge "Kanto-licensed Tsugaru ships," licensed by the Hōjō to ply their trade between Kamakura and Tsugaru from the beginning of the fourteenth century, reminds us of this often unrecognized source of Hōjō wealth. Such ships could also be found in Hōshōtsu Harbor in Etchū and Tagarasu Bay in Wakasa, both on the Japan Sea coast north of Kyoto. Even though it was directly opposed to the agrarian fundamentalist policy that formally characterized the shogunate, the Hōjō family exploited the maritime trade and distribution system for its own profit.

In fact, politics from the late Kamakura through the early Northern and Southern Courts period was characterized by a tense struggle between these two political lines. This ideological split played an important role in the well-known Shimotsuki Incident of 1285 in which Adachi Yasumori—a representative of the shogunate's vassals and advocate of agrarian fundamentalist policies—was defeated in a coup by Taira no Yoritsuna—a representative of the Hōjō family vassals. This was a turning point for the shogunate, which then shifted from trying to suppress the bandit and pirate networks to trying to incorporate them within its systems of control.

The Hōjō family also came to monopolize trade and diplomatic relations with the Asian continent by the beginning of the fourteenth century. Until that point, aristocratic families such as the Saionji and a number of shogunate vassals had sent their own trade missions to China, but by the end of the thirteenth century, as virtually all important harbors became Hōjō family holdings, they were supplanted. Thus, the Hōjō family sought to bring domestic and foreign commercial and financial networks in the islands under their direct control. In the end, their policies aroused the intense opposition of other maritime powers in the islands.

At the beginning of the fourteenth century, the "pirates" of Kumano staged a major rebellion in western Honshu. We do not know many details of the incident, but it appears that the Kumano Shrine purveyors, who wielded great power over an area that included the Kii Peninsula, the Inland Sea, and northern Kyushu, rose up against the Hōjō family's tyrannical control. In response, the Hōjō family mobilized troops from fifteen provinces to put the rebellion down. The fighting lasted two or three years. The mobilization of troops from fifteen provinces matches in scale the mobilizations undertaken to put down the famous Jōkyū Disturbance of 1221 and the battles against Kusunoki Masashige at the time of the Kamakura shogunate's demise. The sheer numbers and time it took to quell the Kumano rebellion gives us a good idea of just how serious and widespread this rebellion was.[5]

The "Ezo" disturbances, in which the maritime powers of Hokkaidō challenged the Hōjō incursions into their area took place at nearly the same

---

5. The Jōkyū Disturbance and the rebellion of Kusunoki Masashige at the end of the Kamakura period are events that would be very familiar to a general Japanese audience. Both would be covered in high school history textbooks, and both have found expression in other cultural forms (plays, paintings, novels, and so on). But the fact that the uprising of the Kumano pirates was on the same scale as these two would take many of his Japanese readers by surprise, since many would not have heard of it before. While Amino is not explicit about it here, one reason is that the first two incidents involved fighting by warriors against other members of the warrior class, with one side being backed by the aristocracy. The rebellion of the Kumano pirates, however, was a civil war fought by warriors on one side and nonwarrior people on the other. This stresses Amino's general point about "rereading Japanese history." The mainstream textbooks restrict their narratives to stories involving the elites—the aristocracy and the warrior class. To the degree that they mention such rebellions as that of the Kumano pirates, they depict them as marginal to the main story line. Amino's insistence that the mobilization to suppress the uprising was as big as the mobilizations to suppress the Jōkyū Disturbance and Kusunoki Masashige is an argument to the effect that neither the Kumano uprising not the pirates were marginal.

time. The rebellion pitted factions of the Andō *uji*—who controlled a commercial network from the Japan Sea to Hokkaido from the Tsugaru Peninsula city of Tosa Harbor—in alliance with the Ainu—who were then quite active in trade—against the Hōjō. This rebellion broke out several times, and the Hōjō were ultimately unable to suppress it before their own fall from power.

Emperor Go-Daigo made his appearance on the historical stage in the midst of this chaos. Go-Daigo employed the military power of these bandit groups to topple the Hōjō family and the Kamakura shogunate. In doing so, he expanded upon the *miuchibito*'s policy of aligning themselves with commercial groups. Even before proclaiming the demise of the shogunate and the establishment of his new imperial government, Go-Daigo attempted to place Kyoto under his personal control by taxing the sake brewers of the city and making all shrine purveyors from Hie, Kasuga, and Iwashimizu Hachiman Shrines his direct attendants. He also ordered that the products of all military steward's fiefs be converted into currency and taxed at 5 percent. This revenue was turned over to Kyoto financiers and lenders to be used to meet government expenses. Go-Daigo also planned to mint coins and issue paper currency. His policies were thus founded on commercial and financial interests rather than agrarian fundamentalist principles. They were also ultimately despotic. Although he did not achieve these goals, their failure was not necessarily due to impracticality, given the frequency with which bills of exchange were traded at the time.

Politics from the thirteenth to the fourteenth centuries was thus characterized by a division between agrarian and mercantile lines. The agrarian line was supported by a system of land taxation that emphasized maintaining warrior control of fiefs and that drew annual tribute from the fields of private and public estates. In contrast, the mercantile line sought to organize the activities of the rising merchants, financiers, and shippers, to build its strength on networks of distribution, and to develop trade to the north and west as well as across the sea.

These two ideological strains came to blows amid the violent transformations of society during this era. The mercantile line gradually came to dominate. By the end of the fourteenth century, Ashikaga Yoshimitsu came close to achieving what Go-Daigo had planned but failed to do. For a period thereafter, agrarian fundamentalism ceded to mercantilism the dominant position in government.

URBAN RELIGION: THE TEACHINGS OF IPPEN

The clash of these two ideologies was not limited to the realm of politics. Religion had to deal with many of the same issues, most notably the problem of evil.

In the early thirteenth century, Shinran, the founder of the True Pure Land Buddhist sect, proclaimed the theory of "evil's advantage." According to Shinran, faith in Amida Buddha's vow to save mankind was the only path to salvation. If even a good man could be reborn in Amida's Western Paradise, Shinran argued, then an evil man had a much greater chance of achieving that rebirth since he would be much less likely to think he would gain a propitious rebirth through his own good deeds. Evil's advantage thus represented a positive approach to evil. After Shinran, Ippen, the founder of the Ji sect, developed a thoroughly universalist theory of salvation in which he claimed that anyone—good or evil, pure or impure, faithful or unfaithful—could be reborn in Paradise if he or she would receive a wooden plaque with the inscription "In the Name of Amida Buddha" on it. Through his belief in the unconditional vow of Amida Buddha, Ippen was able to face and accept what society at the time called evil. For this reason, his supporters included the evil bandits as well as the wealthy merchants and financiers who called themselves virtuous men. Many women also became believers of Ippen's credo at a time when they were increasingly being stigmatized as impure. A great many became nuns and roamed the country with Ippen's group. Ippen's supporters also included many outcastes, or "nonhumans," as I discuss in further detail in chapter eight.

What is important for our discussion here is that Ippen's teachings spread quickly in such urban settings as port towns. As an examination of *The Picture Scroll of the Holy Man Ippen* shows, Ippen's evangelical work covered a broad area. This, of course, would have been impossible had transportation networks not been stable. Ippen is also known for his attempt to distribute wooden plaques to six hundred thousand people. Considering the population of the islands at that time, this was a tremendous task that would have been possible only after urban areas, where people gathered in large numbers, had developed.

Ippen is also known for the *nenbutsu* dance, a kind of religious ceremony performed on a special stage that would be constructed in areas where people gathered in large numbers in the hope of attracting a significant audience (fig. 18). This method of proselytization was predicated on the existence of urban spaces. Indeed, a reading of a document called "A Record of Ji Sect Buddhism" shows that many of the people converted by Ippen's group were "saved" in urban spaces such as ports and markets.

The Picture Scroll of the Holy Man Ippen, which was painted in the late thirteenth century, differs from earlier picture scrolls, which usually depicted agricultural scenes. Through the scroll's depictions of a number of urban scenes, we get a view of one of the major social currents of the time, the growth of urban spaces. Indeed, Ippen's teachings constitute a truly urban religion; its adherents were primarily urban denizens.

Yet from an official standpoint these people were evil and impure. The monks of major temples and shrines, aristocrats, and warriors—particularly those who supported the agrarian fundamentalist line—all saw Ippen's preaching and the composition of his followers as "the work of goblins," as activities, in other words, that had to be censured. Two contemporaneous works, a picture scroll called *The Picture Book of Goblins* (*Tengu sōshi*) and a poetry collection called *A Mirror of Pastoral Life* (*Nomori no kagami*), illustrate this position, harshly criticizing the fact that Ippen included "impure" women and nonhumans in his traveling corps. These texts explicitly depict Ippen's sect as a licentious, mendicant group supported by evil bandits that welcomed polluted outcastes and women.

Figure 18. Dance hut in a center island at Seki Temple. Monks of the Ji sect are performing a *nenbutsu*. From *The Picture Scroll of the Holy Man Ippen.* Source: *Ippen hijirie,* from the collection of the Tokyo National Museum.

RELIGIOUS SOLICITORS AS TRADERS AND ENTREPRENEURS

During the early Kamakura period, other religious figures, such as Shinran and Nichiren, adopted the same tactics as Ippen, purposefully going to preach among the nonhumans and bandits. Monks from the Ritsu and Zen sects also sought to save the nonhumans as a positive response to new developments in society. In addition, there were monks who, even though they wielded great power in the management of *shōen* estates, linked themselves to the Hōjō family's aggressive pursuit of commercial and distributive power and thus came to function as venture capitalists. How, exactly, did they do this?

The monks of the Ritsu and Zen sects first obtained the permission of the Hōjō family, or the imperial court (if they were in the west), to travel the country soliciting contributions for temple construction or some such religious project. Originally these religious solicitors (*kanjin shōnin*) had to walk from province to province and house to house soliciting donations from individual families. But by the Kamakura period they were constructing checkpoints (like tollbooths) in harbors and post towns, collecting their "contributions" as a kind of transportation tax. Another method was to employ provinicial constables, with the permission of the Hōjō family or the imperial court, to collect ten *mon* in cash from every house in a particular region as a contribution. This forced contribution was known as "roof beam money." By the fourteenth century, religious solicitors were thus accumulating capital through obligatory contributions at checkpoints and the activities of constables. The accumulated capital was sometimes immediately put to the use for which it had been solicited, such as the repair of temples.

However, from the fourteenth century on, such funds were occasionally used to construct large trading ships—*karabune* or "Chinese ships"—which were sent to China on trade missions to earn even more money (fig. 19). Because these vessels were called Chinese ships, many have assumed that they were built in and operated from China. However, while that may have been the case with many, these ships were not exclusively Chinese in origin. I believe that the Shin'an wreck, which I discuss in chapter seven, was probably constructed in the Japanese islands. The ship was made of Taiwanese red pine, a southern tree, so there are some who argue that the ship was built in China. But a great deal of Japanese cypress was crossing the ocean to China for use in construction there from the thirteenth century on, so it is not inconceivable that materials from southern China would have made their way

Figure 19. Rented ship from the Kamakura period. From *The Picture Scroll of the Holy Man Ippen*. Source: *Ippen hijirie*, from the collection of Shōjōkōji.

to the Japanese islands. In fact, we have already been able to confirm that some *karabune* were constructed in northern Kyushu.

Nevertheless, construction of such a large, sturdy ship would require the organization and mobilization of a variety of tradesmen. It is here that I find support for my hypothesis of the Shin'an wreck's Japanese construction. The construction of large ships at the time was undertaken by professional sailors known as net attendants (*gōshi*) or net masters (*gōsu*), who were contracted to organize ship's carpenters and blacksmiths and hire sailors for the trip across the ocean. The recovery of the Shin'an wreck has produced not only large numbers of coins and porcelain but many wooden tablets (*mokkan*) (fig. 20). These tablets contain the names of what appear to be Japanese people, such as Iyajirō, so we know that there were many sailors from the Japanese islands onboard. The ship's crew also included a *gōsu* and a religious solicitor. Assuming that this ship began its trip from the archipelago, it was probably loaded with such goods as pearls, swords, gold dust, and mercury when it left.

When the Hōjō family dispatched a religious solicitor on a trip to China, they sent him with goods from Hōjō lands to be sold in exchange

Figure 20. Notes on wooden tablets (*mokkan*) from the Shin'an wreck. Top: net attendants (*gōshi*). Bottom: religious solicitor (*kanjin hijiri*) Kyōsen. From the collection of the National Museum of Korea. Photograph courtesy of Shūkan Asahi Hyakka, ed., *Shintei zōho Nihon no rekishi*, vol. 9.

for an enormous amount of porcelain and Chinese coins. The religious so-licitor would bring these back to the Japanese islands and travel from prov-ince to province selling the pottery for profit, using the coins themselves as capital. We know that the solicitor on board the Shin'an wreck was work-ing for the temple of Tōfukuji in Kyōto, so it is likely that the Shin'an wreck was a Tōfukuji-owned *karabune*. There were also *karabune* employed by the Hōjō family to gather funds for such temples as Kenchōji, Shōchōjun'in, and the Great Buddha in Kamakura. Since the Shin'an wreck was working for a Kyoto temple, it is unclear whether or not it was dispatched on orders from the Hōjō. I personally believe that the ship was dispatched by Emperor Go-Daigo, but in any case the ship's mission was clearly frustrated by its sinking.

If the ship had been able to return safely, its profits would have been used for a large-scale construction project at Tōfukuji. Such construction would have required that the religious solicitor mobilize a labor force of non-humans and "riverside people" as well as temple carpenters, blacksmiths, plasterers, shinglers, coppersmiths, casters, stone cutters, and other such craftsmen. There is really no appropriate academic term with which to de-scribe the monk who could have organized and mobilized such an array of workers, but if we were to use a contemporary referent, we might describe these men as half venture capitalist and half construction contractor. It is im-portant to remember that the Ritsu and Zen Buddhist sects were particularly active in this capacity. We should also recall that Emperor Go-Daigo and the Hōjō had the political power to protect, support, and impel these monks along these paths.

The disturbances of the Northern and Southern Courts period consti-tuted a watershed for Japanese society. After that era, commodity circula-tion, currency, and a credit economy developed on a scale unlike anything before, driving politics and religion in new directions. That is why I see this period as representing a major turning point in the history of civilization in the Japanese archipelago. Moreover, since people in Japan, the Ryukyus, and Hokkaido began to formulate a sense of their own identities at this time, one can also say that this was a turning point in the ethnic history of the islands.

THE FORMATION OF VILLAGES AND TOWNS

As these disturbances came to an end in the fifteenth century, the close trade relationship between the Japanese archipelago and the Asian continent grew even closer, largely as a result of Ashikaga Yoshimitsu's mercantile policies. Trade relations also expanded to a wider area. At the beginning of the fifteenth century, ships from Palembang in Sumatra, known to Japanese as "southern barbarian ships," entered the harbor of Obama in Wakasa. These ships did not arrive in Obama by accident but came on regular, annual visits.

The official ambassadors on these ships brought documents addressing Shogun Ashikaga Yoshimitsu as the "king of Japan." On one of these occasions, the first elephant ever seen in Japan was brought as a gift to the king. Yoshimitsu reportedly saw the elephant once, but since he was not able to care for it he had it sent back to Sumatra. Be that as it may, the transport of an elephant all the way from Sumatra shows how securely Japan was incorporated into the pan-Asian trading sphere, which even included Southeast Asia. The Ryukyuan kingdom, which was first established in the late fourteenth century, was founded on this kind of trading activity, with Ryukyuan ships plying the maritime trade routes in all directions.

We know, too, that relations with Northeast Asia were quite close. Tosa Harbor in Tsugaru was, as mentioned earlier, deeply engaged in trade with areas all along the west coast of the Japan Sea. However, it also appears to have been engaged in trade with Northeast Asia. Therefore, our understanding of fifteenth-century life in the Japanese islands must take into account the close trade relationship with all of East Asia.

Such conditions as the proliferation of urban spaces, the entrenchment of a cash economy, and the spread of a manager-contract system for *shōen* estate and government lands contributed to the stability of the fifteenth century and promoted the formation of a number of self-governing villages and towns. While the form of the *shōen* system remained as a legacy of earlier times, Japanese society was shifting to what might be called a village and town system. These settlements were generally governed autonomously, the city of Sakai being the most famous example. Many villages also began to operate on the village contract system (*mura-uke sei*), whereby the village rather than an overlord contracted with the government for the collection and payment of the annual tax. This suggests that the inhabitants of villages and towns had accumulated the necessary skills to manage affairs that had previously been the domain of specialized estate managers.

When Japanese society entered the Warring States period in the fifteenth and sixteenth centuries, a number of small regional states ruled by feudal lords and built upon this village and town system engaged in violent struggle with each other. What has largely been ignored in our studies of this period is the surprising degree to which "rulers of the sea"—pirates, merchants, and shippers—strengthened their organizations and increased their activities.

For example, traffic on Lake Biwa had long been heavy, but transport on the lake during this period was controlled by pirates from the town of Katada. These pirates had bases in all the ports and inlets on the lake, and when anyone sailed on it they always took a pirate from Katada onboard with them. Since these people were sought out by the shippers themselves, they were paid a gratuity, which functioned as a kind of transport tax to Katada. This in turn provided a guarantee of safe passage. Indeed, the *Honpukuji Temple Memoirs*, written by a True Pure Land monk named Myōzei, noted that if a ship flew the banner of Katada it could cross the lake safely. However, if a ship tried to cross the lake without paying a gratuity, its cargo would be impounded by Katada. This made the people of Katada the equivalent of pirates, for if a ship did not pay the toll, they would not only attack it and impound the cargo, but they would kill everyone onboard, even children. Such rumors undoubtedly helped spread the word that safe passage would be assured only if deference were paid to the pirates.

CUSTOMARY LAW OF THE SEAS

At the beginning of the fifteenth century, a Korean diplomat named Song Hŭigyŏng wrote a record of a trip he made to Japan. His text provides a rich account of the customs and society of western Japan at that time. The text also contains precise information on pirates. Son's description of his embassy's stay on the island of Kamagari in the province of Aki on the Inland Sea resembles the situation in Katada. If boats coming from the east carried an eastern pirate, then western pirates would not touch the boat, and the same held true for the reverse. Kamagiri Island served as the border between the eastern and western halves of the Inland Sea and as the contact point between the pirates of each region. Son wrote that he paid seven *kanmon* to an eastern pirate on Kamagiri for safe passage to the west.

This kind of practice was common on the seas at the time. The various regional maritime powers maintained contact with one other, and as long as checkpoint tolls and warning fees were paid, passage within the linked territories was safe. The affirmative term for these maritime powers at this time was *kaizokushū* (buccaneer). In other words, the term *pirate* was not used in a derogatory manner. It was the accepted term of use among the people I am now calling rulers of the sea. The same situation held for mountain roads, although the affirmative term was not *mountain pirates* (*sanzokushū*) but *mountain yeomen* (*yamadachi*).

In order to maintain control over their territories, these groups built fortresses on islands and capes overlooking entries to the harbors or waters through which all boats necessarily passed. These were both defensive posts and watchtowers for the observation of passing ships. For example, on the tips of the Taichi and Shio Capes, there are mountains known as castle mountains (*shiroyama*). During the Edo period, these mountains functioned as whaling lookout points. When whales were spotted out to sea, the watchmen would light signal fires to inform the whaling bosses. The whaling bosses would then use handheld banners to guide the boats and help them surround and capture the whales. This fishing method can be traced directly back to the practices of the pirate organizations. As on Lake Biwa, there would be no trouble if deference were paid, but if a ship attempted to pass without payment, men in the lookout would light signal fires. A number of small boats from the pirate leader would then surround the offending ship on all sides and impound the cargo.

The Inland Sea and Japan Sea regions had a high concentration of such pirates. There were also many of these lookout posts near harbors in Hokkaido, such as the Katsuyama Fort in Kaminokuni. Most Japanese think of a castle as signifying a mountain fortress in inland regions. However, to truly grasp the nature of fortresses in Japan, we must consider these coastal fortresses in the same terms as the inland mountain castles.

When I first went to Okinawa in the winter of 1993, I found that the castles there, called *gusuku*, all overlooked the sea. These castles closely resembled the ocean fortresses of Honshu. Moreover, these *gusuku* were sometimes also located on sacred land known as *utaki*. In fact, the same was often true of fortresses in Honshu, Shikoku, and Kyushu, where capes were considered sacred places and deities were worshipped there. The "first rice" offered there in worship by passing ships may have been the origin of checkpoint tolls.

In this way, the networks of merchant and local maritime powers became more tightly organized in the fifteenth and sixteenth centuries. Accordingly, it was at this time that customary law for shippers was codified. In the archaic past, any object that approached on the ocean from afar was seen as belonging to the deities, to be used, therefore, by temples or shrines. We also know from documents that customary practices existed to deal with ships that struck reefs or were otherwise wrecked. These customs were finally written down in the sixteenth century in a text known variously as the "The Greater Law for Shipping" (*Kaisen daihō*) or "Shipping Customs" (*Kaisen shikimoku*), which was composed of thirty-one items. Ten more items were added to these codes in the Edo period, and the text was copied and carefully maintained in harbors and ports throughout the islands.

It is not clear who compiled these laws or how. Based on form alone, the common claim that it was issued by Hōjō Yoshitoki in 1223 or by emperor Go-Horikawa appears to be false. These codes were probably written in the sixteenth century when someone gathered information regarding customary law among shippers and wrote it down. People from Bōnotsu in Satsuma, Urado in Tosa, and Hyōgo in Settsu clearly had a hand in their compilation, with the people from Urado playing an especially important role.

There was a similar move to codify merchants' customary practices. Such documents stressed "the history of the commercial way" and referred to previous "merchants' decisions." None of these codification's of customary merchant law survives today, although we can see traces of such documents in genealogical texts such as *The Principles of the Scales* (*Hakari no honji*) and *Important Affairs of Renjaku* (*Renjaku no daiji*). However, much work remains to be done on this topic.[6]

By the sixteenth century, feudal warlords had taken control of every region, having established small estates and drafted their own laws. Yet the networks of merchants, financiers, and shippers remained independent of the feudal lords. They maintained their own customary laws, which they had compiled themselves, and actively maintained their relationships outside the Japanese archipelago. It would take the interdiction of foreign trade by the Tokugawa shogunate in 1638 to bring this to an end.

6. For a further discussion of this, see Amino Yoshihiko, "Chūsei shōnin no sekai" (The World of Medieval Merchants), *in Rettō no bunkashi* (Cultural History of the Archipelago), no. 9 (Tokyo: Nihon editā sukūru shuppanbu, 1992).

CHAPTER FIVE

Rethinking Japanese Society

THE TERM *FARMER*

In the process of the fifteenth-century transformations I have described, a derogatory view of agriculture formed in Japanese society quite contrary to the aims of agricultural fundamentalism. As I have repeatedly emphasized, the term *hyakushō* did not mean farmer until modern times. From ancient times, there has been a different word for farmer: *nōmin*. A close examination of historical documents will also turn up another word for farmer, *nōnin*, which was used surprisingly far back in time.

The first known use of *nōnin* is in the ancient history *A Record of the Latter Ages of Japan* (*Nihon kōki*) in an entry for the year 811. It also appears in official documents of the Grand Council of State in 824. Moreover, in a text called *The Way of Household Instruction* (*Teikin ōrai*), we find the following statement: "If there is land that should be developed, summon farmers (*nōnin*) and have them develop it." If we skip forward to the end of the Edo period and examine the local almanac compiled by the Mōri clan, *A Report on the Customs of the Bōchō Region* (*Bōchō fūdo chūshūan*), we find statistics on *hyakushō* divided into households of farmers (*nōnin*), merchants, blacksmiths, and so on. It is clear from this that *hyakushō* did not refer strictly to farmers. Instead, *nōnin* was the word used for farmers from ancient times through the early modern era.

Here we come upon an important question. In a fifteenth-century poetry contest picture scroll called *The Songs of Thirty-two Tradesmen (Sanjū-niban shokunin utaawase)*, we find a farmer (*nōnin*) listed among the "people of the various trades." This is the only example of a farmer appearing in any poetry contest picture scroll. We should note that this scroll was made at a time when the trades it depicted were beginning to be denigrated. It begins with a pairing of a *senzu manzai*[1] and a picture preacher[2] and goes through a range of performers, such as bell ringers,[3] monkey trainers, and bird catchers. At the time this scroll was probably produced, all of these people were considered debased. Indeed, the introduction to the scroll contains the statement, "we thirty-odd people are of despicable stature."

An aristocrat produced the scroll, whose contents were represented as a command performance of song making by members of the trades just beginning to be stigmatized. What is of interest to our present discussion is that the farmer is paired with a garden sweeper. The sweeper with whom the farmer is paired was originally a riverside dweller[4] who worked on construction projects, including garden construction. In effect, then, farmers are treated here as one of the stigmatized.

One of Japan's most famous garden designers, Zen'ami, was known as a gardener for the shogun (*kubō oniwamono*). Gardeners in the service of the emperor were known as *kinri* gardeners.[5] In general, garden people (*oniwamono*) were riverside dwellers who had connections to court nobles. Despite these illustrious connections, there is no doubt that by this time they had come to be despised. The reason why garden sweepers and farmers are paired in this scroll is probably that both work with the soil. In ancient times, it was believed that causing a change in nature produced a state of pollution. By the fifteenth century, simply tampering with the earth was considered polluting, so farming was understood to be filthy work.[6] Thus, from the perspective of this picture scroll, farmers were despicable.

The late-fifteenth-century *Honpukuji Temple Memoirs* provides us with corroborating evidence. The *Memoirs* was composed by a man named

1. *Senzu manzai* were itinerant people who made their living going from house to house setting up a portable shrine at the entry gate and praying for the good fortune of the household. Since this practice does not appear to have been specially requested by the people of the household, the *senzu manzai* may be seen as a form of beggar.
2. *Etoki* were popular preachers who traveled with picture scrolls depicting various Buddhist scenes. They would gather an audience and preach a Buddhist sermon by explaining the contents of the picture.
3. Like the *senzu manzai* and the picture preachers, bell ringers were itinerant people who chanted Buddhist sutras while ringing a bell or banging a small gong.
4. See chapter eight for a detailed discussion of riverside dwellers.
5. The *kinri* in *kinri gardeners* suggests someone who has access to forbidden interior spaces.
6. When Amino writes about pollution, he is not referring to environmental pollution, as contemporary usage understands it, but to the anthropological notion of pollution: a state of physical and

Myōzei, a priest of the True Pure Land sect temple Honpukuji in the town of Katada on the shores of Lake Biwa. The text relates the activities of the famous monk Rennyo[7] during his visit to Katada as well as miscellaneous town matters. It is an extremely valuable document for understanding the true character of life in those times.

Related to our discussion here, Myōzei observed in the *Memoirs* that "there is no harder work than working in the fields." In contrast, blacksmiths, coopers, grinders, and carpenters were all depicted in the *Memoirs* as rich. According to Myōzei, "even in bad years" these people "do not starve." Myōzei's *Memoirs* reveals in several places that he considered merchants and artisans to be better than farmers.

In the letters of Rennyo, we find an early example of the use of the term *samurai-peasants-artisans-merchants* (*shi-nō-kō-shō*), which we associate with the Edo period class structure. Interestingly, Rennyo uses the character for talent, also pronounced *nō* for the second occupation (peasant) rather than the usual character for agriculture. We may also note that he did not seem to view samurai as occupying the highest position. For Rennyo, *nō* (farming) was performed by people "based in production" who submitted themselves to tilling the soil. He also evaluated commerce very highly: "Morning and night they endeavor to sell, sometimes riding on the rough seas, never turning away from the risk that they will encounter terrifying waves." In his description of artisans, however, he writes that they "revel in the arts and seduce people; they fill books with lies and oddities and troll the floating world." This would seem more appropriate to performers than artisans, but in any case this is a far different stance regarding these classes than that of the Tokugawa shogunate.

Nevertheless, at the time there were certainly members of the True Pure Land sect who viewed agriculture as one of the lowest forms of work. At the very least, we could say that farming was not a respected occupation. Instead, it appears that a high opinion of commerce and manufacturing was perhaps more common among True Pure Land adherents. The True Pure Land sect appears to have been in the vanguard of the mercantilist politics that emerged in the fifteenth and sixteenth centuries.

---

spiritual defilement. People get dirty when performing many kinds of tasks, but the point is that some are seen as reflecting on the character of the person who performs the task. Today, gardeners and garbage collectors may both get equally dirty from a day's work, but gardeners do not face the stigmatization that garbage collectors do. See chapter eight for more details.

7. Rennyo (1415–94) was the eighth abbot of the True Pure Land Shin sect and one of its great proselytizers and organizers.

Until recently, scholars have seen the *ikkō ikki* insurrections of this time as provincial and peasant uprisings, sometimes going so far as to call them "peasant wars." It is true that the *ikkō* insurrections toppled the *shugo* governor of Kaga Province and that the insurrectionists declared Kaga "a land held by the *hyakushō.*" But historians' representation of Kaga as a "kingdom of farmers" is a mistake based on our present-day presumption that *hyakushō* meant farmers. Inoue Toshio was far closer to the truth when he looked for the main base of support for the True Pure Land sect among seagoing folk: fishermen, wealthy shippers, and warehousers.[8]

THE CLASH OF MERCANTILISM AND
AGRICULTURAL FUNDAMENTALISM

In fact, most of the bases of the True Pure Land sect from the fifteenth century on were in urban areas. The town of Katada, once the largest city on Lake Biwa, was one such base, even serving as Rennyo's headquarters for a while. Rennyo also claimed that until he established a practice hall in the town of Yoshizaki, in Echizen, the town was a place "of foxes and badgers," meaning that it was utterly rustic. In fact, it is likely that Rennyo established a hall there because Yoshizaki was well located to function as a port. Yamashina, the site of the temple of Honganji,[9] was also an urban site. Another important base of the True Pure Land sect, Ishiyama, is actually a section of Osaka, so naturally it was urban also. Nagashima, in Ise, was a city surrounded by rivers and the ocean, as was Hiroshima, and both were strongholds of the sect. If we go on to look into the Hokuriku region, we find that most of the big True Pure Land temples and practice halls were located on the coast along shipping routes.

We also find a huge True Pure Land temple in the mountains of the Noto Peninsula in a village called Yanagita. This may seem an exception to our rule. However, Yanagita was not a simple mountain village but a place where a kind of lacquerware known as *gōrokunuri* was produced in great quantities. Due to its character as a site for craft production, Yanagita can be

---

8. See, for example, Inoue Toshio, *Yama no tami, kawa no tami: Nihon chūsei no seikatsu to shinkō* (People of the Mountains, People of the Rivers: Life and Faith in Medieval Japan) (Tokyo: Heibonsha, 1981); and *Ikkō ikki no kenkyū* (Studies of the Ikkō Rebellions) (Tokyo: Yoshikawa kōbunkan, 1968).

9. This was the headquarters of the True Pure Land sect.

considered to have had an urban character. Furthermore, large numbers of merchants and craftsmen lived in the precincts of True Pure Land temples in places like Kaizuka in Izumi Province and Imai in Yamato Province, making the temple itself the center of a town.

We must be careful here to remember that by the fifteenth century Japanese society was undergoing a major transformation. Fear of the deities and pollution was waning, and stigmatization of such people as nonhumans, riverside dwellers, courtesans, and gamblers was beginning to permeate society. The religious position of the Ji sect—which held that there is no difference between good and evil and that everyone has to be saved—gradually lost its power over these stigmatized people. In the fifteenth century, more and more of these groups associated themselves with the True Pure Land sect, which pointedly contrasted good and evil and positively proclaimed support for "evil."

It appears that the Ji sect bases were taken over by the Ikkō movement[10] in the fifteenth and sixteenth centuries. Just like the Ji, the True Pure Land sect was a thoroughly urban movement. In fact, the Nichiren sect, another of the new Buddhist sects of the Kamakura period, was also based in urban areas. The reason why the Nichiren sect's Lotus Sutra movement and the True Pure Land sect's Ikkō movement struggled so violently against each other during the Warring States period is that they were both trying to expand their bases in the same areas.[11] When Christianity was brought to Japan in the sixteenth century, it adopted the same evangelical strategy. As a result, the Christian missionaries of the sixteenth century felt that their greatest competition was the Nichiren and True Pure Land sects. Religions that targeted urban areas received their support from "mercantilist" powers. These merchants and shippers were, like the *wakō* pirates,[12] linked to areas outside the archipelago, and they possessed a vast trading network that extended from Southeast Asia to South America.[13]

However, in opposition to this interregional network, local warlords such as Oda Nobunaga sought to unite all the small regional states in the

10. The Ikkō was a True Pure Land sect movement promoted by Rennyo.
11. For a description of these struggles, see Mary Elizabeth Berry, *The Culture of Civil War in Kyoto* (Berkeley: University of California Press, 1996).
12. These were pirates who operated in the seas between Japan, China, and Korea.
13. Amino's son, Amino Tetsuya (a professor of Latin American history at Tokyo University) has uncovered documents in Spain pertaining to a Japanese settlement in Peru in the sixteenth century. This is what Amino is referring to when he writes of networks extending to South America.

archipelago and to rule "Japan" as a single country. This drive to unify the country came into direct conflict with the mercantilist religions, resulting in the famous collision between Oda and the Ikkō sect at Ishiyama. Toyotomi Hideyoshi and Tokugawa Ieyasu's later conflicts with Christianity had the same roots. In order to reunify Japan, the warlords felt compelled to reassert themselves on the issue of land-based tax revenues. The direction taken by the warlords meant the revival of ancient Japan's "agrarian fundamentalism," as we see in Hideyoshi's attempt to solidify the system of land taxation (based on the annual rice tribute of the *kokudaka* system) by making warlords throughout the country submit land survey registers to the emperor. Tokugawa Ieyasu took the same path when he established the final shogunate of Japanese history in 1603.

As a result, the attempt to reunify and stabilize Japan on the basis of agricultural land came into direct conflict with those who sought to build networks of commercial circulation on the sea and who aimed to build trade networks that extended beyond the Japanese islands. This conflict ended with the victory of the "agrarian fundamentalists" in a great bloodletting. The network of the seafarers was shattered. The unified country of Japan, for which the ocean was now a *border*, was revived.

This victory also resulted in the early modern state. Under this state, the mercantilist valorization of commerce was suppressed and agrarian fundamentalism became the orthodox principle of society. With the revival of agrarian fundamentalism as a governing principle, the idea that *hyakushō* were farmers began to take root. Our image of Japanese history has been formed on the basis of this belief. But when we reexamine history by looking at forms of production other than agriculture, we find a very different image of Japanese society coming to the fore.

A NEW HISTORICAL IMAGE

As I describe in chapter seven, in the latter half of the Kamakura period coins circulated widely and something approximating a credit economy developed. We have evidence of the deployment of financial capital, commercial trade capital, and even large-scale capital invested in construction projects in this period. While this may be a bit of an exaggeration, I believe this activity can be seen as having a capitalist character.

Evidence of such conditions can likely be found on the Korean Peninsula and the Chinese mainland. But the agrarian fundamentalism of the Confucian thought, centered as it was in China, exerted a tremendous influence on the entire East Asian region. As a result, we have overlooked an important aspect of the social life of our past.

For example, there is a strong oceangoing strain in Korean society, particularly in the islands along the southwestern coast. When in the thirteenth century the Mongols attacked the Koryŏ dynasty in Korea, the Korean military unit that held out against them the longest, the Sambyŏlch'o, had its base in the southern islands, including Jeju-do. It was probably particularly skilled in naval battles.

However, when we look at the entire course of Korean history, we see that people with a link to the ocean, including fishermen, have been denigrated and relegated to nearly outcaste status. The Korean Peninsula was even more thoroughly permeated with Confucianism than was the Japanese archipelago, and so an intense agrarian fundamentalism may have been the source of the denigration of coastal peoples. Nevertheless, if we dig a little deeper we find that Korean society also had a fairly strong nonagricultural productive aspect to it.

We know that commerce and trade have flourished in China, especially south of the Yangtze River, since the Song dynasty. Still, there is much room for further research. For example, an oceangoing people in southern coastal China called the Dan, a minority group that has been subjected to some discrimination, has received little scholarly attention. Moreover, the ocean has been important not just for minority groups but for all those in China who have ventures on the sea. If we reconsider the trends in Japan with an eye toward movements on the Korean Peninsula, the Chinese mainland, and Southeast Asia, our grasp of Asian history will change considerably.

In the sixteenth and seventeenth centuries, the governments of Japan, Korea, and the Ming, then Qing, dynasties in China all adopted what we have commonly called an exclusionary policy. Each state undervalued and denigrated its society's commercial and industrial elements, a condition that persisted until the modern era. The same kind of historiographical mistakes that we have been making in Japan have been made throughout the East Asian region under the sway of Confucian-style agrarian fundamentalism.

I recently inquired into scholarship in Korea and was told that, indeed, there have been very few studies of oceangoing peoples or nonagricultural production. China appears to be the same. It seems that most people have leaped to the conclusion that nonagricultural production was of little importance in Asia. East Asian societies as a whole have consistently underestimated their own nonagricultural and commercial aspects up to the present day. What kind of new images of society or the state will come into view when we finally correct this evaluation? Of course, to return to the Japanese case, the task of rereading historical documents has just begun, so it will take some time before a new understanding of society develops. In anticipation of that day, I would like to examine several historical problems that continue to be surrounded by confusion.

WHAT CAUSED FAMINES?

Famines have been gravely misunderstood. They first became a serious problem around the thirteenth century. I am not denying that there were poor harvests in ancient times as well. However, famines first had a decisive social meaning, that is, for the first time the government had to directly confront this problem, during the famous Kangi (1230) and Shōga famines (1258). Other great famines in Japanese history include the Great Kanshō Famine in the fifteenth century and the Kan'ei, Enpō, Kyōhō, Tenmei, and Tenpō famines of the Edo period.

These famines originated in severe climatic changes that brought about bad harvests, but how a bad harvest developed into a famine is a question that has not yet received sufficient attention. We must take a fresh look at the actual conditions of a famine. For example, we have in *A Record of Myōhōji* a very detailed account of conditions at a temple in the region of Fuji Yoshida, Kai Province, from the latter half of the fifteenth century to the early sixteenth century. According to this text, there were occasional small-scale famines when the price of rice, wheat, millet, and other grains were high. When prices were low, the world was said to be well off, but when the price of food rose, people starved. The text makes use of an interesting term, *seni kekachi*, which refers to shortages of coins caused by attempts to rectify currency problems by rejecting "bad coins" at market.[14] In other words, the removal of bad coins

---

14. Without a centralized mint, the currency situation in medieval Japan was often chaotic. Much of the currency used in Japan in the fourteenth century was Song Chinese copper coins. Since there was frequent reminting of coins and several different precious metals were in use, on occasion the

from circulation caused a shortage of coins, so that even if prices were ostensibly low, there were no coins with which to buy commodities.

Most scholars have read *A Record of Myōhōji* as an account of an extremely poor area subject to frequent famines. Even today Fuji Yoshida is an area with very few rice paddies. According to the conventional wisdom, which equates the lack of rice paddies with poverty, the entire prefecture of Yamanashi has always been poor. So, when *A Record of Myōhōji* notes a coin shortage (*kekachi*) when "things got tight," scholars have assumed that there was a famine in Yoshida because it was poor. Somewhat tautologically, this poverty was assumed in turn to have derived from the fact that there were few rice paddies there. However, as noted above, famines occurred *when the price of grain was high*. This region had to *purchase* its food supplies from elsewhere, which is why people became rich when grain prices were low.[15] How did the people of this area earn their cash? Large numbers of pilgrims to Mount Fuji came to Yoshida, which was at the foot of the mountain, and paid for their lodgings in cash. In other words, in the fifteenth and sixteenth centuries Yoshida was an urban area.

Famines generally occur first in these kinds of urban places. Indeed, Yoshida became famous at the end of the Edo period for the social disruptions caused by insufficient food. According to Yamaguchi Keiji, the disturbances in Yoshida, like the Kamo uprisings in Mikawa Province, were perpetrated by "rice-purchasing farmers" (*shokumai kōnyū nōmin*).

This phrase strikes me as very odd. Yamaguchi presents us with the image of rice-growing farmers who also have to buy it, forcing one to conclude that they were extremely poor farmers. But is it not more likely that these people were not farmers? Yoshida had been urban since the medieval era, so these were "rice-buying city dwellers" who were starving. The same was true for the riots on Mikawa, where people living on both the coast and in the mountains had to buy their food. Unless you recognize this, you cannot truly understand either these famines or these riots.

I was recently reading the documents of the Tokikuni family on the Noto Peninsula and came across a document from 1681 in which four

government would intervene in the market and declare a number of the circulating coins "bad." When these were withdrawn, prices would rise, as usable currency became scarce.

15. The key point here is that grain prices were high, not that grain was necessarily in short supply. As Amino will explain, the one constant about Yoshida is that there was always a short supply of local grain, so if famines were caused by short supplies then Yoshida would have experienced constant famine. Amino wants to pursue the causes of famine in conditions of commercial exchange, not agricultural production.

atamafuri of the nearby coastal village of Sosogi submitted a petition asking for rice rations since they had been "driven to desperation" by starvation. Certainly, there were bad harvests around this time. Had I read this document ten years ago, I would have assumed that these were impoverished farmers asking for famine rice rations. But, having come to understand that I could not assume that *atamafuri* were poor farmers, I realized that I had to investigate what kind of people these four *atamafuri* were. In fact, one of them was from a wealthy family that owned two ships and traded in salt. There is no evidence whatsoever that these were poor people. Rather, they engaged in nonagricultural production and possessed *monetary* wealth.

Sosogi had long been an urban-type settlement whose inhabitants engaged in salt production and shipping. When there was a bad harvest and rice prices rose, these inhabitants were unable to buy food. So, they had to petition for rice rations or emergency silver with which to import food from other regions. They were not starving because they were chronically poor people scraping by on the product of a few rice paddies.

If what I have just described is true, then a primary reason why famines occurred from the early thirteenth century on was the phenomenal growth of urban areas throughout the country, which began about that time. Famines first appeared in urban places. Those of us who experienced World War II may remember that there was little starvation in the food-producing areas of Japan. It was the city dwellers—the ones who had to buy their food—who first went hungry.

As for the great famines of the Edo period—the Kyōhō, Tenmei, and Tenpō as well as the devastating famines that were restricted to northern Honshu—none happened simply because the northern Honshu region, for example, was poor. We need to thoroughly reinvestigate whether farm village districts were truly devastated by these famines. It may turn out that northern Honshu had far more urban characteristics than we previously thought. There is cause to believe that poor harvests wreaked such damage because much of the region was engaged in other forms of production.

Famines are the major symbol of the poverty and cruelty of the Edo period. However, the overall trends may well have been in the opposite direction. An increasing number of famines in the Edo period did not mean economic stagnation and grinding poverty. Instead, Japanese society experienced expanding urbanization and increasing density in the urban population. This is why a famine could have such a devastating effect on an entire region. We might well take the severity of famines as an indication of how much urbanization had advanced.

WHAT WAS FEUDAL SOCIETY?

The members of my seminar and I recently had an opportunity to examine an Edo period writing practice book at the Kamikaji family household in Outer Noto.[16] We were looking at a section from 1700 when we found the following sentences: "For the past three or four years, the people have been struggling without cease, some even dying of starvation. We ask in your wisdom that you grant us funds for food." In fact, there were no famines around the time this sentence was written. Since this was a collection of sample sentences for use when villagers wrote petitions, this was merely practiced as an example of what to write in hard times. Since these were evidently stock phrases in village petitions, we should be wary of taking at face value appeals from villagers claiming that many were on the brink of starvation. One occasionally finds this in the medieval era as well, so one must not underestimate villagers' shrewdness when reading documents.[17]

We need to revise our definitions of feudal society in light of the above. Our understanding has been that the lord's control of farmers constituted the basic production relationship in feudal society. This has been the case not only for the Edo period, but for the Kamakura, despite clear differences in social organization and territorial administration before and after the reunification efforts of Nobunaga and Hideyoshi.

The late historian Araki Moriaki argued that the medieval era was a "patriarchal family/slave" society, with full-fledged feudalism only coming into being in the early modern era.[18] According to Araki, the medieval era was more backward than feudalism, essentially a slave society. However, since Araki believed that the family-owned slaves of the medieval era were put to work at farming (that is, they were agricultural slaves), his basic view

---

16. This was a book in which local villagers learned how to write by copying set phrases and sentences. Unlike today, they did not learn to write by memorizing a full set of Chinese characters. Instead, minimum literacy was achieved by copying out the kinds of phrases that would be necessary for the documents they would have to produce.

17. See an essay by Kitsukawa Toshitada on this practice book, "Shiryō to shite no teshūhon" (Writing Practice Books as Primary Sources), *Rekishi to minzoku* (History and Ethnos) 12 (1995).

18. Araki Moriaki, *Nihon hōken shakai seiritsu shiron* (On the Establishment of Japanese Feudal Society) (Tokyo: Iwanami shoten, 1984).

of both eras was really not so different. Nor was Araki alone in this approach. The widespread idea that Japanese society in both the medieval and early modern eras was feudal, in that it was founded upon the slave-like control of farmers by feudal lords, is the one that is presented in school textbooks today.

One of the premises of this viewpoint is that the lords bound farmers to the land by force rather than economic means. By depriving them of freedom of movement, the lords were able to collect a land tax. Yet, one of my main arguments has been that not all *hyakushō* were farmers, indeed, that many *hyakushō* were sea-going people, or mountain-dwellers, or merchants and artisans. Many of those who were not farmers did not need the land to survive. This relatively high proportion of *hyakushō* who did not hold land was not only difficult to tie down, but had to move around to make a living. In such a case, are the concepts of noneconomic restrictions and forced ties to the land in fact effective concepts for understanding this history? Is it not simplistic to claim that the lords could bind villagers—people who were engaged in a variety of forms of production, who were intelligent and possessed a high degree of managerial knowledge—to the land and control them with nothing more than the threat of violence? This much, I believe, has been made abundantly clear in my discussion to this point. For example, in the medieval era territorial lords possessed land that they managed themselves. Agricultural lands called *shōsaku* and *tsukuda* were situated in the immediate vicinity of the lord's headquarters. The lands surrounding the headquarters were farmed by his own servants, while the lands beyond were farmed by other villagers. The prevailing image is of a medieval lord unable to pacify the surrounding populace by mobilizing wealth generated from his own lands. In the early modern era, the lord and his military vassals, the samurai, moved to urban castle towns, thus effecting a separation of farmers and warriors. Shogunal control was maintained by the organizational manipulation of urbanized lords. This conventional wisdom is by no means completely erroneous, but it does require major revision. Upon reexamination, I think it highly unlikely that we will be able to continue to say that medieval society was simply a feudal system based on farming villages or that early modern society was a feudal system centered on agriculture.

I base my contention, first of all, on the fact that a highly active sea transport system had developed in the Kamakura period. Beginning in the latter half of that period, commodities were circulated on such a scale that credit transactions became common. How could a ruling class extract tax revenues and control such a mobile and fluid society while sitting in their headquarters?

I would argue that for the most part medieval lords were not very skilled at controlling commerce and distribution. Single-minded in their emphasis on "agrarian fundamentalism," since basic taxes were levied on land, they failed to grasp the potential of the era's developing economy. Nevertheless, because of the degree to which commerce and distribution developed in this period, they were unlikely to have been merely disinterested. Rereading historical documents with this in mind will lead to all kinds of new insights.

Although I discussed this somewhat earlier, I would like to provide a few more examples. Recall again the conventional view of *shōen* estates. They were large, private landholdings and essentially large-scale agricultural operations. Prominent and powerful local families owned and managed these agricultural operations, but in order to protect their rights of private ownership they "commended" these lands to high-ranking court nobles in the capital.[19] The higher the rank of the nobility in the capital the more vigorously would local families compete to commend their lands to them. As a result, court nobles would naturally accumulate holdings throughout the country.

But to believe that court nobles could acquire landholdings throughout the country without making an effort is unrealistic. Without a doubt, the accumulation of *shōen* estates proceeded in accordance with some form of intention, plan, or strategy. If we reexamine the geographical distribution of *shōen* estates in this light, we will see that there was nothing accidental about their accumulation. The intentions of the temples and shrines, the imperial family, the Fujiwara regent family, and the other nobles are revealed in the way estates were accumulated. We can thereby uncover their strategies as a ruling class.

THE HOLDINGS OF THE SAIONJI FAMILY

Shrines, such as Kamo Shrine, attempted to acquire estates and pasture lands along the coast; their holdings were located along the Inland Sea and in ports and harbors of the northern Japan Sea. Many of the pastures of Ise Shrine could be found along the Pacific coast, while estates and subsidiary shrines

---

19. This was a favored course of action because when commending the land to a court noble the commending party would usually be named the local manager by that noble. The noble would rarely if ever make any claims upon the management of the estate as long as revenues accrued to him.

of the Iwashimizu Hachiman Shrine dotted the Inland Sea coast and the west coast of the Japan Sea. The same was true for the imperial family, the Fujiwara regents, and the Taira *uji*, as discussed earlier. One of the most interesting cases I've investigated recently is that of the distribution of the holdings of the Saionji family. This aristocratic family held the post of *mōshitsugi*—"the service desk"—representing the "monarch of the east" (the Kamakura shogunate) to the "monarch of Kyoto" (the emperor). From the perspective of the emperor, the Saionji were the diplomats through whom the imperial government conducted its "foreign relations" with the shogunate in Kanto. It was an immensely wealthy and powerful family.

When we look into the distribution of this family's holdings (fig. 21), we find that, first, they had villas on two rivers—at Makijima on the Uji River and at Suita at the entrance to the Yodo River. They had administrative offices at both of these villas and employed a variety of tradesmen, including boatmen. The Saionji family also owned a number of pastures covering the area from Lake Ogura to the Yodo River. These pastures were created by putting up fences on land enclosed by a bend in the river. The Saionji pastures operated like the famous Kinto pasture near the capital, where horses and cattle were raised to be offered as tribute to the imperial court's Bureau of Horses and to the stables of the retired emperors. Like the Taira at the end of the Heian, the Saionji served as the hereditary directors of the retired emperor's stables in the Kamakura period. As such, they had the right to appoint officials to the Left Bureau of Horses and to acquire pastures in the Lake Ogura–Yodo River and Kawachi regions.

Horse packers and teamsters were attached to these stables, so the Saionji also acquired control of these transportation workers. Since the pastures were located along rivers, they were always supplied with docks. They thus formed the point of contact between land and water transportation networks. In this way, horses and cattle were always paired with boats, demonstrating the strong links between pastures and water transport.

Other holdings were scattered along the banks of the Uji River, Lake Ogura, and the Yodo River. For example, the Toba Palace, a large imperial villa, was located at the confluence of the Kamo and Katsura Rivers near the Yodo. The Saionji managed the Toba Palace for the imperial family, and as a result its lands also came under their control. Since the Yodo fish market was located on these lands, the Saionji controlled the most essential part of the Yodo River. In fact, all of the estates neighboring Toba Palace were under the management of the Saionji.

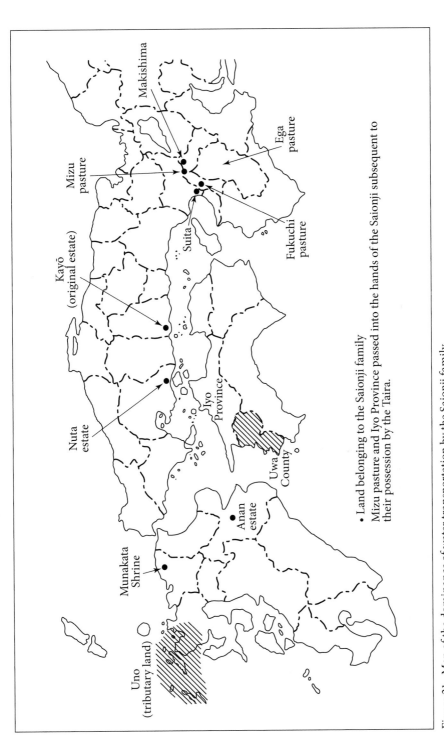

Makishima

Ega
pasture

Mizu
pasture

Fukuchi
pasture

Suita

Kayō
(original estate)

Iyo
Province

Nuta
estate

Uwa
County

Anan
estate

Munakata
Shrine

Uno
(tributary land)

• Land belonging to the Saionji family
Mizu pasture and Iyo Province passed into the hands of the Saionji subsequent to
their possession by the Taira.

Figure 21. Map of the dominance of water transportation by the Saionji family.

When we look at all the waterways from the Yodo River to Osaka Bay and the Inland Sea, we find that the Saionji had holdings in the area of Settsu and Harima, both of which were entrances to the Inland Sea. Furthermore, they possessed holdings in key ports such as the Kayō estate in Shimotsu Harbor in Bizen Province and the Nuta estate in Aki Province. The Nuta estate is famous for its marketplace, and the area as a whole was well known as a major base for fishermen.

In addition, the Saionji family held the hereditary post of governor of Iyo Province, located on the edge of Shikoku nearest Kyushu. Apart from an interim during the Kenmu Restoration, Saionji family members continued to staff that post throughout the Muromachi period. The Saionji base in Iyo Province was Uwa District, the same area where Fujiwara no Sumitomo made his headquarters in the tenth century.[20] The Saionji also held the Anami estate in Bungo Province, just across the straits from Uwa District. Whoever controlled this area controlled the Bungo Straits, which served as the passage from the Inland Sea to northern Kyushu.

Saionji possessions also included the famous Munakata Shrine in Chikuzen Province, which had such close ties to the continent that for two generations the wives of the head priest were Chinese, and Uno no Mikuriya, which had been the base for the famous "masters of the sea," the Matsura band. The Matsura District boasted many harbors and inlets, and its pastures produced not only horses but the famous Mikuriya cows, which were sent to the capital as tribute every year because the Saionji family managed the retired emperor's stables. To sum up, the Saionji family had holdings that allowed it to control river and ocean transportation routes from the Uji River, just south of the capital, through the Inland Sea to northern Kyushu.

As mentioned earlier, Saionji Kintsune sent a trading mission to China using his own capital and importing 100,000 *kan* of copper coins in the middle of the Kamakura period. The Saionji family was clearly tremendously wealthy, but wealth alone was not enough. It was able to conduct this kind of trade because it controlled important points of waterborne transport in the archipelago. As this makes clear, certain aristocratic families of this period were quite careful to control key points in transportation routes. Later the

20. Fujiwara Sumitomo was a court noble who staged a revolt against the imperial court in the tenth century and attempted to construct a new kingdom that included territory in western Japan and southern Korea. See chapters two and four.

Saionji became one of the *daimyō* families of the Warring States period, constructing such castles as the Matsuba in Uwa. Even superficial investigations of the Matsuba Castle have yielded a good number of Chinese celadon porcelains; more serious archaeological digs would surely turn up much more.

THE LORDS' INTEREST IN OCEAN TRANSPORT

The situation just described was not limited to the Saionji family. Whoever held the posts of head of the Left Bureau of Horses or director of the retired emperor's stables was able to control the pastures of the Yodo River and the Uno Mikuriya domain of Hizen Province. The governor of Iyo Province could control the entrance to northern Kyushu and the Inland Sea. So, combining the posts of head of the Left Bureau of Horses and the governorship of Iyo Province meant being able to control these vast ocean transport networks. The Taira family was the first to acquire these posts, and Kiso Yoshinaka and Minamoto no Yoshitsune, the famous protagonists of *The Tale of the Heike*, followed suit. Control of the transportation networks of the west through these two posts was crucial for those who wished to oppose Minamoto no Yoritomo's control of the "Eastern Country" at this time. We have further evidence of the importance of these ocean routes when we note that when Kiso Yoshinaka was offered the post of governor of Echigo Province, he refused it, demanding instead the governorship of Iyo. He actively sought to acquire and control this post and other *shōen* estates and government lands. There was nothing accidental about the distribution of his holdings.

Not surprisingly, many aristocrats and warriors vigorously competed with each other whenever a certain *shōen* estate or government post opened up somewhere, employing myriad schemes and going to all kinds of lengths to acquire it. The local lords that we have been calling feudal lords—that is, the shogunal vassals and military stewards—did not rule their territories by passively sitting in their headquarters at the center of a concentrically structured domain.

For example, the Kobayakawa family had its main base in Sagami Province, where it built the family home. It also possessed such holdings as the Nuta, Tsū, and Takehara estates in Aki Province (present-day Hiroshima). The Kobayakawa had maintained an interest in the sea from the time when they were based in Sagami, but eventually they gave up their Sagami home and moved to Aki Province, in the process becoming "lords of the sea."

The Miura was a Kamakura era shogunal vassal family whose original base was on the Miura Peninsula, an important point in sea transportation networks. From the beginning, this family was consciously concerned with controlling sea transport bases. First, the Miura became military governors of provinces that had strong connections to the sea, such as Kawachi, Izumi, and Tosa. They also became military stewards of Munakata Shrine and Kanzaki estate in Hizen Province, a key point in sea transport facing the Ariake Sea. These possessions were distributed in a way that appears to have had Pacific Ocean transport and links to the Asian mainland in mind. Since the Hōjō had an even greater interest in sea transport, they and the Miura carried on an intense rivalry over the control of these networks.

The military stewards and shogunal vassals of the Kamakura period were all keenly aware of ocean routes and mountain roads. When ocean travel and trade became even more active in the Muromachi period, with the increased circulation of goods, military governors became even more sensitive to such issues. There are, however, very few studies of Muromachi era military governors or the Edo period lords who followed in their footsteps that take such issues into account.

Yet the fact that the Date family of Sendai possessed an outpost at Itako on Lake Kasumigaura, well outside its domainal boundaries, was no doubt due to its desire to control important points on water transport routes. In a similar vein, the ten-thousand-*koku* domain of the Hijikata family was established on the Noto Peninsula at the beginning of the Edo period.[21] While the Hijikata were not vassals of the Tokugawa family (*fudai*),[22] they were extremely close to Ieyasu, founder of the Tokugawa shogunate. The ten-thousand-*koku* domain of the Hijikata appears insignificant in comparison with the million-*koku* domain of the Maeda family, which covered the provinces of Kaga, Noto, and Etchū. In fact, the Hijikata domain on Noto, which is scattered in different locations within the Maeda domain,

21. See the discussion of the Hijikata in relation to the Tokikuni family in chapter one.
22. All warlords (*daimyō*) during the Edo period were divided by the shogunate into three types: *shinpan* (collateral families of the Tokugawa), *fudai* (warlords who served Tokugawa Ieyasu as his vassals and thus owed their positions and land to him), and *tozama* (warlords who possessed territories independently of Tokugawa Ieyasu and who either joined forces with him or were defeated by him at the final battles of the Warring States period). The Hijikata received their lands on Noto in a form reminiscent of the way *fudai* warlords received their lands. In fact, the Hijikata lands on Noto were known as *tenryō* or shogunate lands. But, they were not vassals of the Tokugawa in the strictest of terms.

has been understood to be indicative of the generosity of the Maeda in granting them such land as they had. The common story is that the Hijikata originally possessed a domain of ten thousand *koku* in Etchū, but the Maeda complained that it was inconvenient to have to pass through the Hijikata domain en route to Edo in fulfillment of its alternate attendance obligations.[23] As a solution, the Maeda are said to have offered the Hijikata land on Noto Peninsula.

This is what I also believed at first, but when I asked a member of the Tokikuni investigation group, Oikawa Kiyohide, to locate all the Hijikata possessions on a map of Noto, we found that their lands were neatly distributed at key points on the coastline. Their occupation of these points means that, although they may have been lords of only ten thousand *koku*, they were by no means insignificant.

Coastal villages and cities had a high proportion of *atamafuri*, so their value measured in *koku* was low. However, the Hijikata systematically controlled a number of crucial ports. It appears that the Tokugawa shogunate drove the ten-thousand-*koku* domain of the Hijikata like a series of wedges into the million-*koku* domain of the Maeda. The Hijikata owed their domain to the will of Tokugawa Ieyasu, not the Maeda. In light of the fact that the million-*koku* domain of the Maeda, the largest domain after that of the Tokugawa family itself, was perceived as a major threat by the shogunate, the distribution of the Hijikata holdings within the Maeda domain makes sense.

The aforementioned Tokikuni on Noto Peninsula was a "dual polity *hyakushō*" family, with holdings in both the Hijikata and the Maeda domains, one hundred *koku* under the Maeda and two hundred under the Hijikata. With the powerful backing of the shogunate, the Hijikata attempted to make all of the Tokikuni family's indentured servants, livestock, and boats subject to their control. In response, the head of the family at that time, Tōzaemon, decided to split the household in two, forming the upper Tokikuni lineage in the Hijikata domain and the lower Tokikuni in the Maeda domain. It was because of the struggle between the Hijikata and Maeda lords that the family is still divided into two households today.

23. In order to secure peace after nearly 140 years of civil war, the Tokugawa shogunate instituted a system whereby all warlords kept their families in Edo near the shogun's palace as permanent hostages while the warlords themselves divided their time between their castles in their domains and their mansions in Edo. This was known as the alternate attendance system (*sankin kōtai*). The routes along which warlords traveled when fulfilling their obligations were predetermined by the shogunate, as were the numbers of attendants and the general costs of the journey.

It is likely that many of the isolated outpost holdings of Edo period lords, such as that of the Date family, were related to important points on transportation routes. If we examine the strategic placement of lords carried out by the Tokugawa shogunate in this light, we are likely to come up with a new understanding of the position and interests of the lords. The lords lived in their castles and controlled their domains, managing their lands as the head of a kind of enterprise. They were able to rule their domains only after they had gathered a number of house vassals who had the management skills to deal with taxation, finance, and personnel. A reexamination of the Edo period from this perspective will yield many new questions.

MERCANTILISM IN JAPANESE HISTORY

One final issue relates to the way the ruling class consciously began, from the thirteenth century on, to tax not just land but entrepreneurs. Emperor Go-Daigo, in particular, attempted to construct a monarchy that relied entirely on the financial support of entrepreneurs. He levied taxes on sake brewers and deposited tax revenues with moneylenders (*dosō*) to use as capital. He used his authority to establish and remove toll barriers, and he took back the right to collect tolls, transport taxes, and port entry fees. Furthermore, he ordered that the value of proprietors' holdings be expressed in terms of copper coins (a value known as *kandaka*), levying a 5 percent tax on their value.

The Muromachi shogunate followed Go-Daigo's example, levying a 2 percent tax on territorial holdings and collecting taxes from sake brewers and moneylenders. Thus, the trend toward actively seeking tax revenues from commercial and financial enterprises began in the latter half of the Kamakura period, from the despotic rule of the Tokusō Hōjō, continuing through the Kenmu Restoration of Go-Daigo, and finally becoming the established system of the Muromachi shogunate. This mode of governance could be called mercantilist in its dependence on commerce to maintain itself.

It is interesting to note that this kind of rule tended to become despotic in Japan. For example, the Kamakura shogunate had an assembly of powerful vassals called the Hyōjōshū (the Board of Inquiry). The basic principle of the shogunal regent's rule was that politics proceeded according to decisions reached through debate in this body. But during the era of Tokusō despotism the Tokusō Hōjō family eviscerated this assembly, almost completely ignoring its decisions, and ruled on its own according to decisions made at meetings of its own vassals.

Go-Daigo did much the same. He broke up the assembly of the highest ranking courtiers in the Grand Council of State, a body that had been in existence since ancient times. In its place, he appointed nobles and officials to official posts who would act according to his desires. With these men in place, he attempted to rule autocratically. Two of the most powerful shoguns of the Muromachi shogunate, Ashikaga Yoshimitsu and Ashikaga Yoshinori, also ignored the assembly of powerful military governors and ruled in an autocratic manner. It seems to be more than a coincidence that all of these polities were monarchies that relied on commerce, distribution, and foreign trade. The absolutist monarchies of the sixteenth to nineteenth centuries in Europe also ignored the assemblies of feudal lords as they built autocratic regimes by relying on commercial sources of wealth. A variety of debates on European absolute monarchy has been employed in analyses of the Meiji state in Japan. But we should remember that this approach to rule had been developed in Japan as early as the late thirteenth century; it did not have to be imported from Europe.

If we look at early modern Japan with this in mind, especially the transition from the late medieval to the Edo period, we find ourselves dealing with virtually unexplored terrain. Undoubtedly, the formal principle of the Edo period was agrarian fundamentalism based on land taxes. But what went on beyond that formal principle is difficult to grasp. The prevailing trend in research has been to point out the "capitalist" aspects of commercial activities and to designate them the foundations of an "economic society." But scholars who argue for this are grounded in the preconception that the *hyakushō* were farmers. When they go on to claim that the overwhelming majority of the population was agricultural, they significantly diminish the force of the economic society.

Just after World War II, Hattori Shisō characterized the Momoyama period as "early absolutism," which was, I believe, accurate.[24] His argument that "absolutism miscarried" in the Edo period, however, was widely ignored. Yet I believe that his theory can be extended and will likely gain further acceptance in the future.

24. Hattori Shisō, *Tennōsei zettai shugi no kakuritsu* (The Establishment of Emperor System Absolutism) (Tokyo: Chūō kōronsha, 1948). See also *Zettaishugi no shiteki tenkai* (The Historical Development of Absolutism) (Tokyo: Fukumura shuppan, 1974).

If we follow this line of thinking, we come up with a truly different perspective on the Meiji Restoration and Japan's subsequent "modernization." The Satsuma, Chōshū, Tosa, and Hizen domains, which backed the Meiji Restoration, were not remote and backward. They were all domains that had conducted maritime trade.[25] It is clear that the Satsuma conducted a secret trade to both the south and the north. Indeed, it is likely that the other domains were doing similar things. We must not underestimate the accumulated volume of commercial and financial enterprises or the growth of capitalist society up to and throughout the Edo period.

It is interesting, for example, that all the commercial terminology used today derives from historical terms used since at least the medieval era. Our term for "market price" (*sōba*) has been in use since the medieval era and is derived from the fact that people gathered in a place (*ba*)—in other words, a marketplace—to decide on prices. The *kitte* of *kogitte* (check) and *kirifu* (ticket) are words that have been used since the Heian period. The word *kiru* (to cut) had great significance; tax orders from that period were called *kirifu* or *kirikudashibumi* (cut orders). Financiers would receive repayment of loans of rice made to governors and officials in the form of these *kirifu*. So *kirifu* and *kitte* were used in the Heian period to mean "bill." *Bill* (*tegata*) is itself an extremely old word, as is *invoice* (*shikiri*). The terms for stocks and bonds are similar. The *kabu* of *kabushiki* (stocks) was used, at the latest, from the Edo period on, and *shiki* was used in the medieval period (although it employed a different character). There are any number of other interesting words from the past still in use today, such as *opening session* (*yoritsuki*) and *closing* (*ōbike*). If we were to investigate these commercial terms in a historical and ethnographic fashion, we would surely make some interesting discoveries.

Since ancient Japanese words are still used as commercial terms today, there was no need to develop translations of Western terms for these activities upon contact with the West. Words already in use were sufficiently comprehensible. This was true not only for commerce but probably for industry as well. Yet research has consistently underestimated the depths of these antecedents in Japanese society. Europe has been perceived as the most advanced civilization, and through such catchphrases as Fukuzawa Yukichi's "Leave Asia, Enter Europe," our eyes have been turned exclusively toward

25. For a recent English-language study of the economic policies of one of these domains, namely Tosa, see Luke S. Roberts, *Mercantilism in a Japanese Domain: the Merchant Origins of Economic Nationalism in 18th-Century Tosa* (Cambridge: Cambridge University Press, 1998).

European models. We have never looked at our very feet for the richness of Japanese society or, for that matter, of Asia. Rather, politicians and academics have sought to break that Asian base apart since the Meiji period.

Economists and historians all use translated words in academic terminology, hardly ever using words like those discussed. The translated academic terms have a very strong agricultural component. The same may be said for all of Asia, perhaps; in any case, we are still trapped in this problematic in Japan.

Now, fifty years after World War II, we are at a point where we should think about agricultural reform. Postwar reforms were based upon the notion that *hyakushō* were farmers, and they were carried out without taking regional differences into account. We still live with this legacy. While the problem of whether or not to import rice is by no means easily resolved, I do not believe we can truly understand all the angles of the issue if we continue to approach it from the perspective of agrarian fundamentalism. If we remain captive to this ideology, we will be unable to formulate appropriate responses to foreign pressures. Our attempts to deal with rice in terms of a self-sufficient food supply misses the point. How accurately do those economists, politicians, and others who oppose the opening of rice markets understand the historical significance of rice in Japanese society? The responsibility of historians in this matter is grave, and I cannot help but feel that debates are being carried on based upon dubious and baseless conventional wisdom.

In order for us to live in an international society, in order for us to fulfill the mission that we truly should, we must have an accurate understanding of Japanese society. We must have an accurate assessment of ourselves. Without that, we crush what should be nurtured, we waste our energy, and we create the danger that we will expend our efforts in ridiculous directions.

In that sense, the study of history has never been more important, nor has there been a time when the field of history has borne a heavier burden. At the same time, this is an exciting period in which new things are constantly coming to light. We are beginning to discern an image of the past that is entirely different from that which we have had so far. It is my deepest hope that young people will confront these problems with ambition.

BOOK TWO

Sacred Space
and the People
on the Margins
of History

CHAPTER SIX

On Writing

LITERACY RATES AMONG THE JAPANESE

The Japanese people use three types of script every day: *kanji* (Chinese char-acters), *hiragana*, and *katakana* (two parallel phonetic syllabaries). These three scripts can be combined into seven kinds of written expression.[1] There are few people in the world who possess seven forms of written expression, each of which can express a variety of thoughts and feelings. This variety of meanings can be expressed because the three types of script each have their own histories and functions. Nevertheless, there has been surprisingly little thought given to the roles these scripts have played in Japanese history and literature, and little exploration of the meanings they have come to possess as systems of writing.

The dissemination of writing in Japan was far more extensive than we have hitherto supposed. Even today, one finds old documents and books in the older houses in farming or fishing villages. Such books might include the *Agricultural Encyclopedia* (*Nōgyō zensho*)[2] or treatises on Confucianism, but one can also find a surprising number of volumes intended for the education

---

1. These seven are (1) *kanji* alone (2) *hiragana* alone (3) *katakana* alone (4) *kanji* and *hiragana* (5) *kanji* and *katakana* (6) *katakana* and *hiragana* (7) *kanji, hiragana,* and *katakana*. The term *kana* is used when speaking of the two phonetic syllabaries together, without making a distinction between the two.
2. This was published by Miyazaki Yasusada (1623–97) in 1697 in ten volumes. Miyazaki based the work on both Chinese agricultural texts and his own experiences and observations.

of women. Of course, the literacy rate among women was relatively low compared to that of men. But literacy among women had reached a level that cannot be slighted. For example, the famous late-eighteenth-century traveler Sugae Masumi found that many of the families that provided him with lodging on his journeys held poetry gatherings in which even the mistress of the household joined.[3] Thus, I think there is little doubt that members of the leading families of the villages, including women, could read and write. There are those who say that the literacy rate was as high as 50 to 60 percent during the latter years of the Edo period, but we can safely say that on average 40 percent of the populace could read.

Ilya Ilyich Mechnikov noted in his *Recollections of the Meiji Restoration*[4] that the literacy rate was extremely high, particularly in the cities and towns. Mechnikov, a Russian who lived in Japan around 1874–75, was astonished to see that rickshaw pullers, stableboys, and young girls working in the tea shops in Yokohoma would pull out books and read whenever they had a free moment. He wrote that in comparison with the various Latin countries and his own Russia, the Japanese had a much higher literacy rate. This is a significant point to keep in mind when considering premodern or modern Japanese society.

Turning to my own experience, I have examined Edo period documents from all over Japan in the course of my research. Although I have been reading and copying these materials for years, it just recently occurred to me to wonder why I was able to read documents from Kyushu when the spoken language there is otherwise so different. Once, four or five years ago, when I was visiting the city of Kagoshima in southern Kyushu, I found myself waiting at a bus stop next to two elderly people who were enjoying a nice chat. Out of curiosity, I began listening in, trying to understand what they were saying. I simply could not follow their dialect. Of course, I understood a few words here and there, but I could not make out the gist of their conversation. I recalled that experience as I was reading historical documents one day, and suddenly I thought it strange that I could read documents from all over the country.

---

3. Sugae Masumi (1754–1829), born Shirai Hideo, left his native region of Mikawa in middle age and traveled throughout the northern areas of Honshu for the remainder of his life. His many writings, left scattered throughout the areas in which he stayed, were collected in the modern era and published as *Records of the Travels of Sugae Masumi (Sugae Masumi yūranki)* in 1966. These writings have since been recognized as an early precursor of modern Japanese ethnography.
4. Mechnikov (1845–1916) was a Russian-born zoologist and biologist who worked in France and visited Japan in the early Meiji period.

As a part of my work at the Institute for the Study of Japanese Folk Culture at Kanagawa University, I visited the Tokikuni household on the Noto Peninsula for one week every summer and fall from the mid-1980s to the late 1990s to examine documents in their possession. It so happened that our group found a couple of documents from the Warring States period (1482–1558) in which a number of local place names appear. We decided to ask some older people from the area about the relationship between the names in the documents and the place names used today. We were soon introduced to a man of seventy or eighty years. He happily answered our questions, but we were able to understand only about half of what he said. I had a similar experience when I went to Tosaminato in Aomori Prefecture. When I arrived at the inn, the owner, who had been drinking, came out to greet me quite jovially, evidently thanking me for coming from so far away, but I could not understand him at all. Some time later it occurred to me that ethnologists have an incredibly difficult job, for in order to carry out their field work they must be able to understand old folks and drunks. An ethnologist working in Japan must also be able to comprehend the different dialects from such disparate regions as Kagoshima, Tohoku, Kansai, and Kanto. They must cull from speech the depths of human feeling and attempt to grasp thereby the deepest layers of Japanese society. On reflection, I realized that I could never be an ethnologist.

The topics with which historians deal are similar to those of the ethnologists. Nevertheless, I can read documents from any region, even though they always have something unique from their place of origin. Until recently, I had never thought to question this phenomenon, but after these experiences I realized that it was important to ask why I can read historical documents from any region. In short, the answer lies in the fact that the lettered society of Japan—the realm of documents—is relatively homogeneous. In contrast, the unlettered society—the world of the spoken word—is far more heterogeneous than we have imagined. Therefore, when we peel away the outer layer of homogeneous, literate society, we reveal an extremely diverse folk society below it. Even today, Japanese society is by no means homogeneous. This kind of relationship between the written and oral worlds is an issue common to many of the world's cultures, but in the case of Japan it strikes me as particularly evident.

This problem of the relationship between lettered and unlettered society in Japan leads us to the question of the relationship between history and folk studies.[5] But the major task we must perform before we can pursue those questions is to consider more completely the functions of the three forms of script in Japan. To that end, we will now look at how historically *hiragana* and *katakana* have been used differently.

THE WORLD OF *KATAKANA*

Documents containing a mixture of *hiragana* and/or *katakana* with *kanji* (known as *kana-majiri*) began to appear around the tenth century. In the late thirteenth century, *kana-majiri* came to comprise approximately 20 percent of all documents. The ratio did not change much during the Northern and Southern Courts period (1336–92), but in the fifteenth century, during the Muromachi period, this percentage rose quickly, with *kana-majiri* comprising 59 to 60 percent of all documents.

These numbers are based on the documents that have survived to the present day, and we should remember that, for the most part, they were intentionally preserved. However, there is another class of documents, which we call *shihai*,[6] that were meant to be thrown away but happened to survive when their reverse sides were used to write another document. The proportion of documents with a mix of *kanji* and *kana* in this class is much higher than the rate just cited for documents that were meant to be kept. Therefore, I think we can say that the *kana-majiri* form of writing was widely practiced from the late thirteenth century on.

However, the increase in the numbers of this kind of mixed script document was principally an increase in "*kanji* with *hiragana*" documents. *Kanji* with *katakana* materials comprise only 1 to 2 percent of all the documents that have survived. This trend becomes particularly apparent after the Muromachi period. If we look at regional documents from the Edo period, such as the more than twenty thousand documents from the Tokikuni household, we do not find a single example of a *kanji-katakana* document. Grammatical

5. Amino is referring to the fact that in Japan both history and folk studies are seen as disciplines that deal with the past. But, while history is understood to do so through written documents, folk studies is understood to be a field that relies on an analysis of spoken material and performative culture.

6. Literally, these are "on the back of the paper" documents. As Amino notes, these were documents written on the backside of paper that had been used for another purpose. They are not exactly palimpsests, but the layering of documents on both sides of one sheet of paper makes them a similar phenomenon. Amino's point is that one only writes on the backside of papers one does not intend to save, so the survival of this class of documents may be seen as accidental.

particles such as *ni* and *wa* were commonly written in *katakana*, but we have not found any written strictly in *kanji* and *katakana*, or just *katakana*, such as can occasionally be found in documents dating from the medieval era. Thus, we can infer that the diffusion of writing took place almost exclusively as the diffusion of *hiragana*.

To what uses, then, was this "minority" class of documents (*kanji-katakana*) put? Basically, *katakana* was used to express in writing words that had been spoken, such as oral testimonies. Moreover, many of the documents from the medieval era in which speech was transcribed turn out to have been on matters related to the deities (Shinto and Buddhist). For instance, *katakana* was conspicuously used in documents recording a vow made to the deities (*kishōmon, kōmon*) or a prayer requesting something from a god (*ganmon*). The same was true for documents recording words received from the gods, such as divine oracles (*takumon*) or records of dreams written immediately upon waking (*mūki*). In other words, *katakana* was deliberately used when the document recorded speech, particularly when it was related to the realm of the divine.

Trial records that contained statements from both the defendant and the plaintiff were often written in a mixed *kanji-katakana* style. This was called the imperial edict style (*senmyōgaki*), and it was also commonly used to record the confessions of defendants. Perhaps the clearest case of *katakana* usage is that of graffiti and anonymous flyers (*rakusho*) and anonymous pledges (*rakusho kishō*), almost all of which were written in *katakana* (fig. 22). The term *rakusho* literally means "writings that have been dropped." According to Katsumata Shizuo, the act of dropping something was significant, for it meant that once it was dropped the object was no longer in the possession of human beings.[7] Instead, "dropped things" were seen as belonging to the deities. Therefore, documents that had been dropped were seen as having entered a realm beyond the powers of humanity, where they took on the character of the voice of the deities.

The same was true for *rakusho* pledges. To take a hypothetical example, suppose that one member of a group has stolen some property from another member and the theft has been discovered. If no one is willing to confess to the crime, the criminal will often be revealed by someone who anonymously writes a *rakusho* pledge in which, swearing to the deities that he or she is not lying,

7. See, for example, Katsumata Shizuo, *Sengoku seiritsu shiron* (The Formation of the Warring States Period) (Tokyo: Tōkyō daigaku shuppankai, 1979); and *Chūseibito no seikatsu sekai* (Everyday Life of Medieval People) (Tokyo: Yamakawa shuppansha, 1996).

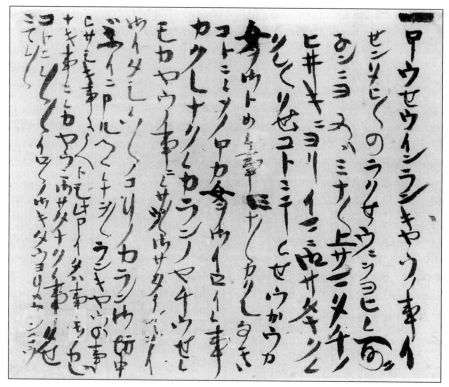

Figure 22. Anonymous flyer (*rakusho*) written in *katakana* from Tōji Temple. From the collection of Kyoto Furitsu Sōgō Shiryōkan.

the criminal is named. Since dropped writings were believed to transcribe the voice of the deities, the institutionalization of this belief produced the *rakusho* pledge. *Rakusho* pledges first appeared in the middle of the Kamakura period, and up to the Muromachi they were almost all written in *katakana*.

Thus, *katakana*'s basic textual function was to record the spoken word. But, while the relationship between *katakana* and the deities was central to the script, the use of *katakana* was not limited to sacred subjects or contexts. *Katakana*, not *hiragana*, was used to write down the names of things and places that had been orally described to the writer. For that reason, one also often finds *katakana* being used in petitions, for example, the petition of Kami village in Ategawa estate, Kii Province, famous for its depiction of the violence of its military steward (with his threat to "cut off ears and noses"). This document, dated 1275, is so well known for having been written in *katakana* that it is sometimes simply called the *katakana* petition. Early in my career, when I taught high school, I treated the *katakana* in this document as a childish and faltering mode of expression, the kind of thing one would get from simple villagers suffering at the hands of a tyrannical constable. From that rough appearance alone, I told my students, one could sense the emotions of the villagers. Actually, most other scholars said the same thing. But on further reflection it does not make sense to say that just because it is written in *katakana* it is faltering. *Katakana* is certainly difficult to read, but it is equally difficult regardless of whether it was written by a villager or an educated priest. Those of us of the wartime generation who learned *katakana* before *hiragana* in elementary school have a tendency to view *katakana* as a childish mode of expression. Thus, we have mistakenly assumed that the *katakana* in this petition indicated that the villagers were unfamiliar with writing in *hiragana* and therefore were unsophisticated.

Since the word used to describe this document as a "petition" literally means "to speak to a superior" (*genjōjō*), it is possible that it was originally read aloud. One further reason why it was written in *katakana* is that the document itself contains a direct quotation of a threat made by the military steward to the villagers: "If you do not turn over the wheat, I will cut off your ears, slice off your noses, and cut off your hair. Do not resist or I'll shave your heads and tie you up like criminals."[8]

In a related area, diaries (*nikki*) in the early medieval era were texts in which the events of the day were written down soon after they occurred. What is noteworthy for us is that many of these diaries were written in a combination of *kanji* and *katakana*. Drawing upon that observation to reconsider the Ategawa petition, it seems to me unlikely that the petition of the villagers of Ategawa estate was submitted through official channels. I make that inference because most villagers' petitions from the Kamakura period that were properly submitted were written in *kanji* alone. The Ategawa petition is a remarkable exception. It may well be, then, that it was written like a diary under conditions in which events had to be recorded immediately after they happened.

Turning from documents to the world of literature, we find that *katakana* was used in many of the books related to Buddhist temples. It was first used in temples to gloss the pronunciation of Buddhist sutras—which

8. To contemporary readers, cutting hair and shaving heads may not sound as devastating as cutting off noses and ears, but, as Amino discusses in chapter eight, clothing and hairstyles in ancient and medieval Japan were considered to be important markers of status and occupation. Losing one's hair could not only be humiliating, but it might seriously damage one's livelihood. For example, the phrase "shave your heads," appears to mean, literally, "I'll turn you into nuns" (*ama ni nashite*). This was a status that signified separation from the secular world and its occupations.

were, after all, written in Chinese—so that the monks could read them aloud. This origin of *katakana* meshes well with its continued use in temple books. Tsukishima Hiroshi has spoken of "the monkish love for *katakana*," and even though *waka* poetry was customarily written in *hiragana*, monks tended to write it in *katakana*.[9] The tenth-century text *Illustrations of the Three Jewels* was written to explain Buddhist teachings to women in a simple fashion, so it was written in *hiragana*.[10] But the version of that text that was kept and transmitted within temples was written in *katakana*. Similarly, the oldest extant copies of *The Tale of the Heike* are the Enkyō, a version held in temples that was also written in *katakana*.[11]

Another genre of texts related to the temples are the transcriptions (*shōmono*) of lectures given by Zen monks on the Chinese classics from the Muromachi period on. We have copies of such books as *Comments on the Records of the Historian* (*Shikishō*) and *Comments on the Analects* (*Rongoshō*). The vernacular Japanese used by the lecturers is transcribed in these books in *katakana*. Thus, Zen monks—and the Confucian scholars associated with them—frequently used *katakana* as late as the Edo period. However, there is no doubt that by the Edo period commoners used *katakana* only on special occasions.

WOMEN AND *HIRAGANA*

Hiragana, clearly the most frequently used of the two phonetic scripts, was first used by women. Long after its invention, it was known as women's script (*onna no ji*), and this association eventually gave rise to a unique style of writing known as women's writing (*onna bumi*). If we also remember that when men wrote letters to women they used a large proportion of *hiragana* characters, we can clearly see that *hiragana* was understood to be feminine.

During the Muromachi period, when the king of the Ryukyus sent private letters to "the king of Japan"—in other words, the Muromachi shogun—

9. See, for example, Tsukishima Hiroshi, *Kana* (Syllabary) (Tokyo: Chūō kōronsha, 1981); and *Rekishiteki kanazukai: Sono seiritsu to tokuchō* (The Historical Uses of Syllabary: Its Formation and Special Characteristics) (Tokyo: Chūō kōronsha, 1986).
10. *Sanbō ekotoba*, was compiled in 984 by Minamoto no Tamenori for Princess Sonshi, who had just become a Buddhist nun. The Three Jewels of Buddhism were: the Buddha, the Buddhist Law (dharma), and the priesthood. See Donald Keene, *Seeds in the Heart: Japanese Literature from Earliest Times to the Late Sixteenth Century* (New York: Henry Holt, 1993), 570–71.
11. Enkyō is the reign name of a three-year period (1308–10), so this is the period in which this text was produced. For an English translation of the text, see *The Tale of the Heike*, trans. Helen Craig McCullough (Stanford: Stanford University Press, 1988).

the letters were written in *hiragana*. We do not know why it was *hiragana* and not *katakana* that came to be used in the Ryukyus—it may have been because women were involved in its transmission. In any case, when the shogun received one of these *hiragana* letters, he would pass it on to one of his consorts and have her write the reply. This example also demonstrates that women and *hiragana* were closely related.

Thus, it is absolutely indispensable to an understanding of Japanese culture that we recognize that women used their own script from very early on. The long-standing tradition of women's literature, from the tenth-century classics *The Pillow Book of Sei Shōnagon* and *The Tale of Genji* to the medieval diaries *The Confessions of Lady Nijō* and *An Account of Takemuki Palace*, was made possible by this fact.[12] I cannot think of any other culture in which women produced such exemplary literature well before the modern era. But the more important question is, What made it possible for women to play this role in Japanese culture? I am afraid we do not yet understand how important this phenomenon was. This question is also linked to the question raised in the foreword—about the origins of modern Japanese villages in the fourteenth century—because the women's literature I just referred to was produced up until the fourteenth century. We still find women's diaries after the Muromachi period, but there is nothing that we can really call literature until the modern era. This is surely related to the social transformation that took place in the fourteenth century.

Setting that question aside for the moment, *hiragana* was first used as women's script and then spread when men began using it as well. From the Heian period through the Edo, most men used mostly *kanji* when writing for official purposes. The aristocracy used *kanji* for all official documents as a matter of course. The warriors did as well, although from the beginning there was something different in their documents that produced a climate of acceptance for the use of some mixture of *kanji* and *hiragana*. To get a sense of the specialized spheres reserved for each script, consider the official decisions on litigation handed down by the Kamakura shogunate. This class of documents, known as "Kanto's orders" (*kantō gejijō*), was written entirely in Chinese characters. Even when these decisions quoted letters and deeds of transfer—I will return to these later, but for the moment I

---

12. Three of these are available in translation: Sei Shonagon, *The Pillow Book of Sei Shonagon*, trans. Ivan Morris (New York: Columbia University Press, 1967); Lady Murasaki, *The Tale of Genji*, trans. Edward Seidensticker (New York: Alfred A. Knoph, 1976); and Lady Nijō, *The Confessions of Lady Nijō*, trans. Karen Brazell (New York: Doubleday, 1973).

wish to note that these documents contained a fair amount of *hiragana*—the scribes took great pains to rewrite the *hiragana*-enscribed sections in *kanji* (*man'yōgana*).[13] The officials of the Kamakura shogunate clearly felt that it was unseemly for *hiragana* to appear in official judicial decisions. The documents produced in the masculine world, the public world, continued to use primarily *kanji* until the end of the Edo period.

That is why men began to use *hiragana* only in private letters. By the end of the Heian period, however, it was also being widely used in deeds of transfer (*yuzurijō*). *Yuzurijō*, documents that were unique to the medieval era, were used to bequeath or transfer assets; they had all but disappeared by the Edo period.[14] We do not really understand why deeds of transfer were often written in *hiragana*. But if I were to hazard a guess, it seems to me that one important expectation of a deed of transfer was that it be written by the issuer himself. This is partly related to the degree to which writing had been disseminated, for it was members of the warrior class who wrote most of these deeds, and it was in the Kamakura period that they learned to write in *hiragana*. So, we might conclude that it was natural for them to write these documents in *hiragana*.

These deeds were necessary at that time because the transfer of assets could not be accomplished solely within the bounds of the relationship between the one who bequeaths and the heir. There were no registration procedures whereby some official body could grant recognition of ownership, and no transfer of property could be carried out without the acknowledgment of a certain portion of the society in which the partners to the transaction resided. So, unless the people of that social sphere could read and understand the document, there would be no point in writing it. The greater popularity of *hiragana* may have been the reason why deeds of transfer were written in it. Whatever the reason, it is worth noting that this genre of document, while creating the conditions for social recognition, was essentially private.

In fact, during the medieval period there was a general tendency for public documents to resemble private letters. Official documents from ancient times did not include such epistolary forms as an address. But the medieval

13. The first poetry collection in Japan, the *Man'yōshū*, was compiled before the invention of a phonetic syllabary, so the scribes who recorded these "Japanese" poems used *kanji* phonetically. This phonetic use of *kanji* (to be pronounced in a Japanese manner, not the customary Japanese approximation of the Chinese pronunciation) came to be known as the *man'yōgana* or *man'yō* syllabary. Amino's point here is that changing the *hiragana* portions of quoted documents into *man'yōgana* would preserve the all-*kanji* appearance of the official documents.

14. We do not really understand why this type of document fell into disuse. That in itself is a problem worth investigating.

era developed a widely used form known as the epistolary style (*shosatsuyō monjo*), which contained the date and the name of the sender as well as the name of the addressee at the end. Another type of document that came to be widely used was the service order (*hōsho*). These were written when a high-ranking person asked his vassal to communicate his desires to the vassal of another high-ranking person.[15] Direct imperial edicts (*rinji*), edicts of the retired emperor (*inzen*), and the instructions (*migyōsho*) of nobles of the third rank or higher all took this form.

As these documents began to be written in *hiragana*, other official documents were as well. This process began in regions outside the political centers of Kyoto and Kamakura, and the group that initiated it was the document-producing class most firmly rooted in such locales: the *jitō* military stewards and the *shōen* estate managers (*azukarisho*). Documents passing from the regions to the capital, and from low rank to high, also began to use *hiragana* relatively early on. These included reports and intelligence from *shōen* estate managers sent to proprietors in Kyoto or Kamakura, appeals from villagers to their superiors on every kind of matter, and so on. What made the rapid rise in the number of these documents possible was the increasing use of *kanji-hiragana* documents (fig. 23).

The use of this kind of document increased exponentially during the Muromachi period, but we can see the incipient signs of it in the late thirteenth century. By the fifteenth century, documents written in a mixture of *kanji* and *hiragana* dominated the written world. For example, 70 to 80 percent of the surviving documents of Niimi estate in Bitchū Province were written in a combination of *kanji* and *hiragana*. Considering that the sheer volume of documents increased tremendously during this period, and that many among them were in *kanji-hiragana*, there can be no doubt that the fourteenth and fifteenth centuries constituted an extremely important epoch for the diffusion of writing in Japanese society.

From the late Kamakura to the Muromachi period, literacy spread to new classes and constituencies, including the lower levels of the warrior class, leading families in the villages, and women, all of whom were able to write documents in a mixture of *kanji* and *hiragana*. For example, the wives

15. This is a somewhat indirect way of describing an indirect mode of communication. Given the intricacies of communication when all the hierarchical forms must be strictly observed, the service order was a way of making requests without involving the high-ranking person who initiated the exchange. In other words, the letter would be written in the style "My master desires of your master that . . ." and then exchanged as if it were a communication between servants rather than their masters.

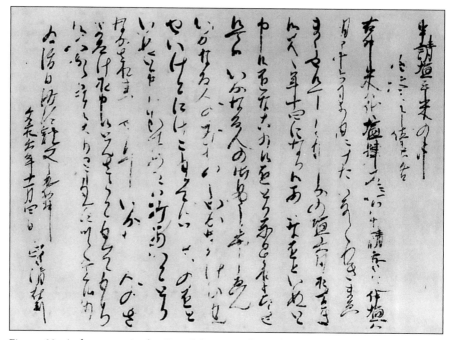

Figure 23. A document in *kanji* and *hiragana* from the Tōji Temple estate. From the collection of Kyoto Furitsu Sōgō Shiryōkan.

and daughters of shogunate vassals and nonvassal warriors[16] were writing letters in *hiragana* in the Kamakura period. We can also confirm examples from literate women in the five home provinces around Kyoto from the upper levels of the villager class.

From the Muromachi period we have the example of a very famous and beautifully written letter by a woman named Tamagaki of Niimi estate (fig. 24).[17] Tamagaki was probably a woman of low status who served under the priest who was chief administrator at Niimi. Some say that she may have been a courtesan. When the priest she served was murdered, she wrote a letter to the estate proprietors at Tōji in truly beautiful *hiragana* relating her thoughts on the incident. As these examples suggest, the spread of literacy among women probably paralleled that among men.

Later, the construction of the governmental system in the Edo period was itself predicated upon the dissemination of writing among the common

16. These were warriors who were not vassals of the shogun in Kamakura.
17. For a further discussion of this woman, see chapter three.

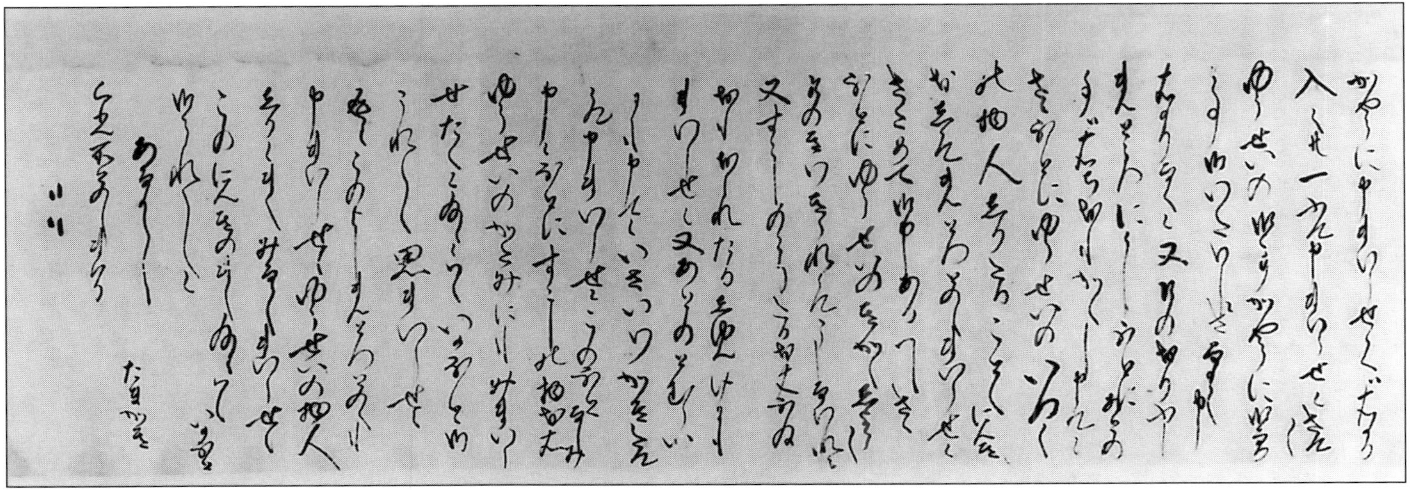

Figure 24. Letter from Lady Tamagaki received by Tōji Temple. From the collection of Kyoto Furitsu Sōgō Shiryōkan.

people. From the beginning, the Edo shogunate's system of rule assumed that there were people in the towns and villages who could read and write.[18] That presumption made this government highly unusual in world history, and it suggests how we might investigate the correspondence between the structure of the Tokugawa state and the high degree of literacy among the populace.

Documents written through the Kamakura period are extremely pleasing to the eye or, as Kasamatsu Hiroshi puts it, "elegant." This is true of the writing not only of the aristocracy but also of the warriors and literate villagers. As we enter the Muromachii period, we find many more documents, but the quality of the writing clearly declines. As a result, these documents are extremely difficult to read. The best example of this is the wooden tablets found at the Kusado Sengenchō excavation in Fukuyama City, Hiroshima Prefecture.[19] Kusado Sengenchō (sengenchō means "town of one thousand buildings") is a famous excavation of a medieval town that is now at the bottom of a river. The tablets recovered at this site are not at all like the magnificent examples found at the recent excavation of the residence of Prince Nagaya.[20] The Kusado tablets are roughly planed wooden strips with characters written on them in hurried brush strokes. These strips were probably much like those used until quite recently to post prices at fish stores. Many wooden strips at the Kusado dig appear to have had something scrawled on them quickly in the middle of a transaction. We can barely read them; the writing is that hard to make out. This suggests to me that the social attitude toward writing changed significantly after the Kamakura period. This is also why I think the process of the dissemination of texts is so important.

I believe that prior to the Kamakura period people had a certain reverence toward writing. This led them to value the beauty of the script itself. But even as that reverence lived on writing gradually became a far more utilitarian matter

18. The ability of villagers to write was presumed because, given the requirement that all warriors must leave the countryside and reside in the castle town of their masters, villages were charged with a relatively high degree of self-governance. Ordered by their lord to pay a certain level of taxes, it was the villagers themselves who gathered tax rice, calculated and recorded its volume, and stored it locally or forwarded it to domainal warehouses. All of these procedures required the production of documents attesting to their completion and recording their details.
19. The original text has a photograph of one of these wooden tablets. For more on the Kusado Sengenchō excavation, see the excavation web page http://www.mars.dti.ne.jp/~suzuki-y/index_e .html (current as of April 2011).
20. Amino is referring to the discovery of thirty-five thousand wooden tablets in Nara in the late 1980s at the site of what was believed to have been the Nara era residence of Prince Nagaya. Amino wants his readers to contrast the Nara period production of the Prince Nagaya tablets with the medieval era production of the Kusado tablets. For a detailed discussion of the Nagaya tablets see William Wayne Farris, *Sacred Texts and Buried Treasures: Issues in the Historical Archaeology of Ancient Japan* (Honolulu: University of Hawai'i Press, 1998), 221–30.

for those who wrote. It was in relation to this growing instrumentalism that the change in writing technique occurred. At the same time, I believe that the growth of towns and villages is deeply connected to the spread of writing and its increasing instrumentality.

I agree with Ishii Susumu that the wooden strips at Kusado Sengenchō are the forerunners of account books.[21] Account books were being independently created in villages and towns no later than the Warring States period. It is also quite clear that the people of these villages and towns kept two sets of books, one for the ruling lord and one for their own use. We have examples of "hidden" account books (*ura chōbo*) from the Warring States era that were different from the "formal" books produced for the lord. Villagers decided for themselves how to divide the tax burden of the yearly tribute levied by the lord. That is why they kept their own books. Significantly, the lords never interfered with the villages' internal bookkeeping.

This system continued into the Edo period when villages autonomously determined how they would pay the yearly tribute levied by the lord. This "village contract system" would not have been possible had the villagers not been able to write or do complex mathematics. This is why I say that the diffusion of writing and the establishment of stable villages were inseparable processes. What was true for villages was all the more so for towns, where even more people had a good command of writing and numbers. It was thanks to these skills that towns and villages maintained a degree of self-governance.

THE STATE AND THE DISSEMINATION OF WRITING

One further point I would like to make about the dissemination of writing is that the motor of this dissemination was not *katakana* but *hiragana*. This is a major issue for our consideration of writing in Japan. *Katakana*, the script most closely related to the world of speech, did not become the script used for "books." *Hiragana*, on the other hand, was intended from the start to be used for writing and reading. So, when we think about how writing disseminated in Japan, we should remember that it occurred by means of *hiragana*, the script intended for reading and writing, and not through *katakana*, the script most closely associated with speech.

---

21. See, for example, Ishii Susumu, *Chūsei o hirogeru: Atarashii shiryōron o motomete* (Opening up Medieval Japan: In Search of a New Theory of Sources) (Tokyo: Yoshikawa kōbunkan, 1991). In English see, Susumu Ishii, *History of Medieval Japan* (Centre for East Asian Cultural Studies, 1976).

This is also related to the way in which writing entered the Japanese archipelago, as *kanji* imported from the Chinese mainland and the Korean Peninsula. The Japanese syllabaries were created out of *kanji* after it had been used phonetically as *man'yōgana*. But more than anything else it was the establishment of the Ritsuryō state that had the greatest significance for the ways in which writing was used and disseminated.

The establishment of the Ritsuryō state had a major impact on all aspects of society in the Japanese islands. For example, the most common elements of male villagers' names during the Edo period, such as *bei*, *zaemon*, *uemon*, and *umanojō*, were all slight variations on names of official posts in the Ritsuryō system. And when it comes to writing, what was truly decisive was the fact that the Ritsuryō state adopted a "documentist" (*monjo shugi*) approach to governance.

By documentism I mean that the Ritsuryō state prescribed that all administration, including those matters that had previously been implemented verbally, would from then on be dependent on documents. The Ritsuryō state put this documentist system into practice in the strictest terms. That meant that anyone living within the state's domain who expected to have interactions with the authorities was compelled to learn how to write. The establishment of this state was, from the perspective of those in the regions, a major event. In a certain sense, one could say that this state was received as a "sacred world" created in the distant capital. Whatever the case, it was a window opening onto the glittering world of civilization. For those in the regions, writing was the link that connected and mediated the relationship between that world and the self. That much is clearly demonstrated by discoveries at several excavations of wooden strips that show traces of *kanji* as it was practiced by candidates for office in preparation for the government examinations.

Tōno Haruyuki has written a fascinating book on these wooden strips called *Ancient Japan as Revealed by Wooden Tablets*.[22] Central to Tōno's book is a set of wooden strips uncovered at the excavation of Heijō Palace in Nara. These strips have inscribed on them repetitions of sets of two or three characters. Tōno has won high praise for performing the laborious task of attributing each of these two- and three-character sets to their original texts. According to Tōno, it appears that candidates practiced their writing

---

22. Tōno Haruyuki, *Mokkan ga kataru Nihon no kodai* (Ancient Japan as Revealed by Wooden Tablets) (Tokyo: Iwanami shoten, 1983).

by copying from a Chinese classic called *Selected Writings* (*Monzen*), which contained most of the questions used on the examination.

These wooden tablets have also been discovered in the ruins of Akita Castle in Dewa Province. It would not be surprising to find these in sites near the capital, but it is noteworthy that they have also turned up at the northernmost outpost of the Ritsuryō state. One explanation for this is that the state ordered the creation of family registries for all areas under its control. It was the district magistrates or village heads who had to write the characters in the registries. That being the case, we can see that in every one of the areas under its control the state produced people who could write. It is worth noting that the writing in the family registries tends to be in a very good hand. The writing in the registry currently in the possession the temple of Shōsōin in Kyoto, for example, is good enough to be appreciated as a work of art (fig. 25). I find it remarkable that an official of the lowest level was able to write characters this well. The characters in the Shōsōin registry leave no doubt that the people of that time were extremely serious about writing, treating it as something very valuable. In succeeding eras, the Heian court and the Kamakura and Muromachi regimes all followed the example of the Ritsuryō state with regard to documentism. The Edo shogunate was perhaps

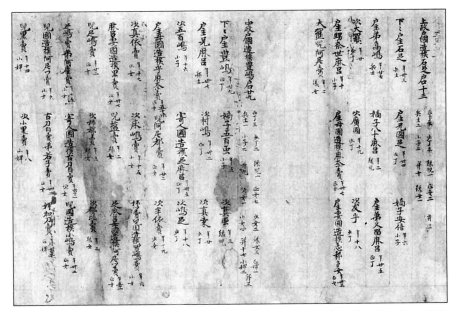

Figure 25. Family registry (*koseki*) of Harube Village, Mihoma Gun, Ono Province, 702. Credit: Treasures of Shōsōin (*Shōsōin hōmotsu*).

the most thorough, and successful, in its application. Whenever the shogunate or the regional lords ordered their subjects to produce a certain kind of document, the people of the villages and towns were able to comply. From the Edo period on, Japanese society began to produce a huge number of documents. This volume was no doubt due to the state's continuing employment of a documentist ideal of governance.

But notwithstanding the state's determination to ground itself in writing, we cannot conclude that writing was simply forced on society from above. Rather, the establishment of the Ritsuryō state called forth a spontaneous movement from below, one that gave birth to *hiragana* and *katakana*. I believe the evangelical Buddhist sects that began to appear around the end of the twelfth century had a particularly important role in the spread of writing.[23] Such major religious figures as Hōnen, Shinran, Nichiren, Ippen, and later Rennyo all wrote a great number of letters in *hiragana*, and even an occasional letter in *katakana*, as part of their evangelical work. The new sects used *hiragana* and the speech-related *katakana* because they deliberately sought converts among the masses. Many prayers and songs that were meant to be sung aloud were written and disseminated in *katakana*. We even find some texts, such as the ones written by monks at the Ikkō sect temple of Honpukuji in Katada, in which dialect is recorded in *katakana*.

This trend continued from the medieval period to the beginning of the early modern era and even included Christian literature produced in Japan. But these religious movements were suppressed by the secular military class. After their suppression, no religion in Japanese society was able to maintain the kind of independent power base that Islam and Christianity enjoyed elsewhere. The suppression of the new religions also deeply affected the subsequent existence of the emperor. But for the issues raised in this chapter the defeat of the new religions resulted in the strengthening of the state's documentist regulation of society, which in turn helped bring about the current state of writing in Japanese society.[24]

I have been working with historical documents for many years now, and I am able to distinguish medieval from early modern documents at a glance.

23. See chapters four and eight for more detailed discussions of these Kamakura sects.
24. This may seem unclear, since Amino has just stated that the new Buddhist sects of the Kamakura era relied heavily on writing, especially in *hiragana* and *katakana*, in their evangelical work. Amino's point is that the suppression of the new religions, which had embraced writing, erased some possibilities for alternative developments in the history of writing in Japan. It particularly leads to his following point that the world of documents in Japan is extremely homogeneous, a homogeneity that derives from the close relationship between writing and governance.

A trained eye can determine whether Edo period documents are from the early, middle, or late Edo without even seeing the date. True experts in Edo documents can come even closer to the precise reign date without seeing the date on the document. I am not that good, but the ability to distinguish general periods holds true for documents from all over the country, regardless of region. Given the amount of difference in spoken dialects, this uniformity among documents is striking.

My good friend Tsukamoto Manabu tried an experiment with Edo period documents for an exhibition at the National Museum of History and Ethnology. He lined up tax levy documents sent from a certain domainal lord to his villages from one period with sales documents exchanged among villagers from the same period. On examination, Tsukamoto discerned that changes in textual styles clearly originated with the domainal lord. Such changes spread very rapidly among the documents written by villagers. When the lord's documents changed, the villager's documents—at least those being sent to the lord—also changed.

This transformation in textual style was especially dramatic in the Meiji period. Styles that had been specific to particular families underwent a drastic and sudden change with the abolition of domains in 1871. As a result, those who can easily read Edo period documents find that documents from the Meiji period are very difficult to decipher. I have a very hard time reading the letters of the Meiji statesman and author of the Meiji constitution, Itō Hirobumi, for example.[25] But the style prescribed by the Meiji state was quickly picked up by village heads and district administrators throughout the country. We must admit that this stylistic change came from above.

A good example of this can be found in the town records of Katada in Ōmi Province. Katada was legally designated as a village during the Edo period, but in actuality it operated as an independent town.[26] The town had a number of elders who took turns keeping the community's daily records. Town records from the entire Edo period still survive today. In the third year of the Meiji period (1870), however, the writing in the Katada town diary suddenly alternates between someone who wrote like a government official and someone who wrote in the old style of the town. Within two

25. Itō Hirobumi (1841–1909) was one of the two most important of the Meiji oligarchs from the 1880s to the end of the era. Itō drafted the Meiji Constitution and served as the first prime minister under the constitutional system.
26. For a more detailed discussion of the difference between a village and a town in the Edo period, see chapter one.

years, the grammatical style of the document had been entirely adjusted to fit the new Meiji style.

As I mentioned earlier, this change was due to the influence of the state and its emphasis on the production of documents. If that is the case, then one might conclude that the Japanese masses were always looking up to their masters, and adjusting their lives to follow their dictates. There is much support for that argument, but we should remember that these changes were taking place in the public realm of official documents. The same kind of situation could not be said to have prevailed in the field of letters or the more private diaries. When we recognize that difference, we find ample reason to believe that there were different trends behind the immediately apparent world of officialdom in the Edo period as well.

So what was behind this homogenization of the world of writing in Japan? On the one hand, we clearly have the power of the state pressing down from above. But, on the other hand, we also have the attitudes of those below, who were responding to that pressure. What I would ask the reader to remember is that the will to respond among those "below" is something with very deep roots in Japanese society.[27] Furthermore, if we remember to always distinguish between the surface world of officialdom and the undercurrents of society, we find that the will of the ruled to respond to the official homogenization became particularly strong from the Muromachi period on. But we cannot forget that this process began with the Ritsuryō state.

It seems to me that we have not given sufficient thought to the state of writing in Japan. Nor have we thought about what kind of changes are likely to take place or what kind of changes will be desirable from here on out. For example, the use of *katakana* suddenly increased in the Meiji period. Legal and military texts all used *katakana*, and elementary education in the Meiji period began with it. But *hiragana* was dominant in ordinary peoples' daily lives, and there was very little literature written entirely in the *kanji-katakana* mixed style. Scholars, especially of the Chinese studies lineage, initially wrote in the *kanji-katakana* style. But this, too, soon disappeared, and almost all scholarship came to be written in the *kanji-hiragana* mix.

27. Amino is pointing out that they were not passively formed by the dictates of those above but actively sought out that relation. This is not necessarily to say that there was a natural and mutual relation among the rulers and ruled but that by actively responding the ruled were working to create the conditions of that relation. In other words, Amino is urging his readers to think of governance as a series of ongoing negotiations between rulers and ruled. Unequal though they might be, Amino believes it is still possible to discern the roles of the ruled in establishing the terms and procedures of governance.

Literature since the Edo period has been written in the *kanji-hiragana* style, whereas Confucian scholars of that era used *kanji-katakana*. Why was it, then, that under these conditions legal and military texts of the Meiji era were composed in a mixture of *kanji* and *katakana*? This question has not yet been resolved, but I suspect that the answer touches upon the very essence of the Meiji state. After World War II, elementary education began with *hiragana*. I doubt that this change was effected after deep reflection on the history of writing in Japan, but I will leave that question up to historians of education.

It seems to me that, particularly in recent years, the realm of written representation has undergone enormous change on a variety of levels. I believe that our discussions on the state of writing in the Japan of the future must be based upon a consideration of the issues I have raised in this chapter—issues of power, ideology, and the historical uses of the scripts with which we write today.

CHAPTER SEVEN

Commerce, Finance, and Currency

THE FLOW OF COINS FROM SONG CHINA

In chapter six, I noted how the social function of writing changed considerably around the fourteenth century. I believe this change is closely related to the fact that coins also began to circulate in the islands with regularity from the late thirteenth century on. Of course, coins had been used in Japan prior to the thirteenth century, with minting having begun in the eighth century. These early coins, made of silver and copper, were known as *wadō kaichin*.[1] The court later minted imperial twelve-sen coins until the middle of the tenth century.

The character of these early coins raises a number of issues for our consideration. To begin with, it is no accident that they were first minted at the same time that the Yamato state was adopting the Chinese governmental system. They were often used to pay taxes in kind (*chō*) and corveé labor taxes (*yō*). But in fact the only place where these coins actually circulated was the Kinai region, which comprised the five provinces surrounding the capital. We have no evidence that they were in use throughout the islands. Furthermore, *wadō kaichin* were not used simply as a method of payment and circulation. They also had magical uses. For example, they were always placed on the foundation when a new temple was constructed. Several coins were

---

1. The name comes from the characters 和同開珎, which were inscribed on the coin clockwise around the center hole.

also usually placed in a corner of a building, as we know from the excavation of the Fuwa barrier in Mino. This kind of placement appears to have had a magical significance. Since society in the islands had not yet experienced the conditions that make currency necessary, the minting of coins came to an end in Japan after the tenth century, just as the power of the central government went into a significant decline. Nevertheless, the fact that this primitive society had coins had critical consequences for the subsequent relationship between coins and society.

There were, however, other items that circulated as currency (in other words, as a medium of exchange). Foremost were silk and rice. For example, records show that silk and rice were used as the measure of the price of land until the middle of the twelfth century. But from that point in time through the thirteenth century coins from Song China flowed into Japan in great quantities. Taira no Kiyomori,[2] in particular, put tremendous energy into developing trade with the Song.

However, just as this process was getting underway, the Japanese islands were hit by a series of epidemics popularly called "the coin pestilence" because of rumors that it was the use of coins that caused their outbreaks. These rumors provide us with evidence that coins were beginning to circulate with greater frequency. But they also show that the tendency to view coins as magical items was still strong. In other words, the idea of coins as a mere medium of circulation had still not permeated society.

Nevertheless, according to Matsunobu Yasutaka, payments that used to be made in silk were almost all made with coins by the first half of the thirteenth century.[3] This trend continued in the latter half of the thirteenth century, as land sales were no longer conducted in rice but in coins. As a result, the importation of Song coins had reached an enormous volume by the thirteenth century. While there are very few examples to give us a concrete sense of the volume of coins that entered Japan, we do have records of a ship sent to Song China by the Saionji family in the early thirteenth century that brought back 100,000 *kan* in coins. A *kan* was a string with 1,000 coins on it,

---

2. Taira no Kiyomori (1118–81) was the head of the Taira clan at the zenith of its power at the end of the Heian era. It was his rise to power that exacerbated growing tensions between regional warrior groups and warriors associated with the aristocracy in the capital, and it was his death that precipitated the events leading to the five years of civil war known as the Genpei wars. Taira no Kiyomori was portrayed as a great villain in the romance of that war, *The Tale of the Heike*.
3. Matsunobu Yasutaka, "Zeni to kahei no gainen: Kamakuraki ni okeru kahei kinō no henka ni tsuite" (The Concept of Money and Coinage: Regarding the Change in the Function of Coinage in the Kamakura Period), in *Rettō no bunkashi* (Cultural History of the Archipelago), no. 6, ed. Amino

so 100,000 *kan* would amount to 100 million copper coins. This enormous volume of coins was most likely placed in the bottom of the ship as ballast.

Not long ago a sunken ship from the same era was raised from the ocean floor off the southwest coast of the Korean Peninsula. The ship, known as the Shin'an wreck,[4] was a rare find, for its cargo was raised almost entirely intact. The ship contained a large number of wooden tablets by which we know that there were many people with Japanese names onboard, including a religious solicitor (*kanjin hijiri*) who was gathering funds for construction work at the temple of Tōfukuji.[5] The ship contained vast stocks of celadon and porcelain, and about twenty-eight tons of Song coins were placed in its keel as ballast, an amount far exceeding the 100,000 *kan* the Saionji family imported. We do not know whether all of this was intended for import into the Japanese islands, but a significant proportion was surely destined for the archipelago. According to the wooden tablets found onboard, the ship sank in 1323.

Documents of the time reveal that a great many ships traveled between the archipelago and the mainland through the fourteenth century. From the latter part of the eleventh century on, ships like these, loaded with copper coins, sailed continuously from the Asian mainland to every part of the Japanese archipelago. Many ships also were sent to the mainland from the islands. The level of intercourse was so high that Chinese merchants and sailors formed Chinatowns in Kyushu ports such as Hakata, Imatsu, and Bōnotsu and Japan Sea ports such as Tsuruga. Most of the goods imported from China on these ships were copper and pottery (porcelain and stoneware). Again, the Shin'an wreck provides evidence of this, for several tens of thousands of unbroken blue and white porcelains were recovered from the wreck (fig. 26).

This volume of imports testifies to the fact that there was a tremendous demand for Song coins precisely at the time when Japanese society was undergoing a major transformation. We have very few extant records of transactions in commodities, but the documents concerning sales of land from this period suggest that value was being measured more frequently in coins in a wide variety of transactions. Coins became the primary medium of finance,

Yoshihiko, Tsukamoto Manabu, and Miyata Noboru (Tokyo: Nihon editā sukūru shuppanbu, 1989), 177–210.

4. The area in which it sank is called the Shin'an Sea.

5. *Kanjin hijiri*, as the reader will see below, were wandering priests who traveled the country collecting donations for large-scale temple construction projects. Tōfukuji was a Rinzai Zen sect temple founded in 1236 in eastern Kyoto by the aristocratic Kujō family.

Figure 26. Blue and white porcelain pots recovered from the Shin'an wreck. From the collection of the National Museum of Korea. Photograph courtesy of Shūkan Asahi Hyakka, ed., *Shintei zōho Nihon no rekishi*, vol. 9.

but, as I shall discuss in further detail below, we should also remember that rice did not lose its function as a measure of value or a means of exchange and payment.

The coins brought back by these ships began to circulate in Japanese society in the thirteenth century—in the early part of the century in eastern Japan and in the latter half in western Japan. The dissemination of coins, however, was not uniform, for eastern Japan—where until the twelfth and thirteenth centuries silk and cloth had circulated as currency—took to coins earlier than western Japan. Since a "bolt" is a unit of measure for silk or cloth, the saying of the time that "ten copper coins will get you a bolt" suggests that silk and cloth were traded for coins.

In contrast, rice was used quite early in the Kinai region and the rest of western Japan as the primary means of exchange and measure of value. At the end of the Heian period, there even appeared rice promissory notes known as *kaemai* (exchange rice). With the appearance of these notes, the rice itself did not have to be transported in order to make rice payments. In other words, these notes effectively fulfilled the function of currency, thereby delaying the adoption of coins in the area.

In the east, however, the Kamakura shogunate authorized the circulation of coins in lieu of silk and cloth in the early thirteenth century. Thus, from the thirteenth to the fourteenth centuries the shogunate began to express the value of annual tribute from stewards "vassals" fiefs in terms of cash: for example, as a "one-hundred-*kan*" holding or a "five-hundred-*kan*" land tribute. Likewise, the Kanto *kuji*, a tax levied on vassals themselves, was also collected in coins.

In this way, we can see the end of the thirteenth century as a period in which a cash economy was developing as coins permeated the Japanese archipelago. In addition, it marked the beginning of a credit economy, with bills of exchange circulating instead of coins. The reason is simple: the large volume of coins used in many transactions was too unwieldy to be practical. Ten *kanmon* in coins—bills of exchange were customarily issued in that amount—were equal to 10,000 coins, quite a healthy sum. One string held 100 *mon*—usually about ninety-six coins—which by itself would be quite heavy. Ten of these made one *kan*, so ten *kanmon* would be 100 strings, which would be extremely heavy (see fig. 27). Transporting actual coins could be dangerous, so safe and portable notes of credit came to be the preferred means of sending payment. We should also remember, however, that these bills of exchange could only work if there was a widespread network of merchants who recognized and honored them.

Figure 27. Coins found in the remains of Namioka Castle. Photograph courtesy of Namioka Town Board of Education, Namioka-machi, Tsugaru-gun, Aomori.

SYMBOLS OF WEALTH

The normal result of a massive influx of coins is inflation. We expect prices to rise, and indeed for a time in the late thirteenth century the price of rice, silk, and other commodities did rise. But, as Matsunobu Yasutaka has shown, prices in general, including those of land, had a tendency to fall in the fourteenth century. Not many historical materials have survived from that period, so there is little that we can say for certain. But Matsunobu believes that the reason prices did not rise was that it was the value of the coins that rose—that is, the demand for coins increased—which would have caused the relative value of other commodities to decline. The late thirteenth through the fourteenth centuries represented one peak in this demand, as we can see from the frequent discoveries of what are called "buried offering coins" (*mainōsen*) or "set aside coins" (*bichikusen*) from that era. The next peak came during the Warring States period and into the first years of the Edo period.

The standard view of buried coins is that they were buried because of some from of social chaos such as war. That is conceivable for the period of the second peak in demand, which was a time of extended civil war. But Matsunobu believes that the peak in coin burials in the late thirteenth and fourteenth centuries represents attempts to accumulate, rather than simply safeguard, wealth. This is a sign that Song copper coins had come to possess great significance.

I am basically in agreement with this. However, I should point out that people at the time considered buried things to be ownerless. Our investigation of the significance of buried coins must take this into account. The fact that coins were buried suggests that they still retained a certain magical significance (to which I shall return in the next section). This is a somewhat different meaning from that attributed to the accumulation of coins after the Warring States period, when burial had ceased to signify the same kind of alienation. In any case, we can say that coins had definitely become a means of accumulating wealth. The fact that coins—which, unlike rice and silk, have no use value—became a symbol of wealth demonstrates that there was a major transformation in the image of wealth. This constituted a momentous shift in the way society understood coins.

In Yoshida Kenkō's *Essays in Idleness*, there is mention of "an exceedingly rich man" who said of coins: "Money should be feared and dreaded like a master or god, not used as one pleases."[6] That is, one should seek to suppress one's desires and single-mindedly save one's coins. For this rich man, the accumulation of coins was itself a virtue. In fact, wealthy people in that period were called "virtuous people" (*yūtokujin*). This gives us a good indication of the way in which society's understanding of coins was changing. Nakamura Naokatsu has called this late-thirteenth-century approach to coins "money worship."[7] By the fifteenth century, coins had become more than just a measure of wealth. They had begun to function as a means of payment and exchange.

There are a number of things that we can say about the fact that coins made the transition to functioning as currency in this manner. In chapter six, I wrote that the dissemination of writing propelled the homogenization of society. Here I believe we can say that the circulation of these round coins with square holes throughout the archipelago (except in Hokkaido and Okinawa) also contributed to the trend toward homogenization. This transformation was an epochal event in the formation of a national consciousness (*minzoku*) in the Japanese archipelago.

Nevertheless, I must admit that there are many things about premodern copper coins that we do not understand. The biggest question relates to the fact that these coins were all from the Chinese mainland—Song, Yuan, and Ming dynasty coins. Yet, there was a great amount of copper being mined and processed in the Japanese islands at that time. So much copper was produced that it was counted among the archipelago's top export items. Casting technology had long been available, and casters were active in Japanese society. So, there is no doubt that the ability to mint coins existed in the islands. Nevertheless, the ruling class in Japan showed no desire to mint coins after the late Heian period. Apart from the administration of Emperor Go-Daigo—a rare exception among emperors in that he planned, but was unable to bring about, the minting of coins and the printing of paper currency—neither the imperial government nor the shogunates (Kamakura and Muromachi) seem to have conceived of the possibility.[8] Why was that? This should be a major

---

6. Yoshida Kenkō, *Essays in Idleness: The Tsurezuregusa of Kenkō*, trans. Donald Keene (New York: Columbia University Press, 1967), 179. The essays were originally written between 1330 and 1332.
7. Nakamura Naokatsu, *Muromachi jidai no shomin seikatsu* (The Life of Commoners in the Muromachi Period) (Tokyo: Iwanami shoten, 1935).
8. This statement only applies to the Kamakura and Muromachi shogunates. The Tokugawa shogunate did mint coins and in fact made recurrent debasements of its coinage a central feature of its financial policy.

topic of investigation in the history of the relations between China and Japan. What might this have to do with the fact that Japanese society already had a government that produced currency (the *wadō kaichin*)? Historians have not yet answered these questions.

Matsunobu calls the society of the fourteenth century "a society that had converted to currency too early."[9] Whether or not that was true, the practical circulation of coins as currency had a decisive and transformative effect on the meanings of trade and finance as well as on the social status of those members of society who were involved in such activities.

HOW DID THINGS BECOME COMMODITIES?

The act of exchanging one thing for another—treating each thing as a commodity—took time to develop the form we know today. In earlier societies, the exchange of goods was conducted within a so-called gift economy. In this kind of economy, relations between people were cemented through the acts of giving a gift and receiving something in return. This was not an exchange of commodities. How, then, did things become commodities?

Katsumata Shizuo suggests that the exchange of one thing for another requires a particular kind of place in which to facilitate the exchange. This is the marketplace. It is only when the particular space of a marketplace comes into existence that things can be separated from a gift economy and circulate in trade. In this sense, a marketplace is a site that must be cut off from the everyday relations that bind people together. If I were to put it my own way, I would say it is a site of disengagement (*muen no ba*).[10] Katsumata proposes that these sites have existed since ancient times. For example, there was an ancient custom that a market can be set up wherever a rainbow appears. This custom appears in the writings of Heian period aristocrats, and there were still traces of it as late as the Muromachi period. In one case, a rainbow appeared in the compound of Fujiwara no Michinaga, the grandfather of three Heian emperors.[11] So, following custom, Michinaga set up a market in his

9. Matsunobu, "Zeni to kahei no gainen," 208.
10. "Muen no ba" is a phrase that comes from Amino's groundbreaking book, *Muen, kugai, raku: Nihon chūsei no jiyū to heiwa* (Disconnectedness, Space, and Markets: Freedom and Peace in Medieval Japan) (Tokyo: Heibonsha, 1978). The fundamental issue of that book was the function of sites outside the control of the state where goods and people circulated in an alternative economy.
11. Fujiwara no Michinaga (966–1027) led the Fujiwara clan at its zenith of power and was the ultimate master of marriage politics, succeeding in establishing five daughters as imperial concubines; he was grandfather to three successive emperors.

compound and allowed merchants to enter and ply their trade. Of course, one never knows exactly where a rainbow touches ground, but this did not prevent the custom from being followed.

According to Katsumata, Japan is not the only place that had a custom of holding a market where a rainbow appeared. He conjectures that this custom arose in the Japanese islands because rainbows were seen as a bridge between the next world and this one—between the sacred and the profane.[12] Conducting trade at this kind of site was believed to please the deities, who resided in the other world. Katsumata's point, then, is that markets in general were established at the border between the world of the deities and the world of human beings, at the boundary of the sacred and the profane.

I agree with Katsumata completely. In fact, markets in Japanese society were usually established in places that marked boundaries (such as riverbanks or the islands in the middle of a river), on the beach (the boundary between the ocean and the land), or in foothills between mountains and plains. A functioning market was seen as a place separate from the everyday world, in large part by virtue of the significance of its physical location. It was seen, in other words, as a place linked to the sacred world, the world of the deities. Upon entering such a place, both people and things were severed from their mundane relations. It was only in an "unencumbered" condition that objects could be exchanged as simply "things in themselves." To put it another way, both people and things became possessions of the deities once they entered the space of the marketplace. Or we could say that in a marketplace objects became ownerless. At the very least, they were no longer seen as emblematic of the person who possessed them. That seems to me to have been the condition that enabled the exchange of objects for other objects.

Since markets in Japan were places where the worldly relations between people were severed, they also became a place for activities such as the bacchanalian revelries known as *utagaki*.[13] During festivals, the everyday relationship of marriage was severed and men and women could freely come into contact with one another, at the festival site, as unattached individuals. What is less well known is that the same principle held true in the marketplace. Thus,

12. There is a more detailed discussion of this notion in chapter eight (as well as in the Foreword), but readers should know that a basic tenet of the ancient Japanese worldview is that there are two planes of existence: the present everyday world and an invisible "other world" that exists close to this one—even potentially overlapping it—but is nevertheless distinct. The borders and liminal spaces Amino writes of in this chapter were understood to be borders between the world of humans and the other world of spirits or deities.
13. Amino returns to *utagaki* in the context of his discussion of medieval sexual practices in chapter nine.

the exchange of objects as commodities became possible only under conditions in which both people *and* things were cut off from their relations in the everyday world (fig. 28).

This severance of objects from human ownership as a precondition for exchange is, I believe, a key to understanding the significance of the buried coins discussed above. Since the area beneath the ground was seen as the "other world," burying things in the ground would mean removing them from the hands of humans and consigning them to the world of the deities. It appears that by burying things in the ground, and thereby making an offering to the deities, people may have been seeking divine permission to use the land or the coins. Or perhaps making something ownerless transformed it into an offering, a sacred possession, and thereby made it possible to reuse it as a form of financial capital.

Important questions are raised if we say that the principle of the market and the modern exchange of commodities were based on the state of disengagement from mundane relations that appeared in the market place. What could account for the change from this market conception, which lasted until the medieval era, to the one with which we are more familiar today? We will come to that.

Figure 28. A market scene from *The Picture Scroll of the Holy Man Ippen.* Source: *Ippen hijirie,* from the collection of Shōjōkōji.

HOW INTEREST WAS TAKEN

The practice of finance raises the same issues. Just how did it come about that things were loaned and interest was charged on that loan? There is nothing natural about it. I do not know how things would look if we approached this on a world historical scale. But if we trace the origins of finance in the case of Japanese society, we eventually arrive at the concept of *suiko*. *Suiko* was a practice intimately tied to rice agriculture. In ancient society, the first rice of the season (known as *hatsuho*) was offered to the gods and kept in a sacred storehouse, which was probably managed by the leader of the community. The next year the rice that had been offered to the gods and placed in the storehouse was loaned to farmers as sacred seed. At harvest time, the farmers would return the amount of rice they had been loaned for seed and add to that "interest rice"(*ritō*) as thanks to the deities. This cycle constituted the basic principle of *suiko*.

Just how this fit into the system adopted from China by the Ritsuryō state is a point of some debate. But, however they meshed, the Ritsuryō state cemented this practice within its governmental system in a practice known as public *suiko* (*kusuiko*). Tax rice stored in provincial government storehouses was originally used as principal. Lent to farmers in the spring, the loan was to be repaid in the fall with interest rice. This interest, called the proper tax (*shōzei*), was used to pay regional administrative expenses.

However, the custom of *suiko* was not restricted to the government. It was also practiced in society at large, where it was called private *suiko* (*shisuiko*). Whether public or private, it is important to remember that this lending relationship was expressed as *suiko*. Interest rice was usually collected at a rate of 50 percent. Both state and private *suiko* strictly abided by the restriction that interest could not be more than double the principal. Interest rates of 50 and 100 percent may appear to be extraordinarily high, but if the interest is collected on agricultural production in kind it is not that high.

Financial activities were conducted as the lending of something owned by the deities, and, through the process of agricultural production, that loan was returned with an extra amount as an expression of gratitude. The initial offering of the first harvest to the deities was still occasionally called *hatsuho* in the medieval period, but more often it was called an offering (*jōbun*). For example, the first products of the harvest offered to Hie Shrine were called goods offered to Hie (*Hie jōbun butsu*), rice offered to Hie (*Hie jōbun mai*), or copper coins offered to Hie (*Hie jōbun seni*). The offerings to Kumano

Shrine were called either Kumano's first grains (*Kumano go-hatsuho butsu*) or goods offered to Kumano (*Kumano jōbun butsu*).

These rice and coin offerings—which, as offerings, had become the possessions of the deities—were then used as capital for loans. We can confirm that loans were widely executed in this form in the twelfth century and that in such cases the act of making a loan was still called *suiko*. This lending of sacred possessions continued after the Muromachi period as well under the name of temple coins (*shidōsen*). By this time, the loans, offered at low rates of interest, were generally made with the coins that had been offered to the Buddhas at temples.

Whatever they were called, whenever human beings made use of something that had been offered to the deities, the return of those sacred possessions was accompanied by interest as a gesture of gratitude to the deities whose objects had been used. Financial activities therefore were carried out in a close relationship with the realm of the sacred. Earlier I mentioned that coins that were buried in the ground became ownerless. We might also see burial as a way of giving the coins to the deities, in which case whoever buried the coins may have meant to consign them to the deities for a time so that they could later be used as financial capital.

Thus, whether we are discussing trade or finance, both were only possible through the construction of a relationship with the sacred world, a world that transcended the mundane. Merchants and financiers were thus set apart from ordinary people, for they were continually in the presence of that sacred world. That is why merchants and financiers in the medieval period took on the physical appearance of people in the service of the deities and Buddhas (i.e., religious workers). In the terminology of the time, people who served the native deities were called *jinin* (or *jinnin*), and people who served the Buddhas were called *yoriudo*. The emperor, who was likened at the time to a deity, was served by people called *kugonin*.[14] The *kugo* of *kugonin* originally meant "food eaten by the emperor and the nobility," but it eventually expanded to include anything used by the emperor. Those people who provided the emperor with the things he needed every day were called *kugonin* or "imperial purveyors." All of these purveyors—to shrines, temples, and the emperor—were considered servants of sacred beings. They even called themselves "slaves of the gods" (*shinbutsu no nuhi*).

14. Following Andrew Goble's usage, I (the translator) would call these people shrine, temple, and imperial purveyors. The reason for choosing the term *purveyor*, despite the more literal translations of "shrine people," "people who approach," and "people who make offerings," will become clear in Amino's discussion of their functions in chapter eight. See Andrew Edmund Goble, *Kemmu: Go-Daigo's Revolution* (Cambridge: Harvard University Press, 1996).

In concrete terms, then, the people who conducted financial activities through lending offerings, from Hie Shrine, for example, were known as the Hie Shrine purveyors. Lower level monks and mountain ascetics put the offerings made to the temple of Enryakuji into circulation as loans, and the Kumano Shrine purveyors and mountain ascetics ran lending enterprises with Kumano's offered goods. At Ise Shrine, it was a group called the *oshi* that used Ise's offerings. It is important to note, then, that financial operations were conducted by people who were recognized as serving the deities in their various forms.

PEOPLE WHO SERVED THE GODS AND THE EMPEROR

The same was true for those engaged in trade. For example, the casters who made the metal lamps used in the imperial palaces were granted in return the right to travel freely throughout the country buying and selling iron and iron goods. Given the weighty title of "lamp purveyors of the emperor's private office" (*kurōdo-dokoro tōro kugonin*), metal casters thus engaged in public trade through their status as imperial purveyors.

Manufacturing and trade were not yet specialized fields at the time, so craftsmen, such as the lamp casters, were also merchants. The cypress craftsmen (*hinonoshi*) who made round wooden boxes (*magemono*) both made the boxes and sold them at market. They were also given imperial purveyor status or else were attached to shrines throughout the islands as shrine purveyors. In short, all merchants from the ancient and medieval eras made their livings as servants to one of the divine entities; performers, in the narrow sense of those who engaged in the performing arts, were in the same situation. Merchant manufacturers, financiers, and performers possessed the status of servants to the deities and emperor because the activities of trade and finance, as well as the performing arts, were seen as having a deep connection to the divine world.

To return to an earlier topic, their status also derived from the character of the spaces in which they made their livings. In those days, purveyors of all kinds moved about from market to market within a particular area or even across the whole archipelago. They naturally had a base somewhere, but many were on the road for long periods of time. In the end, the places through which they passed—the roads, harbors, and anchorages—and their destinations—the markets on riverbanks, beaches, and foothills—were all liminal places. The liminality of these spaces can be seen in customs other than those related to market activity. For example, it was the custom in those days that any incident that occurred within a marketplace had to be resolved within that space. Grievances could not be carried to outside authorities for redress. The same turns out to have been true for roads. Even in the case of murder, the parties involved had to resolve the situation at the site itself, and relatives of the victim could not launch a vendetta against the murderer once everyone had left the scene of the crime. Traveling in such places, itinerant purveyors adopted attire that distinguished them from ordinary people. Mountain ascetics, as Buddhist monks, were naturally very easily distinguishable. But shrine purveyors also wore yellow robes to signify that they traveled as servants of the deities.

As mentioned above, shrine, temple, and imperial purveyors occasionally called themselves slaves of the deities, slaves of the bodhisattvas, or temple slaves. As a result, historians have treated them as people of extremely low status, as being, in fact, slaves. But closer investigation reveals that during the medieval era these so-called slaves were occasionally of the same high class as vassals of the shogun. From the perspective of their own society, therefore, these people were in a position comparable to that of the warrior class.

These groups have not yet been precisely situated within a world historical framework. Doing so will help us understand them better, for Japan was not the only society that had servants of the deities or slaves of the sacred. They could also be found in societies with divine kingship. For example, the Incan empire had slaves of the deities—slaves of the sun god and slaves in the service of the Incan emperor.[15] In Japan's case, there were women known as court servants (*uneme*) as far back as archaic times. Shamans (*miko*) in Japan were of a similar status. We also know that a similar group of workers at Kashima Shrine were known as divine menials (*shinsen*). The problem for us today is the use of the character *sen* (賤) in reference to these people. Our modern sense of the character is that it means "base" or "despised." But it would be a mistake for us to employ our modern sensibility and conclude that ancient menials were socially despised.

The class system of the Ritsuryō state designated five kinds of menials, known literally as the five colors of baseness (*goshiki no sen*). Four of these groups—public slaves (*kunuhi*), government slaves (*kanko*), private slaves (*shinuhi*), and domestics (*kenin*)—may justifiably be called slaves, either state or privately owned. But the fifth class of menials were the tomb guards

---

15. In the Incan world, female slaves were called *akurya* and male slaves, *yanakona*.

(*ryōko*), who stood guard over the imperial tombs. These people were classified as menials, but they could not be called slaves in the same sense. Later,
in the medieval era, we find that tomb guards had the same status as shrine
purveyors and were considered "slaves of the gods." Notably, it was *because* of
this status that they were granted special rights and engaged in commerce. We
must thus think of menials who were in direct attendance on the deities, like
those whose function it was to guard such sacred spaces as the graves of the
aristocracy, as having possessed a character that was radically different from
the way a modern sensibility understands the term baseness. Even though
they may have been called slaves of the gods, they were in fact people with a
status comparable to that of warriors. Some even received court rank.

As a consequence, the status of purveyor groups was explicitly distinguished in a variety of ways from that of the common people, who were
known as *hyakushō*. The homes of shrine workers (i.e., the houses that
formed their base of operations) were exempted from the duties levied on
the homes of commoners. There were even cases in which purveyors were
granted tax-exempt paddy land from which they could draw income. In addition, their privilege of free travel granted them exemption from the transportation taxes collected at barrier gates, river crossings, ports, and harbors,
thus making it possible for them to move freely about the country. That is
one more reason why these people wore the yellow or persimmon robes
characteristic of monks when they traveled: to distinguish themselves from
ordinary people.

They also distinguished themselves by the unusual things they carried:
remarkable staffs, sticks, and so forth. Shrine purveyors who sold fish carried
sacred buckets on their heads into which offerings to the gods were usually
placed. It was believed that if an ordinary person laid a hand on a purveyor—
on his possessions, or on his person so as to cause injury or death—the
offender would be subject to a terrifying divine retribution. In addition, sites
where the corpse of a shrine or imperial purveyor was found were considered
sacred places, now possessed by the deities. Therefore, whenever the villagers of a *shōen* estate that was owned by a temple or shrine failed to submit
their yearly tribute, the purveyors (not warriors) would be mobilized to act as
bailiffs and collect the tribute from the villagers. We even find cases in which
the purveyors put on demons' masks or carried statues of the buddhas with
them to intimidate the villagers into turning over the tribute.

Whatever the activity, the shrine and imperial purveyors lived a separate existence from that of the commoners, their status provided for in the

state system itself. I believe we should call this the purveyor system, although this term has not yet achieved currency in the academic world.

FROM THE SACRED TO THE PROFANE

In sum, until the early part of the medieval era—the twelfth and thirteenth centuries—commerce and finance were conducted by these purveyor groups because commercial activities could only be carried out in a relationship with the deities. Their involvement was based on the magical character of commerce. The contemporary problem of the group known as "discriminated people" (*hisabetsumin*, or *burakumin*) is related to this condition because there was another group in ancient Japan that had shrine purveyor status. These people were known as "nonhumans" (*hinin*) or "dog shrine purveyors" (*inujinin*). Female entertainers such as courtesans (*yūjo*) and dancers (*shirabyōshi*) also had a social status comparable to that of the divine servant groups up until at least the early part of the medieval era, but I will discuss these groups further in the next chapter.

The special character of commercial activities and of those who participated in them underwent a major transformation in the latter half of the thirteenth century as the increased circulation of copper coins created new conditions for commerce. In contrast to the earlier financial practice of *suiko*—in which the possessions of the deities were loaned out—loans of coins simply for the sake of earning more coins in interest became more common in the late thirteenth century. One could call this a more worldly use of coins, signifying the fact that financial activities were becoming more secular.

Of course, not all financial activities were immediately secularized. It is well known that the most important financiers of the Muromachi period were the *dosō* moneylenders.[16] Originally, many of these moneylending institutions were managed by monks from Enryakuji temple or purveyors from Hie Shrine. These institutions began to appear in the Kamakura period, and the principal they originally used for their loans were offerings to the deities. In particular, the *dosō* moneylenders were characterized at first as divine

16. *Dosō* literally means "earthen storehouse" and referred to the thick-walled, white-plastered storehouses in which these institutions kept their caches of coins and objects handed over as security for loans. Since many loans were made on the basis of movable collateral, these institutions are sometimes called pawnshops. But their activities were more varied than a modern pawnshop, and the scale of their loans may have been much greater, making them more like banks. In general, they will be referred to in this book as moneylending institutions.

storehouses, which were even considered to be a kind of disengaged space. For example, in time of war anything placed within a *dosō* storehouse was considered safe. *Dosō* storehouses never entirely lost this character, but in the Muromachi period the managers of these storehouses began increasingly to make private loans of coins. The debt cancellation edicts (*tokuseirei*) of the Muromachi period were aimed at bringing an end to this form of private lending.[17] The period also saw the continuation of previous kinds of financial activities, such as the lending of the deities' rice and the Buddhas' copper coins (*shidōsen*), but the debt cancellation edicts of the Muromachi period did not apply to these kinds of loans.

In this way, financial practices gradually took on more of the secular character that a modern sensibility can understand. Nevertheless, the reaction against interest money (*rizeni*) loans also grew stronger, often culminating in debt cancellation uprisings (*tokusei ikki*) in which people would demand the cancellation of cash loans and the return of pawned goods. In that sense, the fifteenth and sixteenth centuries were an epochal period in which the prior relationship between finance and the sacred realm gradually changed and finance settled into a secular practice. Merchants and tradesmen were also affected by this secularization. One sign of this was the fact that a distinction between merchants and artisans slowly emerged at this time. In a related development, shrine and imperial purveyors retained their status but the meaning of that status was undermined as the act of commercial exchange gradually became seen as secular.

We can explore this transformation by considering an example involving artisans. From the latter half of the thirteenth century, a genre of picture scrolls developed that was known as tradesmen poetry contests (*shokunin utaawase*).[18] These scrolls depicted several kinds of skilled workers arranged in pairs. In the

17. The Japanese term *tokuseirei* literally means "decrees of virtuous government" and were essentially general cancellations of most debts. These decrees are found periodically in the late Kamakura period, although most took place in the Muromachi.
18. The third volume of *The Cambridge History of Japan* defines *shokunin* as "a general term for those engaged in nonagricultural occupation, that is, artisans. Entertainers were sometimes included in this category." While most scholars follow the convention of translating *shokunin* as "artisan" (for lack of a smoother alternative), I am uncomfortable with the way that tends to restrict our notion of this group to those who work in handicrafts. Since one of the major thrusts of Amino's reinterpretation of Japanese history is to argue that our modern understanding of premodern terminology is trapped in modern-day conceptions, I am tempted to break with convention and use a broader, albeit more clumsy, translation. Thus, I am going with "tradesmen" and "skilled workers" to distinguish *shokunin* from the more restricted group *kōgyōnin*, which I am translating as "craftsmen." With tradesmen and skilled workers, I hope to suggest the concept of a person who possesses a polished skill but one that need not be restricted to material production. This also has the merit of avoiding the white-collar connotations of today's use of "professional."

standard format, each member of a pair creates a poem, and then the poems from each pair are evaluated by a judge. In effect, these scrolls feature a variety of tradespeople whose crafts are represented in song and picture. This genre became quite popular and was widely disseminated in the Edo period under the rubic of "an illustrated catalog of tradesmen" (*shokunin tsukushi*).

When these scrolls first appeared in the late thirteenth century, they were produced in a way that revealed a relation to the deities. One example of the early form of this genre is the *Tōhoku-in Poetry Contest*. This scroll depicts a poetry contest held among a gathering of tradesmen and women for a memorial service (*hōe*) at Tōhoku-in Temple. Another early example is a scroll called the *Tsurugaoka Bird Release Poetry Contest* (*Tsurugaoka hōseikai utaawase*), which depicts tradesmen reciting poetry while gathered at Tsurugaoka Hachman Shrine for a bird-releasing ceremony. Both of these scrolls therefore take the form of a poetry contest among skilled workers held in conjunction with a sacred event at a sacred site.

In these poetry contest scrolls, the tradesmen and women are placed in pairs, seated left and right, and there appears to be a logic to the way certain occupations are paired. For example, one often finds blacksmiths paired with carpenters. When we look into why these two were paired, we find that blacksmiths in those days were more closely associated with making nails and clamps than with making swords. Since blacksmiths were associated with construction they were often attached to temples and shrines and given the status of shrine or temple purveyors. Since the blacksmith was a construction worker, he was paired in the picture scrolls with the most important worker on a construction site, the carpenter.

Thus, each pairing of trades in the scrolls was based upon a logical relationship between the two. What is particularly interesting is that in the *Tōhoku-in Poetry Contest* scroll we find a shaman paired with a gambler. The fact that a gambler is included in a picture scroll of tradesmen at all reveals the different mind-set of society before the thirteenth century. Most likely the pairing here has to do with the way in which each one communicates the will of the deities: the gambler through the roll of the dice and the shaman through spirit possession. It is in this sense that these two are paired as skilled workers. But how are we to understand their place in this gathering of people who might otherwise simply be labeled artisans? On the one hand, gambling was something that was subject to social condemnation. On the other, it was placed in the same domain of activities as the drawing of lots, which was common in so much communal activity. In either case, gambling was considered to be a form of artistic practice that had its own "Way" (*dō*). We know from documents of the time that there was something known as a "Way of gambling." We know, too, that at the end of the Heian period there were positions in the headquarters of the provincial government of Kaga for "the director of the dice" and "the director of the shamans." We can also confirm that there was an office that oversaw dice players, gamblers, and shamans in the imperial government in Kyoto. In fact, the famous picture scroll, *The Picture Book of Hungry Ghosts* (*Gaki sōshi*), depicts a scene in which shamans were present when the wife of a retired emperor gave birth (fig. 29). The shamans—whose job was to become possessed by any evil spirits that might otherwise possess the mother—were seated behind a Buddhist ascetic who had been brought in to pray for a safe birth. A *sugoroku* board (a kind of backgammon board) was placed next to the shamans. The shamans then "gambled" by playing the game and rolling the dice. This was also practiced by commoners, but such gamblers and shamans had a particularly close relationship to the imperial palace. Gamblers and shamans can thus be seen as types of skilled workers, forming a natural pair in the tradesmens' poetry contest scrolls. We can also see that the other "tradesmen"—handcraftsmen, merchants, and performers—were understood via their relationships with the deities in scrolls produced in the thirteenth century.

Figure 29. Shamaness and a board game from *The Picture Book of Hungry Ghosts*. Source: *Gaki sōshi*, from the collection of the Tokyo National Museum.

However, scrolls produced in the fifteenth century, such as *The Songs of Thirty-two Pairs* and *The Songs of Seventy-one Tradesmen*, still portray a great number of tradesmen—handcraftsmen, merchants, and performers—but the opportunity for their gathering no longer has anything to do with the deities. In particular, in *The Songs of Thirty-two Pairs* the tradesmen call themselves "base" (*iyashiki mono*) and the contest is presented as a gathering of those whose occupations have become socially stigmatized. This is inextricably bound up with the issue of discrimination, which is discussed in greater detail in the next chapter, and this scroll indicates to us that a portion of the professional class had become denigrated by the fifteenth century.

In *The Songs of Seventy-one Tradesmen*, the now stigmatized commercial and performing tradesmen are clearly divided according to their *appearance* rather than their function. For example, they are divided according to whether or not they wrap their faces in cloth or wear an *eboshi* cap (see fig. 30). Female professionals are also distinguished according to the styles of headgear, coiffure, and makeup that marked their occupations. In this manner of dividing the tradesmen, these fifteenth-century scrolls are quite different from their thirteenth-century predecessors. The fifteenth-century poetry contest picture scrolls clearly attempt to realistically depict the tradesmen's work itself. For handcraftsmen, the scrolls show their tools and working styles, while for merchants the scrolls show their wares and their selling styles. On that point alone, we can see that commerce, handicraft production, and performances were being separated from their sacred functions and becoming more secular.

All of this points to the fact that during the disturbances of the Northern and Southern Courts period Japanese society underwent a major change in the structure of authority. Along with that social transformation, those tradesmen who had based their distinction from ordinary people on their direct relationship with the gods (thereby becoming sanctified themselves) were no longer able to maintain their special privileges. That is why in the fifteenth century these merchants and craftsmen frequently appealed to such temporal powers as military governors (*shugo daimyō*) to maintain their privileges. Thus, the fourteenth century constitutes an epochal period in the transformation of the conditions of commerce, trading, and finance as well as of the existence of the people who were involved in those activities. And there is no doubt that the increased flow of metal currency, discussed in chapter three, had a deep connection to this transformation.

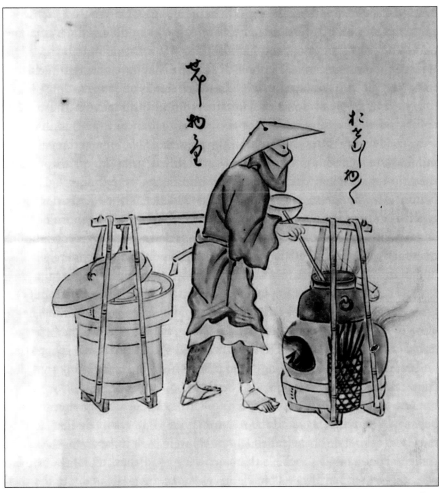

Figure 30. A man with a mask from *The Songs of Seventy-one Tradesmen*. Source: *Shichijū-ichiban utaawase*, from the collection of the Tokyo National Museum.

THE ROLE OF NEW BUDDHIST SECTS IN KAMAKURA

Our attempt to understand this transition raises an important problem at this point. That is, it is precisely during this period of change that the Buddhist sects known as the Kamakura New Buddhist sects came to play a major role in society. For example, during the Kamakura period the Saidaiji branch of the Ritsu sect achieved great popularity due to two of its

with contributions known as kindnesses (*shi*) and through the commercial activities of their surrounding "temple towns."

Why it was that so many of the new Kamakura Buddhist sects operated in this way remains a major question in need of further investigation. As the character of commerce, trade, and finance—which had been supported by the old, magical authority of the deities—changed during the major social transformation of the fourteenth century, the new Kamakura Buddhist sects appear to have begun to confer a new kind of sacred meaning on commerce and finance. It appears that the new sects attempted to fulfill the same function in Japan as the European historian, Abe Kin'ya, has suggested Christianity fulfilled in Europe.[23] That is, in a society based upon a gift and reward economy, finance and the exchange of commodities came to take place at a site or according to a method that was related to the founder of a monotheistic religious sect rather than an earlier, more generalized notion of divinity.[24]

In fact, an examination of the overall conditions of faith among tradesmen and merchants reveals that their connection to the new Kamakura Buddhist sects remained extremely strong from the Edo period on. I believe the time has come for a reconsideration and reexamination of the state of religion in Japanese society from this perspective. Even if we do not go in the direction of Max Weber's *Protestantism and the Spirit of Capitalism*, we can find in the relationship between the new Kamakura Buddhist sects and commerce, finance, and handicraft production issues that Japanese society shares with Weber's work.

But in Japanese society the new religious groups—including Christianity, which was introduced in the sixteenth century—were bloodily suppressed in the sixteenth and seventeenth centuries by Oda Nobunaga, Toyotomi Hideyoshi, and the Edo shogunate. As a result, these groups were unable to establish an independent power base. Why did things turn out this way? This may in fact be the most important issue in the overall history of Japanese society.

---

23. Abe Kin'ya, *Chūsei o tabisuru hitobito: Yōroppa shomin seikatsu tenbyō* (People Who Traveled in the Middle Ages: A Portrait of the Lives of Commoners in Europe) (Tokyo: Heibonsha, 1978).

24. The difference may appear subtle at first, but Amino frequently contends that the new Kamakura Buddhist sects represented the possibility of the generation of a monotheistic style of religious belief in Japan because of their emphasis on exclusive worship of Amida Buddha or the *Lotus Sutra*.

After the disturbances of the fourteenth century,[25] the emperor completely lost his power, and even his authority was greatly diminished. The answer as to why the emperor survived despite all this may be related to the question of why a monotheistic religion never took root in Japan. In the end, the fact that this kind of religion was suppressed and was unable to sustain itself as an independent religious authority is also closely related to the technological condition of merchants, financiers, and artisans in the subsequent course of Japanese history.

In the class system of the Edo period—which was anchored by the four main classes of warrior, peasant, artisan, and merchant—handicraft producers, merchants, and financiers were not ascribed high social status. Even though the merchants had a great deal of power, they had the lowest status. Moneychangers were also subject to social stigmatization. It may be worth considering the idea that the decline in social status of commercial activities and the people who participated in them was inseparably related to the suppression of monotheistic religions. But we must also consider the relationship this has with the style of capitalism found in Japan in the modern period. That is beyond my abilities, but if we are to fully and clearly understand the particularities of Japanese society, we will have to make the effort.

25. Amino is referring to the Kenmu Restoration of Emperor Go-Daigo, which overthrew the Kamakura bakufu in 1336, subsequently split the imperial line into the Northern and Southern Courts at the hands of Ashikaga Takauji, and established the Muromachi shogunate.

CHAPTER EIGHT

Fear and Loathing

DISCRIMINATION IN THE ANCIENT PAST

Research on the discriminated groups (*burakumin*) in Japan, particularly on medieval nonhuman (*hinin*) and riverside dwellers (*karwaramono*), has made great strides in recent years. This research has not only uncovered a number of new documents, but, as in Niunoya Tetsuichi's *Kebiishi* (*The Imperial Police*), it has also concretely shown how the state and religious organizations (temples and shrines) controlled nonhumans and riverside dwellers.[1] It has also become clear how the *miyagomori* of the Gion Shrine in Kyoto and the *sarugaku* dancers should be included in the broader category of discriminated people in medieval Japan.[2] In addition, Kuroda Hideo, Kawada Mitsuo, and Hotate Michihisa have used pictorial evidence to reveal the

1. Niunoya Tetsuichi, *Kebiishi: Chūsei no kegare to kenryoku* (Imperial Police: Pollution and Power in Medieval Japan) (Tokyo: Heibonsha, 1986).
2. Sarugaku is defined in the *Cambridge History of Japan*, vol. 3, *Medieval Japan*, as a type of early medieval theater involving music, dance, and other kinds of entertainment. It was a precursor to Noh theater, which developed in the fourteenth century. It is not entirely clear who the *miyagomori* were, but, as Amino notes later in this chapter, they seem to have been a lower caste of shamans who performed *sarugaku* and completed other tasks for shrines. From pp. 110–11 of the original: "According to Niunoya Tetsuichi, the lower caste shamans, known as *miyagomori* (residing within the shrine), who performed *sarugaku* dances and picked tea, should probably be included in the broad meaning of nonhumans. The *miyagomori* in particular later ran cheap tea houses. After the Northern and Southern Courts period, they fulfilled many of these same functions as teamsters and *inujinin*."

concrete conditions under which nonhumans lived.[3] There has also been excellent research on the major cause of discrimination, the concept of pollution (*kegare*), by Miyata Noboru in the field of ethnology and Yokoi Kiyoshi and Yamamoto Kōji in history.[4] Furthermore, there have been several recent studies on the efforts by the Ritsu, Zen, and Ji sects to bring salvation to the nonhumans and on the relationships of specific religious figures with a variety of nonhuman groups.

Researchers are divided regarding the social position of nonhumans in ancient and medieval times. The dominant interpretation of nonhuman status is that of Kuroda Toshio, who argues that they occupied a "status outside the status system."[5] Kuroda believes that nonhumans originally had an existence that was completely alienated from society. Oyama Kyōhei, on the other hand, argues that they were essentially of the same status as villagers (*hyakushō*).[6] I believe that nonhumans were different from both common villagers and bonded servants and that they possessed the same status as the shrine and temple purveyors discussed in chapter seven. They also shared certain characteristics with skilled tradesmen. I should warn the reader, however, that my interpretation has not yet achieved full acceptance in the academic world.

In our approach to the question of discriminated groups in Japanese history, let us first consider a form that is different from class discrimination: discrimination against the physically handicapped and those afflicted with terrible diseases. If we go all the way back to primitive society, we find no evidence of such discrimination in the Jōmon period (10,000–300 B.C.). The average life expectancy at birth during the Jōman period is believed to have been seventeen years—suggesting extremely harsh living conditions. Human remains containing evidence of such conditions as harelip, leg damage, and so on demonstrate the existence of physically handicapped people during the period. According to some archaeologists, the Jōmon era was a time when

---

3. Kuroda Hideo, *Sugata to shigusa no chūseishi: Ezu to emaki no fūkei kara* (Form and Gesture in Medieval History: From the Landscapes of Pictures and Picture Scrolls) (Tokyo: Heibonsha, 1986); Kawada Mitsuo, *Shinran to hisabetsu minshū* (Shinran and the Outcaste Peoples) (Tokyo: Akashi shoten, 1994); Hotate Michihisa, *Chūsei no ai to juzoku: Emaki no naka no nikutai* (Love and Dependency in Medieval Japan: Bodies in Picture Scrolls) (Tokyo: Heibonsha, 1986).
4. Miyata Noboru, *Kegare no minzokushi: Sabetsu no bunkateki yōin* (An Ethnographic History of Pollution: Cultural Factors in Discrimination) (Tokyo: Jinbun shoin, 1996); Yokoi Kiyoshi, *Mato to ena: Chūseijin no sei to shi* (Target and Placenta: Medieval Life and Death) (Tokyo: Heibonsha, 1988); Yamamoto Kōji, *Kegare to oharae* (Pollution and Purification) (Tokyo: Heibonsha, 1992).
5. Kuroda Toshio, *Jisha seiryoku: Mō hitotsu no chūsei shakai* (The Power of Temples and Shrines: An Alternate Medieval Society) (Tokyo: Iwanami shoten, 1980).
6. Oyama Kyōhei, *Nihon chūsei nōsonshi no kenkyū* (Studies in Medieval Japanese Agriculture) (Tokyo: Iwanami shoten, 1978).

simple survival was extremely difficult. The evidence of physical handicaps in remains from the time suggests that human life itself was so highly valued that discrimination against those with physical difficulties may not have existed.

There is evidence, however, that in Japanese society from the Yayoi period on certain classes of crime called crimes against heaven (*amatsutsumi*) and crimes against the realm (*kunitsutsumi*)—such as mother and son incest, bestiality, and activities that obstructed agricultural production—were also considered forms of pollution (*kegare*). But by the late seventh century, it appears that, *in principle,* there was no thought of excluding the handicapped from the community, as later happened to those who suffered from Hansen's disease (leprosy).[7] In fact, when the Ritsuryō state was founded, the imperial government earnestly attempted to implement the idea that everyone in the land should be listed in a household registry. Rather than providing separate entries, the early household registries recorded the existence of those stricken with severe diseases or injuries (who were designated as disabled [*haishitsu*]), and those with the most severe debilities (who were designated as invalids [*tokushitsu*]), along with the entries for other members of the family. These people were not subject to taxation, and a caretaker was to be assigned to them.

In its zealous attempt to place every person in the realm into a family registry, the early Ritsuryō state also doggedly pursued itinerants who had fled their homes. So, from the standpoint of the government system there was no tolerance for the existence of those who had fled their communities. For that reason, exclusionary discrimination was neither possible, at least as far as the system was concerned, nor demonstrable, as far as we can tell from surviving records.

However, as I mentioned in chapter seven, the Ritsuryō state established *within its system* the statuses of the "five colors of baseness." A distinction was made between the base groups and the commoners and officials (known as "the good people" [*ryōmin*]). Slaves in the service of the bureaucracy or the state were called official menials (*kanko*) and public slaves (*kunuhi*). Privately held slaves were called domestics (*kenin*) and private slaves (*shinuhi*). Of these four groups, official menials and domestics were allowed to form families (which would then receive a separate listing in the registries). In any case, these four groups of debased people were slaves, having lost their freedom

7. Amino admits that it is not clear how the diseased and handicapped were treated in actual practice. His point here is that not only was there no clear principle for excluding these people but there were clear examples of exclusion.

due to criminal acts or unresolved debts. Even though they were not laboring slaves in the sense of those in ancient Greece or Rome, they were "unfree people" possessed by a particular master.

Moving from the ancient to the medieval era, we still find a caste of unfree people called "indentured servants and slaves" (*genin*), but most scholars acknowledge that medieval indentured servants and nonhumans lived completely different lives. If that was the case, then the four groups of debased people in the Ritsuryō state may have been clearly distinguished from free subjects but they were not necessarily stigmatized as the medieval nonhumans were.[8]

Scholarly opinion is sharply divided on the fifth of the five colors of baseness of the Ritsuryō state—the *ryōko*—whose mission it was to guard the imperial tombs.[9] It appears that they were considered the closest to "good people," in other words, to officials. We do not really know, however, why they were included within the category of debased people since they were in proximity to officialdom. One of the prevailing theories is that their inclusion among the debased was related to the pollution that arises from death. The argument is that the tomb guardians were stigmatized as a group because of their connection to the polluted space of graves. In fact, there are some who believe that these tomb guardians were one ancestral source of today's stigmatized *burakumin*. But an examination of the condition of graves and tombs in those days shows that they were sacred sites and not polluted places that had to be avoided. As sacred places, they had to be strictly guarded.

I touched upon this in the previous chapter, but it should be recalled that even in the Middle Ages, the guardians of the mausoleum of Fujiwara no Kamatari had tremendous authority and pride.[10] Indeed, they had attributed to them the special powers of the servants of the gods, that is, the shrine and temple purveyors. Tomb guardians, like the various purveyors, were also involved in commerce. Theirs was not the existence of outcastes but of sancti-

---

8. In other words, if the nonhumans did not derive from the four slavelike groups of the debased peoples, then the discrimination against nonhumans did not derive from a relation to slavery, as is commonly held, but from something else. Amino's point, I believe, is that stigmatization of nonhumans, which was the key form of discrimination in the early modern period, was different from caste-based discrimination such as that applied to slaves. Drawing this inference back in time, then, his argument is that the fact of slavery itself did not generate discrimination, so we cannot infer that the "four debased groups" suffered stigmatization. The subtle difference in the modes of discrimination, between one that is status based and one that is based on the magico-religious notion of pollution, is the crucial concept of this chapter.
9. See the related discussion of this group in chapter seven.
10. Fujiwara no Kamatari (614–69) was the founder of the powerful Fujiwara clan, which dominated court politics throughout most of the Nara and Heian periods.

fied guardians of a holy site. But if that were so, then why were these people given a base status?

The shrine menials (*shinsen*) at Kashima Shrine appear in just one document of the archaic period. It is clear that these people were in direct attendance on the gods, but since they had greater military skills than commoners, they were mobilized by the Ritsuryō state to fight against the peoples of northeast Honshu, then known as Ezo. This may count, then, as one further distinction from the outcastes who appeared from the seventeenth century on. These people as a whole—the tomb attendants and shrine menials—were distinguished from the common people by the fact that they were in direct service to sacred things. The fact that they were accorded base status was due to the Ritsuryō state's imitation of the Tang Chinese system, not a reflection of their actual position in society.

Tomb guardians were in a position similar to the shrine, temple, and imperial purveyors. That is, in their service to the native deities and Buddhas they may have been characterized as menials or slaves, but in fact they had special rights. Therefore, when we consider the problem of discrimination in ancient times as a matter of status, we should recognize that there were two kinds of distinction. One was found in the distinction between slaves and good people. The other was the distinction accorded those people who were in service to sacred beings whose power exceeded that of normal human beings.

BUDDHIST HOSPICES FOR THE SICK AND ORPHANED

The Ritsuryō system, under which everyone was supposed to be recorded in a register, began to fall apart in the eighth century. The government's regulatory power weakened, and the number of vagrants and absconders began to rise. Among these, people with serious diseases, people with no close relatives (such as orphans), and others suffering misfortune became a major political problem. Responding to a growing need for relief, the government established hospices known as *hiden'in* and *seyakuin*.[11] Not only were these facilities constructed in the capital, but there are archaeological traces of hospices established near the government outposts in each region. When the

---

11. The effort of the Ritsuryō state to provide relief at these hospices was in part related to Empress Kōmyō's embracing of Buddhism.

Ritsuryō state established the official regional temple system (*kokubunji*), it also paired relief facilities with official temples in each provincial capital.[12]

Put this way, it looks like the Ritsuryō state did nothing but good works. But the attempt to include everyone in a registration system was more for the purpose of levying heavy taxes than providing relief. And it was because of the state's attempt to increase the tax burden that incidences of vagrancy and absconding rose. Therefore, we should keep in mind the intent of the Ritsuryō state to control the population when evaluating its actions. In any case, when the abandoned children and orphans who had been raised in the hospices grew up, they were attached to the family registers of a normal person's household. Thus, at least during the Nara period, it would appear that these people were not subject to discrimination simply because they had grown up in a hospice.

When the capital was moved to Heian (Kyoto), hospices were built at the far eastern and western ends of Ninth Avenue. We have evidence that they retained their function through the ninth century. During this period, we know that people raised in the hospices were added to the household registers of the capital, given the new surname of Maraji, and granted one house per family registry. When those without relatives gave birth to their own children, they established an official household and were thereafter treated the same as other commoners. However, if all were given new names, then it would be possible to know at a glance that they came from a hospice. This may have become a source of later discrimination.

By the end of the ninth century, the government faced a fiscal crisis as the Ritsuryō system weakened. As a result, it could no longer support the hospices. All government agencies faced this crisis, so all of the artisans attached to these agencies were forced to fend for themselves in their own independent groups. Or, to put it another way, the artisanal classes distanced themselves from government regulation and began to freely form their own groups. The same was probably true of courtesans (*asobime*).[13] The singers and performers in the Office of Female Dancers and Musicians of the Bureau of Music, one of the agencies in the Ritsuryō government, and the lower grade maids serving in the women's quarters of the imperial palace prob-

12. The system, which was established in 741 by order of Emperor Shōmu, provided that an official Buddhist temple be built in every province, subject to the overall control of the headquarters temple, Tōdaiji, in Nara.
13. The same two characters for *courtesan* are variably glossed in the original with three pronunciations: *asobime*, *ukareme*, and *yūjo*. There may well have been differences in the detail and historical circumstance of each pronunciation, but for the sake of translation I am rendering all of them as *courtesan*. It is important to note that *courtesan* does not strictly imply prostitution. While sexual work may have been a part of the function of courtesans, it was not necessarily true of all

ably formed female entertainers' associations. Handcraftsmen and shamans (*miko*) were attached to the regional government outposts as well, and it is possible to confirm the traces of an organization of courtesans (*ukareme*) in the city of Dazaifu in northern Kyushu during the Nara period. So, it is likely that there were professional associations that included courtesans in every region. These craft and entertainment associations appear most clearly in the tenth and eleventh centuries. As the ninth century fiscal crisis pushed tradesmen out of the bureaucracy and into their own associations, the people of the hospices (except for those with the most debilitating diseases) found themselves forced to resort to similar means to support themselves.

In the latter half of the ninth century, a great famine left so many dead and sickened from starvation that the banks of the Kamo River in Kyoto were strewn with bones and corpses. This kind of famine occurred from time to time from ancient times through the sixteenth century. Documentation shows that in order to deal with the disaster the government ordered the people of the hospices to remove the dead from the riverbanks. It was from the time of this late-ninth-century famine, then, that the government first granted them a stipend and put them to work disposing of the dead. However, since commoners in the capital and low-level officials in the headquarters of the Middle Palace Guards (*hyōefu*) and the headquarters of the Inner Palace Guards (*emonfu*) were also made to do some of this work, we can see that it was a task that was not yet exclusive to the people of the hospices. The origins of the gradual separation of the people of the hospices from the communities of commoners to work with the disposal of the dead and at funerals may be found during this period. Nevertheless, since people from hospices were included in the family registers of commoners, it is not possible to directly link the early Heian hospices and the communities of discriminated groups that appeared later.

THE PROBLEM OF POLLUTION

In the tenth and eleventh centuries, it was impossible for the government and its regional outposts to support the sick and orphaned. Moreover, by this time Kyoto had outgrown the classic Chinese model of a capital—that is, one containing only the aristocracy, bureaucratic officialdom, and the small number

---

of them, nor was it the primary task of most of them. The term *courtesan* (and the more awkward *female entertainer*) connotes a wider range of possible activities and a clearer sense of the professional skills involved than does our modern notion of prostitution.

of merchants needed to support a market. Kyoto had become a full-scale city in which all kinds of people lived. With this development, pollution became a serious problem for the city and particularly its leading citizens, the aristocracy. Determining the precise nature of pollution during this time is itself a problem. I agree with Yamamoto Kōji's notion that it was connected to the fear and uncertainty that arose in human society when the state of balance between human beings and nature was disrupted or lost. While that is a viable definition of *pollution* in general, the people of ancient society distinguished among a wide variety of specific forms. For example, death was considered a loss that caused death pollution (*shie*). At the opposite end of human life, birth, which was also held to be a disruption of an existing state of balance, caused birth pollution (*san'e*). Pollution could also arise from animals whose existence was closely tied to that of human beings, such as dogs, horses, and cows.

Pollution was not limited to purely biological conditions. Conflagrations, the grand expression of the power in fire that can escape the control of human beings, gave rise to a form of pollution known as destruction by fire (*shōbōe*). There was also a kind of pollution specific to the commission of a crime (*tsumie*). Of course, murder was connected to death pollution, but even theft was considered a form of pollution. It was believed at the time that objects themselves were closely tied to human beings, so the intentional removal of a thing from its owner in the act of theft was believed to cause a particular kind of pollution. As I will discuss below, major changes made in nature by human means, such as cutting down a large tree or moving a large stone, were seen as causing yet another kind of pollution.

People who entered a site that had been transformed by any of the above forms of pollution would become polluted and would have to seclude themselves for a certain period while it was removed. Since the deities (*kami*) and the emperor were seen as beings whose existence was affected by changes in nature, a serious crisis would ensue if the deities or the emperor became polluted.[14] To be specific, if the emperor were polluted, vital religious and state

14. Western readers may be prone to think of emperors in strictly political terms and deities as not subject to human conditions, which would make this passage difficult to understand. In ancient Japan, the emperor was understood principally as an *arahitogami* (a deity personified), and the deities were understood to be spirits apart from humans but by no means omnipotent. The deities resided principally in "the other world," a kind of parallel universe, but they also had an important impact in the temporal world. The deities were particularly associated with natural processes such as the growth of plants and the flow of wind and water. The emperor, as an embodied deity, was

ceremonies could not be conducted, and all political activity would come to a standstill. A state of imperial pollution actually occurred on occasion at the end of the Heian period. While this kind of fear of pollution probably goes back to the very earliest society of the Japanese archipelago, this nervous avoidance of pollution grew to enormous proportions and became systematized in Kyoto, with its large, densely concentrated population.

This anxiety stemmed from the belief that pollution could be communicated under certain circumstances even to the deities. For example, when a case of birth or death pollution occurred in a closed space, such as one surrounded by a fence and gate, the entire space became polluted. This state can be called primary pollution. If someone entered that space not knowing that it was polluted and then returned to his or her home, that home would also become polluted. This is a state of secondary pollution. If someone else then entered a space in a state of secondary pollution and then, unwittingly, returned home, that home would also become polluted to the third degree. There was no fourth degree of pollution, but the first through the third were all considered pollution in gradually diminishing levels. All levels required purifying rituals, and a system for recognizing and dealing with communicable pollution was developed by the government. Yet, interestingly enough, pollution was not considered communicable in open spaces such as riverbanks and roads. For example, one would not become polluted if one came across a dead body lying on the riverbank. It may well be that the riverbanks became a funerary site for that reason.

THE EMERGENCE OF NONHUMANS AND THEIR LABOR

Groups labeled nonhuman first appear in historical documents at about the same time as this fear of communicable pollution began to spread among the aristocracy of Kyoto. The title "chief of the nonhumans" appears in a document from the latter half of the eleventh century, so we can surmise that at

---

the primary intermediary between the world of the humans and the world of the deities. Therefore, his (or, occasionally, her) primary function was understood to be conducting the ceremonies necessary to maintain the balance in the universe between the temporal world and the world of the deities. As the people of the time saw it, becoming polluted would prevent the emperor or the deities from performing their crucial functions and thus would result in natural disasters. The close contact of the nobles with the emperor explains why Amino discusses this as a particular problem for the aristocracy.

the time there were already groups that had their own independent organizations. The severely diseased and orphaned—who had formerly resided at the Buddhist hospices but now had to fend for themselves—were surely among these groups. As I noted earlier, these independent organizations were groups of people whose vocation—I choose to call it a vocation—was purifying polluted spaces. Over time, they came to be called nonhuman (*hinin*).

Limiting our discussion to those who appear in historical documents, these nonhuman groups were particularly conspicuous in Kyoto and Nara. As provincial government headquarters, especially in western Japan, began to take on the appearance of towns around the eleventh and twelfth centuries, however, nonhuman groups also began to show up in the regions. Since many kinds of people took part in purification work, it is impossible for us to treat them as a homogeneous group. I will therefore discuss them one at a time.

The most conspicuous of these professional purifying groups (the one documented in the greatest detail) were those people simply called nonhumans. We have a fairly clear understanding of their life conditions from around the twelfth and thirteenth centuries. One of their main bases in Kyoto was on the hill leading up to Kiyomizu Temple, on the southeast side of the city, which came to be known as "The Quarters" (*shuku*). The same Chinese character (宿) served for post towns in general, making it difficult to distinguish between the two in writing. However, in the Warring States period a new Chinese character (夙) that was pronounced the same way was used to orthographically distinguish the bases of nonhumans from the other post towns. The quarters below Kiyomizu became known as "The Headquarters" (*honshuku*) where the chief of the nonhumans, who controlled not just the nonhumans of Kyoto but all those living throughout the Kinai region in communities known as "outposts," resided.[15] Another group of nonhumans, which appears to have been opposed to the Kiyomizu group, was headquartered on the Nara Hill in Yamato Province. This latter group, known as the Kitayama Quarters, was a powerful association associated with the temple of Kōfukuji and Kasuga Shrine.[16] It also controlled a series of nonhuman outposts scattered throughout the Kinai region.

15. Kinai refers specifically to the five provinces surrounding the ancient capitals on the Yamato Plain. Today, the Kinai region corresponds to parts of Osaka, Kyoto, Nara, Hyōgo, and Wakayama Prefectures.
16. These were, respectively, a Buddhist temple and a Shinto shrine in Nara. Both were associated with the aristocratic Fujiwara clan.

Each outpost also had its own leader. The word used for these leaders, *chori*, later became a generalized term of discrimination, just as the word used to differentiate nonhuman *shuku* from other post towns later became a derogatory term. However, at the time the same term was generally used to designate the head of any group of people, such as the head of a temple. Courtesans, to take another example, were also characterized by a hierarchy based on seniority. The same kind of organization existed in Buddhist monks' associations and trade guilds. So again, we find nonhumans working within a general, not a distinct, model.

While the Kitayama group was closely linked to Kōfukuji, the nonhumans of Kiyomizu Hill were closely tied to the temple of Enryakuji and Gion Shrine. Among the latter were people who sold strings for archers' bows. In later eras, these people were called string sellers (*tsurumeso*), but at that time they appear in documents as *inujinin*. Their name is a result of the word *dog* (*inu*) added as a prefix to the term for shrine purveyor (*jinin*). The group was composed of shrine purveyors at Gion Shrine and temple purveyors at the Shakyamuni Hall of Enryakuji. But *inujinin* were not restricted to these two sites. These two *inujinin* groups were simply the most famous. A close look at historical records shows that there were *inujinin* groups at shrines in other regions. It is clear, for example, that there were *inujinin* at Tsurugaoka Hachiman Shrine in Kamakura, a rare case for eastern Japan.

As far as we know, the work for these *inujinin* and nonhumans was primarily concerned with funerals. Documents from the Muromachi period show that the nonhumans of Kiyomizu Hill were in charge of the funerary biers upon which corpses were carried to the funeral grounds in Kyoto. As a reward for their work, *inujinin* and nonhumans had the right to goods offered to the deceased at funerals. If we recall the activities of the people of the hospices during the early Heian period, we may surmise that nonhumans fulfilled the function of purifying death pollution going back to the Heian period.

In addition, these people also had the task of purifying other forms of pollution, such as that arising from crime and punishment. For example, capital punishment was carried out by released prisoners. Buildings that had been polluted by the commission of a crime within their walls or by the commission of a crime by their owners were commonly torn down, and this was done by *inujinin*. For Kyoto, the demolition was carried out by the Kiyomizu group. For example, a picture scroll called *Pictorial Gleanings of*

Ancient Virtues (*Shūi kotoku den'e*) depicts *inujinin* destroying the grave site of a holy man named Hōnen during the government's suppression of Hōnen's Pure Land sect (fig. 31).[17]

Documents from the Muromachi period show that riverside dwellers and nonhumans were employed to deal with afterbirth.[18] Young people these days know very little about afterbirth. Since most people are now born in a maternity clinic, we do not have to worry about where to dispose of the afterbirth. But in an era when people were born at home, disposal was a significant problem. In Kyoto and most of western Japan, people were extremely concerned about

Figure 31. An *inujinin* destroying the Tomb of Hōnen, from *Pictorial Gleanings of Ancient Virtues*. Source: *Shūi kotoku den'e*, from the collection of Jōfukuji. Photograph courtesy of Bukkyo University.

17. Hōnen (1133–1212) was defrocked and banished from Kyoto for heresy (he advocated the exclusive practice of *nenbutsu*, calling on Amida Buddha for salvation at the exclusion of all other Buddhist prayers and practices). One of his disciples, Shinran (1173–1262), was also banished, and several others were executed. This marked the beginning of an extended government suppression of the Pure Land sects led by Hōnen and Shinran. The campaign to suppress Pure Land doctrines and practitioners was propelled by many of the major Buddhist institutions, particularly the Tendai monastery on Mount Hiei. The scene Amino refers to in this picture scroll depicts an episode in that suppression campaign that took place after Hōnen's death (thus the destruction of a small building at his grave).

18. Because these documents date from the Muromachi period, Amino cautiously notes that we do not know how far back this custom dates.

"birth" pollution. For example, during the Muromachi period, nonhumans took the afterbirth of the shogun's family to distant mountains for burial.[19] These examples serve to demonstrate that the "skilled labor" of these groups was the purification of various kinds of pollution.

FEAR OF SPECIAL POWERS

While these nonhuman groups were quite diverse, they shared the characteristic of being unable to live as, and among, commoners. As stated earlier, we know that the category of nonhumans came to include orphans, the handicapped, lepers, and other people who were unable to live normal lives. But it also appears that not all lepers had to enter these groups. In the latter part of the Kamakura period, it appears that one leader of a nonhuman organization forced lepers out of their homes and into his group. A priest of the Ritsu sect who had worked for the relief of nonhumans stopped this practice and forced the leader to vow to leave the decision to enter the group up to the individual.

Nevertheless, it is undeniable that the gravely sick or handicapped—in other words, those who were unable to move about freely—were frequently included among the nonhumans. We know from such picture scrolls as *The Picture Scroll of the Holy Man Ippen* (*Ippen hijirie*) that these people begged for a living. Yet according to Buddhist thought in this era, begging was considered a method of spiritual training for those who turned their backs on the secular world. It was a widely held article of faith that donations to beggars were equivalent to virtuous acts toward the Buddha. Nonhumans took to begging in this sense of a religious practice. But since begging also generated income, it had to take place in a clearly marked area, just as commerce had to take place in the particular space of the marketplace (fig. 32). It seems likely that the leader of the nonhumans mentioned above tried to force lepers into his group in order to increase the number of beggars and therefore the organization's income.

19. Ethnologists note a general difference between customs related to afterbirth in western and eastern Japan. In western Japan, including Kyoto where the Muromachi shoguns resided, the afterbirth was carried far away and buried in the mountains where no one would come in contact with it. In eastern Japan, the afterbirth was customarily buried in the entryway of the family home in the belief that the treading of many feet across the doorway would toughen the spirit of the children whose placentas were buried there.

Figure 32. Beggars from *The Picture Scroll of the Holy Man Ippen*. Source: *Ippen hijirie*, from the collection of Shōjōkōji.

Inujinin and nonhumans were also involved in the performing arts. For example, *inujinin* pulled and led the floats in the Gion Festival.[20] Today, the Gion Festival features a number of very tall floats called mountain floats (*yamaboko*). But in ancient times, the procession of the Gion Festival probably consisted of a series of tall poles upon which, it was believed, the gods would descend from the heavens. We have very early images of released prisoners carrying strange long poles with vines attached that are probably the precursors of the Gion floats. During the Muromachi period, the *inujinin* were known to approach the emperor and give performances as part of a realm-purifying ceremony and a ritual prayer for the long life of the imperial clan. This custom continued until the Edo period. These examples point to the fact that nonhumans had important roles to play in the purification of the realm and prayers for long life, which they fulfilled through the performing arts.

It has commonly been believed that the use of the Chinese character for dog (pronounced *inu* in Japanese) in *inujinin*, or the use of the prefix *non* (*hi*) for nonhumans (*hinin*), reveals that these people were excluded and ostracized from the communities of commoners. From this, it has been supposed

---

20. The Gion Festival is perhaps Kyoto's most famous city festival. It takes place in July and involves a parade of huge floats that circles the downtown section of the city. The festival is associated with Gion Shrine, one of the shrines that Amino repeatedly mentions as containing a famous organization of shrine purveyors.

that nonhumans and *inujinin* constituted a society outside of society or a status outside of the status system—in other words, outcastes. But considering the actual conditions we just covered, it was not likely to have been that simple. A somewhat different approach must be taken, beginning with the recognition that the core of these nonhuman organizations was constituted by commercial artisans and performers. Temple and shrine purveyors were clearly given status within society, just as tradesmen were.

Nonhumans became temple and shrine purveyors because of the social fear of pollution and because nonhumans were seen as having the special ability to purify people, places, and things. Fear of pollution at the time derived in part from a utilitarian problem: once a person came into contact with communicable pollution, he or she would have to remain confined at home for a long period of time. Beyond that, fear of pollution was probably tied to fear of the power of nature, a power that far exceeded that of human beings.

In short, people at the time did not just avoid and despise pollution; they feared it. They had similar feelings about those who had the power to purify polluted sites, in other words, nonhumans. Because they performed a special function that went beyond the powers of a normal person, nonhumans were accorded the special status of temple or shrine workers and recognized as direct servants of the native and Buddhist deities. This fear of and respect for those linked to higher powers extended to beggars as well, for they were seen as incarnations of Buddhist deities. As a result, disrespect toward beggars was believed to result in divine punishment. This idea was first propagated to support the spread of Buddhism, but it also contributed to the idea that beggars had special abilities to purify scenes and states of pollution. In time, these special powers became linked to a fear of their very persons. Finally, returning to the question of social status, we should keep firmly in mind the fact that nonhumans were seen, like other tradesmen, as temple and shrine purveyors. In other words, they were people with skills.

NONHUMANS IN THE SERVICE OF THE GODS

The term *nonhuman* itself, the propensity for nonhumans to present themselves as slaves of the gods, and their association with pollution, beggars, and the sick have led many to view nonhumans through a contemporary lens as stigmatized. But nonhumans had pride in their special skills. For example,

Imperial Police Agency such as Prison Guard of the Left and Prison Guard of the Right. By the late Kamakura period, they had organized themselves into something like a guild—known as the Servants of the Four Posts in reference to the four guard offices under the imperial police—with their own system of leadership. Since the Imperial Police Agency was directly answerable to the emperor, we can situate released prisoners as yet another group in direct service to a sacred being.

The actual appearance of this group is portrayed most clearly in *The Pictorial Biography of the Holy Man Hōnen.* In the scene in which the monk Anraku is beheaded on the banks of the Kamo River near Sixth Avenue in Kyoto, they are the heavily bearded men holding long halberds and standing behind the police officers (fig. 33). We cannot tell what kind of hairstyle they had, but I believe their hair was not bound up in a topknot. In this scene, they are not wearing folded *eboshi* hats but completely cover their hair in standing *eboshi* hats, and they are quite lavishly dressed. They were undoubtedly the men who beheaded the prisoners.

Released prisoners also carried out punishments such as the destruction of houses (as did the *inujinin*) and participated in the capture of criminals. In other words, their work was probably comparable to that of detectives during the Edo period. Moreover, they participated in the procession at the Kamo Festival, carrying their halberds and wearing their gaudy clothing. Their clothing got so outlandish at this festival that it eventually became an issue that had to be addressed in the laws for aristocratic households (which employed them). In any case, in fulfilling all of these functions their tasks closely resembled those of the *inujinin*.

Interestingly enough, during the Northern and Southern Courts period the *hōmen* were given allotments of indigo taxes as a salary (this practice probably goes back to the Kamakura period). They received the materials for indigo dye from wholesalers. During the Edo period, indigo dyers were a stigmatized group. This later discrimination appears to have been connected to the *hōmen* in some way.

PEOPLE WITH CHILDREN'S NAMES

Although we do not know many individual nonhumans' names, riverside dwellers and many comparable nonhumans (that is, all except those who

Figure 33. Released prisoners (*hōmen*), with heavy beards, behind imperial policemen (*kebiishi*), from *The Pictorial Biography of the Holy Man Hōnen*. Source: *Hōnen shōnin den'e*, from the collection of Chion'in. Photograph courtesy of Kyoto National Museum.

dressed like monks) generally had the suffix *maru* attached to their names. The same is true, without exception, for all the released prisoners whose names we have been able to identify. In the late Heian period, when released prisoners were still generically called "leg-ironed," we know, for example, of a Kuroyu-maru. We also know of an important executive officer in the released prisoner organization of the Kamakura period named Kunimatsu-maru. And we have records from the Northern and Southern Courts period of released prisoners named Teimatsu-maru, Yoshimitsu-maru, and Hikosato-maru.

Depictions of cows in ancient picture scrolls all show animals with terrifying faces. They are painted with glaring eyes, often charging, brandishing
their horns, and dragging their herders behind them. In the picture scrolls,
cows do not appear to be gentle creatures. This suggests that the dominant
social image of cows was that they were nearly wild and not easily controlled
by humans. While the same can be said for horses, horse drivers are not as well
documented as cow herders. Horse drivers appear in Heian period documents
and are fairly well understood in the Muromachi period. There is a documentary gap, however, during the Kamakura. Since we know that cart drivers were
also cow herders, it seems certain that horse drivers were also affiliated with
the stables of the imperial family or the Fujiwara regents. We also know that
they were occasionally called imperial stable purveyors (*miumaya yoriudo*).

Insofar as they appear in picture scrolls, the styles of those who attended
horses are fairly distinctive. For example, there are pictures of boys galloping
on horses, with their ponytails flapping in the wind. As above, their appearance
and hairstyles were different from those of the common people because they
fulfilled similar functions to those of *inujinin*. The association with animals
and children receives further support from the fact that cormorant fishers also
let their hair flow free, and monkey trainers had the appearance of children.

The thread that ties all of these examples together is the medieval view
that wild or nearly wild animals possessed powers exceeding those of humans. Those people who dealt with such animals were seen as having special
powers unavailable to common people. This view likely extended to the activities of those riverside dwellers and purifiers who dealt with the carcasses
of horses and cows. Quite unlike the view in later eras of animals as four-
legged beasts, people of the ancient and early medieval eras saw them as having an existence that exceeded that of humans. Even if we cannot quite call
them "sacred beasts," to slaughter these animals was to risk the punishment
of the Buddha. Thus, riverside dwellers who were able to deal with animal
carcasses safely were understood to be able to do so because they were sanctified, because they existed on the edge of the sacred realm.

FROM SANCTIFICATION TO LOATHING

Let us return for a moment to the problem of children's names. The suffix
maru was attached to the names of many things besides humans. Hawks
and dogs were given names with *maru*, as were suits of armor and helmets.

Musical instruments such as flutes, reeds, and flageolets were given names with the *maru* suffix, as were boats. In short, all kinds of things were called "something-*maru*." Why this was so is still a matter of debate. There are some who say that *maru* was used to name beloved things. Others argue that people whose name carried that suffix were slaves or servants. But these seem like insufficient explanations to me.

Rather, I believe we need to take note of how these things called *maru* existed on the border of the sacred and profane worlds. Hawks and dogs, because they were used in hunting, were certainly seen as existing on the border. At the time, the world of sound was thought to be connected to the deities; sound called them forth and pleased them. Musical instruments were clearly a way of mediating between the sacred world of the deities and the profane world of humanity. The same may be said for boats. People risked their lives when they went out onto the ocean, so it is understandable that they would want to give ships some kind of magical power. The same was true for the swords and armor, to which soldiers entrusted their lives on the battlefield.

The fact that these various items were given children's names is intimately related to the society's view of children themselves. In short, children were believed to exist on the border between the sacred and the profane. In fact, near the end of the Heian period, records indicate that the accusation of a child was sufficient cause for arrest by the imperial police.[27] The common saying that "until the age of seven a child is with the gods" gives us a clue to the reason why children were presumed to be inherently truthful. That is, whatever children said was taken as an expression of the will of the deities. I believe that the custom of giving certain adults, objects, and animals children's names is related to this belief in the borderline existence of various classes of beings and objects. Thus, until the early part of the medieval era, anything with a child's name was considered at least partially sacred.

The discriminatory word *eta* (greatly polluted) first appeared in a picture scroll from the latter half of the thirteenth century, the *Tengu sōshi* (*The Picture Book of Goblins*).[28] The *eta* in the scroll is also called a child and is drawn with freeflowing hair. The *eta* child is also shown killing a bird on a riverbank (fig. 35). The scroll's text states that the bird is a goblin (*tengu*) that

27. An example of this may be found in *The Tale of the Heike*, where it is reported that Taira no Kiyomori retained a troop of young boys employed as spies in Kyoto. What made them effective, according to Amino, was not simply their ability to slip into places unnoticed, but the presumed truthfulness of their statements.
28. *Eta* is the word used to describe outcastes that is probably most familiar to non-Japanese.

Figure 35. *Eta* boy killing a bird, from *The Picture Book of Goblins*. Source: *Tengu sōshi*, privately owned. Photograph courtesy of Chūōkōron-Shinsha, Inc.

had taken the form of a kite, and that the *eta* child had captured and killed the bird with bait. The text further describes esoteric Buddhist incantations and "*eta* disembowlers" as things that are terrifying to goblins. As stated earlier, riverside dwellers were known for removing the entrails of cows, so this may have been a specific reference to them. Thus, riverside dwellers, or *eta*, were presented as having the power to exorcise goblins. This power of non-humans in general deserves special attention.

I must reiterate that this is the earliest appearance in writing of a discriminatory word (*eta* meaning "greatly polluted") in reference to these people. The scroll was produced sometime in the 1290s, marking the early stages of a shift toward the use of a clearly discriminatory appellation for nonhumans and riverside dwellers. A dictionary of ancient terms complied in the latter half of the Kamakura period explains that "purifiers are called *eta*" because "*eta*" is a slurred pronunciation of *etori*, meaning "procurers of food for animals." The entry ends by noting that "they are evil people whose bodies are polluted from killing and selling animals." This clearly reveals a trend within society toward stigmatizing nonhumans and riverside dwellers.

There are many debates as to why this shift occurred, but I believe it had to do with a change in views concerning pollution around this time. The fear of pollution that had held sway in earlier eras began to dissipate. In its place, there grew an aversion to pollution as simple filth. I believe this shift was the result of changes within Japanese society in the relationship between humans and nature. As people began to see nature more clearly, the fear of pollution diminished. Accordingly, those who dealt with pollution also lost their claim to special skills. The fear with which they had been regarded was superseded by loathing.

However, the transformation was quite complex. The end of the thirteenth century was an era of great intellectual tension over the question of how to view "evil" and pollution (as well as the nonhumans, women, and others most closely related to pollution). While the tendency to despise, debase, and reject "greatly polluted" people as evil represented one end of the spectrum, there was also a counter claim that those associated with pollution, such as nonhumans and women, could be saved through the power of the Buddhas. The Buddhist priest Shinran claimed in a famous dictum that "if a good man may be saved, how much more so an evil one." That is, Shinran held that it was the very people associated with pollution who were most representative of the human condition.

An intensely strained relationship between these two trends developed in the late thirteenth and early fourteenth centuries. We can get a good sense of that tension by examining the contrast between *The Picture Book of Goblins* and *The Picture Scroll of the Holy Man Ippen*, which were produced at about the same time.

THEMES IN *THE PICTURE SCROLL OF THE HOLY MAN IPPEN*

The Picture Scroll of the Holy Man Ippen is famous for its depiction of an unusually large number of nonhumans and beggars in contrast to other scrolls of its time. There is a later *Illustrated Biography of the Holy Man Ippen (Ippen shōnin ekotobaden),* from the Northern and Southern Courts period, that also shows many beggars and nonhumans, but they are drawn in a stereotypical and unanimated fashion. In contrast, the beggars and nonhumans in the picture scroll are each drawn individually, more true to life than in any other extant scrolls, even including beggars who moved around in wheeled huts and some who walked in wooden clogs on their hands (fig. 36).[29]

To date, discussions of this scroll have focused on the beggars, non-humans, and *inujinin*, identifiable by the cloth covering their faces. But if we look at the scroll more closely, we will also find a considerable number of people who appear to have been closely related to nonhumans and beggars, including many who look like children, without the familiar *eboshi* hat, their hair flowing freely or tied in a ponytail. When we broaden our examination of *The Picture Scroll of the Holy Man Ippen* to include these childlike figures, hitherto unnoticed details begin to reveal themselves.

Turning first to a portion near the end of the scroll, two scenes immediately preceding the final image of Ippen's memorial chapel are shown in figures 37 and 38. Figure 37 shows the same scene, not from the best-known copy of the scroll (from Shōjōkōji), but from an unusual, sketched copy (in the collection of Miedō). The two are very similar, but they differ in some important respects. Both show that after Ippen's death some *inujinin* (again, the ones with their faces covered with cloth wraps) attempted to follow him into the afterlife by drowing themselves. In figure 39, there are two monks from Ippen's sect, Jishū, flanked on the left and the right by two *inujinin* who are watching two others move off into the water. I think it is very significant that the final scene of this scroll shows nonhumans (here *inujinin*) attempting to

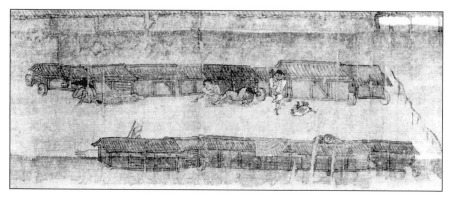

Figure 36. People moving on a cart with a hut, from *The Picture Scroll of the Holy Man Ippen.*
Source: *Ippen hijirie*, from the collection of Shōjōkōji.

29. In the original Japanese, Amino points out that the latter type of beggar was reportedly seen in Osaka until relatively recently.

Figure 37. A monk of the Ji sect attempting to drown, from *The Picture Scroll of the Holy Man Ippen*. Source: *Ippen hijirie*, from the collection of Shōjōkōji.

Figure 38. An *inujinin* attempting to drown and two *inujinin* watching, from *The Picture Scroll of the Holy Man Ippen.* Source: *Ippen hijirie*, from the collection of Shōjōkōji.

Figure 39. An *inujinin* attempting to drown and two *inujinin* watching, from *The Picture Scroll of the Holy Man Ippen*. Source: *Ippen hijirie (Miedō-bon)*, from the collection of Zaidan Hōjin Maeda Ikutoku-kai.

follow Ippen into the other world. This final scene offers the key as to why the scroll depicts so many beggars and nonhumans.

Let us shift to the scene of Ippen's dying hour, which takes place just before the scene discussed above (see fig. 40). Ippen is lying on his deathbed on the left. We can clearly see three *inujinin* among the many people who have come to pay their respects. In the Miedō sketched version of this scene, there are five *inujinin*, one of whom is crying. Note as well that next to the three *inujinin* there is a man with a ponytail and beard. We have no idea what kind of man he is, but I believe he has some relationship with the *inujinin*. The Kamakura era dictionary referred to earlier claims that the "greatly polluted" cannot go about among the common people. But in this scene those *inujinin* who were later to be labeled "greatly polluted" have come along with many commoners to witness Ippen's passing.

Figure 41 also shows many people who have come to witness Ippen's final hour. I believe that all of them belong to a group like the nonhumans. The man with some kind of scroll attached to his umbrella is said to be an *etoki* (a Buddhist layman who delivers popular sermons using pictures). The man in the lead has a topknot, so it is unlikely he is a nonhuman. But the others, such as the one carrying the basket or the one wearing a headband, are probably from some kind of nonhuman group.

Figure 42 shows the scene immediately preceding that shown in figure 40: the scene of Ippen's final sermon. Ippen is lecturing on the left, while

Figure 40. Three *inujinin* at the deathbed of Ippen, from *The Picture Scroll of the Holy Man Ippen*. Source: *Ippen hijirie*, from the collection of Shōjōkōji.

the people shown in the figure are located in the far right corner. The three *inujinin* shown on the bottom may be the same three that appear in the next scene. Considering the continuity of the tale form, this seems likely.

The upper half of figure 42 shows a number of characters, who are usually taken to be beggars and nonhumans, encamped immediately outside the grounds of a shrine. One among these has an extremely large nose, is holding a rounded fan, and has something strange hanging from his waist. There are also some people with ponytails or headbands, and on the far left are what appear to be beggars in small huts. While there are many things of note in this picture, we should observe in particular that the three *inujinin* are facing Ippen and listening to his sermon with looks of true concern. Yet these three are not standing among the rest of the people listening to the sermon.

Taking these five scenes into consideration and following them in the order of the scroll (from figs. 37 to 42), we can see that the painter has depicted an emotional drama. The *inujinin* who have followed Ippen as

Figure 41. A crowd gathering at the deathbed of Ippen, from *The Picture Scroll of the Holy Man Ippen*. Source: *Ippen hijirie*, from the collection of Shōjōkōji.

Figure 42. Three *inujinin* and a group of nonhumans and beggars, from *The Picture Scroll of the Holy Man Ippen*. Source: *Ippen hijirie*, from the collection of Shōjōkōji.

he nears death still show signs of restraint by staying outside the grounds during his final sermon. But upon his death they give up that restraint and enter the grounds to mix with the people and see Ippen off to Paradise. In the end, one among them is so distraught at the loss that he attempts to follow Ippen into the other world by drowning himself. In other words, the painter of the scroll shows in a number of frames the emotional story of how the *inujinin* bound themselves to Ippen and followed him everywhere, including into the afterlife.

VIEWING THE PAST IN PICTURE SCROLLS

Of course, this is not the only theme of *The Picture Scroll of the Holy Man Ippen*, but it can be considered one of the most important. I believe that one of the goals of the painter of this scroll was to convey Ippen's efforts to save the nonhumans. It is for that very reason that the painter so persistently depicted nonhumans in a variety of guises. When we go back through the scroll from this perspective, anticipating the climax, we can catch a number of things that have rarely been noticed before.

Figure 43 is a detail from a scene in Ippen's final journey in which he performs a memorial service at the shrine to Sugawara no Michizane in the town of Shizuke on Awaji Island. It clearly shows Ippen preaching his doctrine to people who are undoubtedly nonhumans, suggesting that his sect intentionally proselytized among them.

Figure 44, a detail from the same scene, shows the exterior of the gate to the shrine. Immediately inside are two *inujinin* and a number of beggars in lean-tos. While it is difficult to determine the exact character of the person we see running toward the gate, it is clear that these nonhumans kept themselves on the periphery of Ippen's group in the position of observers.

When we take into consideration the cumulative effect of the direct proselytizing to nonhumans in figure 43, the position of the nonhumans in figure 44 relative to Ippen (similar to that in the scene of Ippen's final sermon, i.e., outside the gate), and the scene depicting Ippen's final sermon, it is impossible to argue that the nonhumans depicted in the scroll had no connection to Ippen and his followers. It makes far more sense to view them and the beggars as followers of Ippen.

Let us go back to an even earlier point in the scroll; to the scene at Ichinomiya Shrine of Mimasaka, shown in figure 45. This scene depicts a

Figure 43. Jishū monk proselytizing to the nonhumans, from *The Picture Scroll of the Holy Man Ippen*. Source: *Ippen hijirie*, from the collection of Shōjōkōji.

visit to the shrine by Ippen and his followers. The text of the scroll notes that Ippen directed those "polluted ones" in attendance to build a structure outside the shrine grounds. It also records that "at this time, the nonhumans remained outside the gate, while the holy man and his followers entered the shrine." The structure he ordered built was a shed for the performance of the *nenbutsu*, although it does not appear in the picture. The reference to nonhumans outside the gate is to the nonhumans and beggars who are erecting a temporary shelter in the top right-hand corner.

However, we should also take care to observe the two people sitting beside the gate, one with free-flowing hair and an umbrella and the other with a headband. Some feel that the one on the right is a woman because of the high-stilted wooden sandals, but I believe it is a man. These two appeared in

Figure 48. A man in boys' clothing speaking to Ippen and Jishū monks, from *The Picture Scroll of the Holy Man Ippen*. Source: *Ippen hijirie*, from the collection of Shōjōkōji.

Some may doubt that these strange men in childlike garb could be the rich worthy men of the text, but consider the example of the so-called children of the capital (*kyōwarawa*) who were found in Kyoto up to the beginning of the medieval era. Some members of this group, who included cow herders and those who had connections with nonhumans, were wealthy. For example, cow herders were also known to drive carts for hire, so it is not surprising that they could accumulate wealth as transport tradesmen. There is evidence that these people may also have been involved in gambling because the "children of the capital" and gamblers often appear together in the literature of the time.

Of course, we cannot tell for sure what the worthy men in the picture were doing or what function the people with them fulfilled. But to insist that it is impossible for the ponytailed men to be the worthy men is to fall into the trap of presuming that nonhumans and childlike figures were strictly lowly people.

Until now, most scholars have seen the beggars and nonhumans in *The Picture Scroll of the Holy Man Ippen* as unrelated to Ippen and his followers. The tendency has been to study the nonhuman figures as if they were simply nonhumans, while Ippen and his followers have been studied separately. But as I read the scroll, the two childlike men are connected to Ippen through the mediation of the nonhumans. Through such scenes, the scroll depicts the gradual conversion of the childlike men and nonhumans to Ippen's sect. The scroll is much easier to understand as a whole when we view both Ippen and the nonhumans together. To further reinforce my point, consider the written text of the scroll after this scene at Jimokuji:

> As they passed through Mino and Owari, they found occasional signs erected by bandits, saying, "Those who wish to attend upon the holy man may proceed to the practice hall without fear. Those without sympathy will meet with retribution" and so on. For three years, they traveled over land and sea, and during that time they never feared high waves day or night, nor did they meet with trouble in the forests.

The "bandits"[30] in this passage were independent, local, armed groups that the government treated as "mountain bands" or "pirates." It is important for our understanding of Ippen's movement that we recognize that the bandits not only protected him but aggressively supported his evangelical work. At the time, these bandits were closely related to the childlike people, nonhumans, and gamblers we have been investigating. Therefore, the text and images at this point in the scroll are naturally linked, with the text underscoring the importance of the nonhumans, who might otherwise appear tangential.

Let us take a look at one more example. Figure 49 illustrates a scene at the market in Tomono in Shinano Province. Although it is not shown in the picture itself, the accompanying text tells us that the good omen of a purple cloud appeared while Ippen and his group were at the market. We can see a group of monks, with Ippen at their head, sitting to the left and looking at the cloud. Immediately behind the monks is a group of beggars with an *inujinin* at its head.

These beggars and nonhumans have conventionally been understood as receiving whatever was left over from the alms given to Ippen. However, in the scene at Jimokuji the *inujinin* is sitting with an extremely conscientious posture, facing Ippen, while the rearmost monk appears to be calling to the

---

30. The term used here is *akutō*, literally "evil parties." For more on these groups, see chapter four.

must also remember that the conditions of Japanese society were quite different from those stipulated by law.

If this was the case, then Frois's sixteenth-century claims that "in Japan, one may divorce whenever one likes. The wife's honor does not suffer, and she may also remarry. In Japan, sometimes it is the wife who divorces the husband" may well be accurate, and these conditions may well have continued into the Edo period. In the Edo period, the formal and legal principle of men's exclusive right to divorce produced such institutions as the temples of asylum. We must be careful, therefore, not to overestimate the strength of women's right to divorce. Nevertheless, Takagi's research has shown us just how great the gap can be between conventional wisdom and the historical facts.

MEN'S AND WOMEN'S SEXUAL PRACTICES

Frois's claims that Japanese women did not value chastity or virginity, and that daughters and wives could leave on extensive journeys without objections from their fathers or husbands, also struck me as dubious at first. But there is corroborating evidence, both textual and ethnological. For example, sometime after Frois a Spanish missionary named Coriado wrote a text called *A Record of Confessions* in which he described women who spoke openly in confession about their many relations with men. In more recent ethnological examples—such as Miyamoto Tsuneichi's *Forgotten Japanese* and *The Lessons of Home* and Akamatsu Keisuke's *Folk Customs of the Anti-Folk*— we find similar evidence of popular sexual customs up until world War II.[4] Miyamoto's and Akamatsu's texts reveal that at least the practice of *yobai* (literally, "night-crawling") continued in western Japan well into the twentieth century.[5]

I have heard testimony concerning this practice myself. Once, when I visited a town in the mountains of northern Okayama Prefecture, in Bitchū

---

4. Miyamoto Tsuneichi, *Wasurerareta Nihonjin* (Forgotten Japanese) (Tokyo: Iwanami shoten, [1960] 1984); Miyamoto Tsuneichi, *Kakyo no oshi* (The Lessons of Home) (Tokyo: Iwanami shoten, [1943] 1984); Akamatsu Keisuke, *Hijōmin no minzoku bunka: Seikatsu minzoku to sabetsu mukashibanashi* (Folk Customs of the Anti-Folk) (Tokyo: Akashi shoten, 1986).
5. *Yobai* was a custom through which unmarried young people in a village could engage in acceptable premarital sex. Its practices varied, but, as the literal translation of the term suggests, the typical practice was for a young man to "sneak" into the bed of a young woman at night. There were many other ways of doing this, however, and, as Amino notes in the next paragraph, it was not always strictly among locals. It typically functioned as a form of courtship. If it continued between one man and one woman for a set period of time, they would usually be recognized as married.

County, some of the older folks there told me they had continued night crawling up until the mid-1950s. The mountains of Bitchū County form a border between Okayama and the Izumo region and, as the people from the village described it to me, men from Izumo would form a defense line in the mountains, anticipating that men from Bitchū would attempt to come night crawling to their village. My Bitchū informants regaled me with tales of their heroics in breaking through the defenses of the men of Izumo to make it over the mountains to the women of the villages on the other side.

Likewise, orgiastic celebrations known as *utagaki* continued to occur in many places until quite recently.[6] According to Miyamoto Tsuneichi, the *utagaki* custom of free sex was also commonly practiced at events such as festivals and popular Buddist services. Miyamoto noted that during the festivals at the Kannon Hall in Tsushima and on saint's days at the Taishi Halls in the Kawachi region, men and women openly engaged in unrestricted intercourse. My Okayama informants confirmed this for me, noting that the custom came to an end only when police arrived to investigate a murder in connection with the *utagaki* in the 1950s. Their testimony strikes me as quite plausible.

The same was true during retreats at temples and shrines in past eras. We occasionally see scenes in medieval picture scrolls in which men and women can be found sleeping together in front of the deities. In one picture scroll, we even see men and women sleeping together using a large board as a headrest (fig. 50). At the time, it would have been pitch dark, but since these are picture scrolls we can see everything clearly.

Documentary evidence can also be found that indirectly points to the prevalence of these sexual practices. In 1261, the priests and attendants at Kasuga Shrine in Nara signed a vow stating that from then on they would avoid "secret assignations with women visiting the shrine or with senior and junior councillors in the vicinity of the worship or greeting hall." The very fact that they had to take this vow suggests that such things were going on at Kasuga Shrine. In another fascinating document, Emperor Go-Uda sent a letter in 1285 to the Iwashimizu Hachiman Shrine ordering that "men and women shall not mix when visiting the treasure hall or spending the night." Emperor Go-Uda's admonition clearly suggests that men and women were regularly sleeping together in the retreat halls, and it is likely that even after this order was issued mixed residence continued.

6. *Utagaki* were bacchanalian events with much singing, dancing, and sexual intercourse. After much discussion, Amino has insisted that "orgy" is the best translation of *utagaki*. In chapter seven, he also mentions marketplaces as a common setting for *utagaki*. Miyamoto, *Wasurerareta Nihonjin*.

Figure 50. Temple visitors sleeping in mixed quarters, using a board as a headrest, from *The Pictorial History of Ishiyama Temple*. Source: *Ishiyamadera engi emaki*, from the collection of Ishiyamadera.

The same was probably true of the festivals and Buddhist services mentioned earlier. Being in the presence of the native deities and Buddhas meant being in a place subject to their power. In places subject to the power of the deities, the relations of the secular world were canceled. As with the *utagaki* that appear in the ancient poetry collection the *Man'yōshū* and various regional almanacs,[7] these were places where men and women were not constrained by their secular relations as husband and wife.[8] As another sign of how different these places were seen to be, there are many stories of pilgrims receiving instruction from children upon visiting a temple or shrine. This was of course also partially based on the belief that children were imbued with the powers of the deities.

---

7. Portions of the *Man'yōshū*, the oldest collection of poetry in Japan, have been translated into English. See *The Ten Thousand Leaves*, trans. Ian Hideo Levy (Princeton: Princeton University Press, 1981). Local almanacs, known as *fūdoki*, featured compilations of local tales and histories. For an English translation of one such almanac, see *Records of Wind and Earth: A Translation of Fūdoki*, trans. Michiko Y. Aoki (Ann Arbor: Association for Asian Studies, 1997).
8. Unlike marriage in the West, which is seen as a union authorized and sanctioned by God, marriage in Japan was considered a secular rather than a sacred relationship.

However, this release from the rules of social propriety was not limited to exceptional events such as festivals or restricted spaces such as temples and shrines. I believe that the act of travel created a similar condition. In *Forgotten Japanese*, first published in 1960, Miyamoto Tsuneichi described young women undertaking long pilgrimages in groups of two and three. What is shocking about Miyamoto's ethnography is that he records how these women could travel with very little money for months on end with complete ease. According to his informants, there were inns that allowed traveling women to stay for free, making it possible for them to take to the road easily. There are also stories of women going quite far to work, picking cotton or planting rice. This was certainly going on in the Edo period, when women took long journeys in the name of pilgrimage (*okagemairi*). Further evidence of this can be found in picture scrolls, where we find many images of women in traveling garb—deep, face-covering, sedge hats (*ichimegasa*); baggy kimonos known as jar costumes (*tsubo shōzoku*); and straw sandals (fig. 51).

Figure 51. Women in travel attire, from *The Pictorial History of Ishiyama Temple*. Source: *Ishiyamadera engi emaki*, from the collection of Ishiyamadera.

Travelers, especially those visiting temples and shrines, were believed to have severed their ties with the secular world, just as if they were on retreat. But the "nonconnectedness" of travelers was not only due to their religious destinations. During the Middle Ages, roads and crossroads were also considered places apart from the everyday world. When an untoward incident took place on the road, its consequences could not be extended into the everyday world. Rather, the custom was that no matter how grave the incident, everything had to be resolved at the site itself. This is supported by a document in the Kamakura era text known as the *Kantō Formulary* (*Kantō onshikimoku*). According to this text, murders that occurred in "mountains, harbors, market towns, and roads" could only be resolved by those who were there. Such incidents could not be carried into the everyday world in forms such as vendettas.

During the Middle Ages, women walking the roads were sometimes victims of incidents known as "taking a woman" (*metori*) or crossroads kidnapping (*tsuji-tori*). Rape was often involved, so at least in principle, such actions were strictly forbidden by law (for example, in the *Jōei Formulary* [1232]). On close examination, however, we see that the punishment stipulated in the formulary was not very severe. In fact, the *Jōei Formulary* even directs that "allowances should be made in the case of monks."

Why is it that allowances could be made for monks, even for such serious crimes as rape and abduction? Kasamatsu Hiroshi surmises that since even low-ranking monks were subject to the rule of abstinence—a restriction apparently felt to be beyond most men's capacities—it was understandable (and therefore cause for allowance) that they might occasionally abduct a woman.[9] Of course, this is only conjecture, but it is not unfounded.

The Muromachi period short-story collection *Otogizōshi* contains a story, the "Tale of Monogusa Tarō," that suggests that monks were not the only ones granted such "allowances." In the tale, the protagonist, Monogusa Tarō, travels to the capital and is told by the owner of an inn that the abduction of an unaccompanied woman walking on the road instead of riding in a palanquin is "permissible in this realm." In other words, female abduction was publicly permissible under certain conditions. Subsequently, Monogusa Tarō goes to visit the temple of Kiyomizu, where he meets a woman traveling alone. In the course of their meeting, Monogusa Tarō solves a poetic riddle

9. Kasamatsu Hiroshi, *Hō to kotoba no chūseishi* (Law and Language in Medieval Japan) (Tokyo: Heibonsha, 1984).

posed by the woman and thus wins her hand in marriage. Although this is not a violent incident, the narrative refers to the encounter as "taking a woman." Thus, we cannot immediately assume that all cases of *metori* were rape. In another case, the protagonist of the late Kamakura diary, *The Confessions of Lady Nijō*, is a woman who, when she leaves the imperial palace to embark on a long journey, finds herself having to have sex with a number of men.[10]

That the custom of taking a woman actually existed, whatever form it took, demonstrates that what men and women did while traveling was quite different from what they did in their everyday world. More importantly, we must recognize that this was sanctioned by society. Might it not be, then, that such contemporary sayings as "one has no shame when traveling" are traces of these customs?

These records help us to see that customs that are inconceivable by today's standards of propriety and common sense actually existed in premodern Japan in a variety of forms. Frois's observations regarding the lack of import given to female chastity and virginity need not be considered outright lies. In particular, his assertions regarding women's freedom of travel can be seen to have been quite possible. So I have come to conclude that on these points Frois's text is not at all inaccurate. The boldness with which he made his claims elicits surprise, but he was apparently faithful in his narrative. It is also important for us to take these facts into account when thinking about historical transformations in women's lives.

On the matter of abortion, Frois depicted Japanese women as extremely cruel. In his view, they placed no value on the lives of children. Coupled with his opinion of Japanese women as sexually loose and unrestrained, the condemnation is clear. Frois despised these attitudes from the standpoint of his Christian morals. Since Japanese society was not regulated by Christian morals, we may set aside his denunciatory tone, but we must recognize the veracity of his observations.

There was no religion in Japan capable of exerting the kind of total influence that Christianity did in regulating people's everyday lives in the West. Thus, at the time, the common practices of abortion and infanticide—in which a woman stepped on the neck of a child she knew could not be

10. *Towazugatari*, literally "A Tale Nobody Asked For," has been translated into English. See *The Confessions of Lady Nijō*, trans. Karen Brazell (New York: Doubleday, 1973). The diary covers events from 1271 to 1306. We can imagine the rarity of the circles in which she moved by the fact that Lady Nijō was a lover of Emperor Go-Fukakusa.

raised—were seen as simply acts that grew out of poverty and the harsh conditions of life.

I believe that poverty alone does not explain these practices. The sexual practices discussed above allow us to reasonably conclude that there were many "unwed mothers." Setting aside the moral dimensions of such behavior, we can see abortion and infanticide as ways in which the women of the time coped with the conditions under which they lived. Moreover, the flip side of the belief that "a child is with the gods until seven" was that a child was not yet considered a human being. Infanticide in the Edo period continued trends of the medieval era. Here as well, most historians have sought an explanation in the travails of life. I am not arguing that we should fail to take into consideration the kinds of poverty that prevailed, but there are many aspects of that society that were not the result of poverty.

In any case, as a Christian missionary, Frois viewed the state of Japanese society with an extremely moralistic attitude. In the future, it would be instructive to explore the attitudes taken toward such problems by such Japanese religious groups as the Ikkō or the Nichiren sect. Whatever their views might have been, these sects were suppressed by secular powers (the military class) from the sixteenth century into the Edo period. Their suppression also had a great deal to do with the subsequent state of society in the Japanese islands.

THE WOMEN OF TARA-NO-SHŌ

There is little doubt that our conventional view of women's lives from the Warring States period to the Edo period is fairly far off the mark. Until recently, we have seen this as the time when the patriarchal family was established and women had no rights and suffered terrible oppression. But we must admit that actual conditions were quite different. When we go even further back in time to explore the state of women's lives before the fourteenth century, the documentary evidence clearly shows that women moved even more widely throughout society than they did in the Edo period. In order to illustrate this point, I would like to take the example of a *shōen* estate I first studied as a student: Tara-no-shō in the Wakasa region. Tara-no-shō was a small estate, but since many of its documents have survived in the possessions of the temple of Tōji in Kyoto, it provides a rare window on the operation of estates during that period.

At first, Tara-no-shō was an imperial territory (*kokugaryō*) said to have been established by a monk named Niu Dewanobō Ungen from the monastery on Mount Hiei. Ungen's grandfather acquired the fields of this settlement and decided to make it his financial base. When his grandfather died, Ungen's grandmother, a woman named Ozuki-no-uji-no-jo (literally, "woman of the Ozuki clan"), passed the land on to the infant Ungen, who was known at the time by his childhood name of Wakamaru. This was near the end of the Heian period, but we know from this example that women had the right to dispose of family territory.

Sometime after the property had been passed to the infant at the end of the Heian period, Ungen's father died. In the official documents concerning his father's death, we encounter for the first time the wet nurse who raised him in the Tara settlement. Around the same time, this wet nurse's husband also died, and Wakamaru was sent to the monastery on Mount Hiei to become a monk of the lowest rank, at which time he received his Buddhist name, Ungen. While on Mount Hiei, he left the management of his property to his wet nurse. This example shows us that women were able to manage property. And it also reminds us that wet nurses—and their husbands—fulfilled important functions in those days. This is a significant point to keep in mind as we examine women's lives.

In the end, Ungen became a vassal (*gokenin*) of Minamoto no Yoritomo (the founder of the Kamakura shogunate) in Wakasa Province. The standard procedure for acquiring vassals in the western part of Honshu was that the governor (*shugo*) would make a list of potential vassals residing in the area to send on to Kamakura for the shogun's approval. In the eastern half of Honshu, vassals would meet with Yoritomo and submit their "registries," thus establishing a direct relationship of service.[11] Since Wakasa was in the west, the governor drafted a list and sent along some thirty-odd names, one of which was Ungen's.

On the same list of vassals was a woman named Fujiwara-no-uji-no-nyō (literally, "woman of the Fujiwara clan"), who was the widow of a warrior named Miyakawa Mushanojo. We must be careful to note that her status was that of a widow, so in a sense she was acting in her husband's place. Nevertheless, it is extremely interesting that this document provides evidence that a woman could become an official vassal of the Kamakura shogunate.

---

11. These registries (*myōbu*) were lists of the lands to which they held title.

In fact, women were not entirely excluded from donning a warrior's armor and acting in a military capacity in the medieval period. We believe that two women well known in tales for their military abilities, Tomoe-gozen and Hangaku-gozen, did indeed exist. Moreover, women not only acted as vassals; in the province of Hizen, there was a female commander (onna jitō) among the Matsura bandits. There are more than a few examples of this, so if it is true that women were able to take on the duties and territory of a constable (jitō), then they may have been able to fulfill any number of functions at this time.

Returning to Tara-no-shō, Ungen soon sank into ruin and came under the protection of the largest vassal of Wakasa, one Nakahara Tokikuni (also known as Inaba Tokikuni). When Ungen accepted Tokikuni's protection, the job of estate manager (kumon) in Tara settlement—the most powerful position within the administration of the estate—passed from Ungen to Inaba Tokikuni's mother, a nun named Nakamura-ni. Again, Tara-no-shō provides us with the example of a woman in a position of high responsibility, this time an estate manager.[12]

The income of the estate manager was provided by a grant of rice paddies and dry fields. Since Ungen was a vassal of Yoritomo, these lands could not be passed on to someone who was not also a vassal. Thus, Tara-no-shō is an example of an estate in which a woman governed territory received from a vassal and acted as the chief administrator. Tara-no-shō was not the only estate where this kind of situation prevailed. Similar situations could be found in many other regions as well.

Among Ungen's lands there was a set of fields, registered as Suetake-myō, measuring about five acres. After Ungen's death, this land became the object of a long-running struggle between two women, the daughter of one of Ungen's house vassals, Fujiwara-no-uji-no-nyō, and Inaba Tokikuni's granddaughter, Nakahara-no-uji-no-nyō. Note that both plaintiffs in this case were women. Since this was designated as land that only a vassal of the Kamakura shogunate could hold, both of these women insisted for many years that they were the daughters of vassals. In the end, Nakahara won the suit, but even the loser, Fujiwara, was named the owner of the land for a short time. Consequently, we must conclude that in the Kamakura period women could be named vassals and be recognized as owners of vassal land.

---

12. The kumon of an estate was the on-site manager who produced and handled documents, assigned tax burdens, and so on. As Amino suggests, it was a position of great importance and potential power.

WOMEN'S SOCIAL ACTIVITIES

In the early part of the Kamakura period, Ungen's Tara settlement became the property of Tōji and finally came to be officially known as the Tara estate (Tara-no-shō).[13] Upon obtaining this territory, Tōji immediately appointed officials to manage the property. The first manager was a monk named Jōen, but after a time the position of manager came to be considered a post that should be passed from woman to woman. As a result, Jōen's female descendants held that position throughout the Kamakura and Northern and Southern Courts periods.

Jōen was of the Fujiwara clan, so his female descendants were all known in the documents as Fujiwara-no-uji-no-nyō (woman of the Fujiwara clan). In the middle of the Kamakura period, a woman who went by the name Higashiyama Nyōbō (Higashiyama's woman) and her daughter, also known as Fujiwara-no-uji-no-nyō, came to hold this office. These women were not managers in name only. Over the years, they struggled to maintain Tōji's rights in lengthy lawsuits with local military constables. Some of the descendants of Jōen even went out on tours of the territory, suspecting that the villagers were not properly paying their yearly taxes. On these tours, they made the villagers carry their palanquins and collected all the taxes due without granting exceptions. In some cases, the villagers complained to Tōji that these women were too harsh. Thus, there was nothing merely symbolic about female management.

Apart from their activities in the field, we should note that these women produced a great many documents, written in *hiragana*, which remain in the possession of Tōji today. It goes without saying that the female managers of the estate and the daughters of vassals could write. But even the Fujiwara woman who was briefly named as owner of the five-acre Suetake fields—who was eventually determined not to be a vassal but a mere villager—was able to write magnificent *hiragana* letters. The documents at Tōji bear this out. Thus, we know that by the latter half of the thirteenth century the writing of letters in *hiragana* had spread even to commoner women.

Around the middle of the fourteenth century, during the Northern and Southern Courts period, a dispute broke out in Tara estate over a couple of fields belonging to villagers. Three women, named Zennichi-nyō,

13. Tōji was the Kyoto headquarters of the Shingon sect, one of the two major esoteric sects of the Heian period. It continued to be a major factor in national politics and one of the area's largest landholders until the Warring States period.

Kannon-nyō, and Wakatsuru-nyō, were among the disputants in this case. These women's names are unlike the clan names described earlier. Instead, they are in the form of children's names. Since these women were involved in a suit concerning the complicated problems of villager ownership, it is possible that many village women were designated as proprietors of such fields by the fourteenth century. Thanks to documents like these, we know that by the fourteenth century women were publicly involved at every level of activity on the estates and imperial lands. Such involvement included appointment to official duties, in payment for which these women obtained and held land in their own names.

We can confirm this from another area of documentation: the family genealogies of the Shinto priests at the first and second shrines in Wakasa Province dating from the Northern and Southern Courts period. Most family genealogies show only the patriarchal line, but the Wakasa documents include the matriarchal line reproduced in great detail. In other words, these genealogies show *both* lines. This was not only true for the Muku clan, which served as Shinto priests, but for many warrior clans of Wakasa, including the Tada and Wakuri.

Perhaps matriliny was particularly strong in Wakasa. Then again, we know so much about Tara estate because so many of the documents showing us these women's activities have survived. Other estates do not have such detailed records, so we might not be able to immediately generalize from the case of Tara. But I believe that at least in western Japan we can infer that conditions in general were similar to those of Tara estate. On what grounds do I say this?

Since Takeuchi Rizō completed his monumental work, *Kamakura Documents*, we now have nearly all surviving documents from the Kamakura period in print. When we look at documents relating to the sale or transfer of fields and residential lands—particularly when we examine the names of the documents' suppliants and addressees—we find a rather high percentage of women's names. This has been statistically confirmed, so we can be sure that women elsewhere also held, transferred, and bought land. I must stress that this can be ascertained from legal records.

However, by the Muromachi period women's rights to ownership of land and property had been undermined. In the Edo period, women did not possess the formal right to own land, although their rights to movable property were maintained. Thus, if a woman's dowry was pawned by her husband, she could press for a divorce. Incidentally, the fact that women in the Edo period maintained their rights to movable property, such as their dowries provides, support for Frois's observations on property and divorce.

Regarding women's relationship to landownership in general, we have been able to confirm that women appear more frequently as the owners of or participants in the sale or transfer of residential land than in similar transactions involving agricultural land. For example, the temple of Daigoji currently possesses a late Kamakura period household register from a harbor near Tomaura (presently Toba) in Shima Province. An examination of this register shows that a great many of the house owners formally listed in the area were women.

In his book *Love and Subservience in the Middle Ages*, Hotate Michihisa has made some interesting observations concerning the close relationship women had to houses and residential land.[14] Hotate has made a careful study of the way in which *nurigome*—later know as *nando* or "storerooms"—of medieval houses were depicted in picture scrolls. Considered the most "sacred place" in the house, these rooms doubled as the parental bedroom and the storeroom for the family's valuables.

Hotate points out that it was women who managed this space. In historical documents, we often find women recorded as "the house woman" (*kajo*); their management of the most crucial spaces in the house may be the reason why they were also called "master of the house" (*ietoji*). In fact, from the Kamakura to the Northern and Southern Courts period, we find that many of the financiers popularly known as lenders (*kashiage*) or money-lenders (*dosō*) were women. This must have had something to do with their position in the home. The late Heian *Scroll of Diseases* (*Yamai no sōshi*) refers to a female moneylender who "lives near the Seventh Avenue bridge in a wealthy home and has much to eat." She is portrayed in the scroll as an enormously obese woman who cannot get around without assistants to help carry her bulk (fig. 52). Other examples abound. In the late Kamakura period, a female moneylender in the port of Obama in Wakasa Province was known as "the matron of the beach." Again, in Yamashiro Province, a woman known as the "woman of the Taira clan" dealt in loans as great as one hundred *kanmon*. I could go on listing women who owned warehouses, but all of this is simply to underscore the fact that the managers of warehouses were generally women.

---

14. Hotate Michihisa, *Chūsei no ai to jujun: Emaki no naka no nikutai* (Love and Subservience in the Middle Ages) (Tokyo: Heibonsha, 1986).

Figure 52. An obese female financier, from *The Scroll of Diseases*. Source: *Yamai no sōshi*, from the collection of the Fukuoka City Museum Matsukata Collection. Photograph taken by Shin'ichi Yamazaki.

This also has to do with the social views of money discussed in chapter seven. The first-harvest rice (*hatsuho*) and money offerings (*jōbun*) made to the native deities and Buddhas were deposited in storehouses. These items in turn were used as financial capital for loans on which interest could be charged. The fact that a major proportion of the managers of these sacred storehouses were women may well have had something to do with the particularities of women's sexual being itself. Hotate Michihisa points out that in the Middle Ages women were often given care of important documents and property, for example, in time of war. Placing these items in the care of women guaranteed a degree of safety. I believe that this, too, had something to do with the particularity of women's sex.[15]

Elsewhere, I have described this as the belief in "women's unconnectedness" that prevailed until the Northern and Southern Courts period. Women possessed powers beyond those of men, and these powers marked them as bound to the sacred. The fact that women were managers and messengers of peace in the midst of upheaval in the secular world points to this belief. Thus, Frois's claim that women would loan money to their husbands was not absurd. It is supported by the fact that women had their own property and engaged in financial activities.

The infamous Hino Tomiko (1440–96) has often been criticized for amassing a fortune by loaning large sums of money to *daimyō* while married to the Ashikaga shogun Yoshimasa. In fact, she was not an evil woman who overstepped her bounds; she may have been just the tip of the iceberg.

THE EMERGENCE OF WOMEN'S PROFESSIONAL GROUPS

The sacred character of women's sexual being was also linked to the issue of their vocations (*shokuno*). For example, we have evidence of itinerant women's groups from very early on. Female shamans, known as "walking *miko*," were active in ancient times. We can also find traces in ancient documents of the origins of courtesans, described as *asobime* (playgirls; fig. 53) or *ukareme* (wandering women).

One well-known ancient example of courtesans is from a record written by Ōtomo Tabibito upon becoming a major counselor in the imperial government. The records note that officials gathered to see him off on the occasion of his departure from Dazaifu, where he had been an officer, to take up his new post in the capital. Among them were a great many courtesans, who exchanged poems with the new major counselor. Judging from the later

---

15. Amino is referring to his discussion in chapter eight of the concept of pollution in ancient Japanese society. According to Amino, the archaic Japanese believed that a state of pollution was caused by a breach in the border between the present world and the "other world" (the world of the gods or the afterlife). Because women give birth, thereby ushering life from that other world into the present one, their very sexual being places them on that unstable boundary. As the term *pollution* suggests, this is a situation to be feared and avoided. But looked at from another angle, the ability to come into contact with that other world without being destroyed is what marks women as possessing a power beyond that of men.

Figure 53. Playgirls (*asobime*) at riverside, from *The Pictorial Biography of the Holy Man Hōnen*. Source: *Hōnen shōnin den'e*, from the collection of Chion'in. Photograph courtesy of Kyoto National Museum.

functions of courtesans, it seems possible that by this time they were already formally associated with the imperial offices at Dazaifu.

In chapter eight, I discussed courtesans in relation to nonhumans. Under the Ritsuryō system, various imperial offices had jurisdiction over different vocational groups; as this system decayed and the offices' functions changed, these vocational groups became independent. It is likely that courtesans followed the same path. The female officials and singers attached to the Women's Quarters of the Palace and the Bureau of Music formed the nucleus of this movement.

From around the tenth or eleventh century, courtesans began to form independent vocational groups under the leadership of a woman. The towns of Eguchi and Kanzaki were the best-known places for these women. In general, courtesans made ports and harbors their base, and in western Japan these women also traveled by boat. Unfortunately, we have no concrete evidence as to whether the many regional groups had any connections among themselves. It does appear, however, that these courtesan groups, organized as they were by a leader, had a seniority system much like that of the merchant and artisanal groups. Puppeteers (*kugutsu*), usually female, were probably organized along the same principles, and in eastern Japan female puppeteers and courtesans overlapped, often locating their bases in post towns. In the east, they appear to have made little use of boats.

At the capital, we see that, despite the decline in the Ritsuryō bureaucracy in the medieval period, courtesans still held a prominent place in the imperial court. In his early Kamakura text, *The Record of the Right*, Ninnaji Omuro explicitly stated that courtesans and female dancers (*shirabyoshi*) were permanently employed in the imperial place. Many aristocratic diaries also reveal that courtesan groups were placed under the jurisdiction of the Bureau of Music and the Office of Female Dancers and Musicians. They were managed by a special officer, organized in ranks, and summoned to participate in imperial rites and ceremonies.

Shirabyoshi dancers and puppeteers were employed under similar conditions. For example, we have clear evidence of an official post called "*shirabyoshi* service" in the early Kamakura period. Thus, courtesans, *shirabyoshi* dancers, and puppeteers were like shrine purveyors: female vocational groups in the direct service of the emperor and the deities. If shrine purveyors possessed the kind of authority I described in chapter seven, then the social position of these female professionals was far from low. Indeed, up until the Kamakura period we have clear evidence that courtesans, *shirabyoshi* dancers, and puppeteers were giving birth to children fathered by the emperor and nobles and that their poetic compositions were being included in imperially commissioned poetry collections. This is not at all what one would expect from a debased group.

This status was not limited to women who were in the business of entertainment. From the late Heian period, we have ample evidence of women who participated in significant numbers in such nonagricultural occupations as craftwork and religious performances, and who consequently became imperial or shrine purveyors. These tradeswomen may be traced back to at least the eighth century. The early Heian era text *Accounts of Miracles in Japan* presents images of women selling flowers and stories of women becoming wealthy by loaning offerings made to the deities (*suiko*).[16] One sermon deals with a woman known as Tanaka Mahito Hiromushinome who loaned

---

16. This is the *Nihon ryōiki*, a collection of 116 stories compiled by the priest Kyōkai around 822. Portions of the collection are available in English. See *Miraculous Stories from the Japanese Buddhist Tradition: The Nihon ryōiki of the Monk Kyōkai*, trans. and ed. Kyoko Motomochi Nakamura (Surrey: Curzon, 1997).

sake and rice as *suiko* in small boxes and measured payments of interest in large boxes. Another story tells of a woman who became wealthy on interest earned from loans she made with cash offerings that had been given to the Buddha at the temple of Daianji.

All in all, there is little doubt that there were a great many female merchants in Japanese society. For example, fishmongers were almost without exception women. Likewise, the vendors from Lake Biwa who sold fish in stalls in the Rokkakuchō section of Kyoto in the early Kamakura period, later becoming imperial purveyors, were all women. The cormorant fishers on the Katsura River near Kyoto, later know as the Katsura imperial purveyors, also included women known as Katsurame, who sold a fish called *ayu*. In addition, female imperial purveyors from Ohara and Onoyama, to the north of Kyoto, sold charcoal and firewood, while others sold *konnyaku*, vegetables, and shrine offerings. At Gion Shrine in Kyoto, female shrine purveyors sold silk and padded garments (*kosode*). All of these examples predate the Northern and Southern Courts period.

As mentioned above, the role of shrine, temple, and imperial purveyors as servants of the deities was clearly linked to their engagement in wide-ranging, intinerant, tax-exempt commerce. Many of these purveyors were women, which leads us back to my argument regarding the sacred character of females. As with the nonhumans, clothing was an important marker of sacred distinction. For example, Katsurame traveled wearing special hats, thereby signifying that they were distinct from women in general. This practice of signifying status difference by means of clothing was also an important element in women's ability to undertake long journeys. In sum, up until the Kamakura and Northern and Southern Courts period, itinerant female merchants were far more active than previously supposed.

THE EXCLUSION OF WOMEN FROM PUBLIC LIFE

So how do we reconcile these facts with the conventional wisdom that women were excluded from public life and lived under conditions of continual oppression?

In recent years, research in the history of the family has made great progress. Prior to these studies, the assumption was that since archaic times Japanese society had been a patriarchal system based on male superiority. However, scholars of women's history such as Takamure Itsue have countered this view, arguing that up until the Northern and Southern Courts period, Japanese society had strong tendencies toward matriarchy.

The most recent research suggests that lineage groups in archaic Japan did not take the form of clans. In other words, there were no clan groups, matrilineal or patrilineal, that operated on a system of marriage outside the clan and in which men and women within the same clan would be considered blood relatives and therefore subject to a marriage taboo. Under such a system, marriage to partners from other clans is necessary. Instead, one of the noteworthy characteristics of Japanese society since ancient times has been a loose attitude toward marriage with close relatives (consanguineous marriage). In the Japanese islands, there appears to have been a dual lineage kinship system under which membership was recognized through both the father's and mother's lines. As a result, the taboo on marriage to close relatives was very weak in Japanese society; the taboo on marriage to those who have the same family name, still strong in China and Korea, simply did not exist.[17] Ancient documents reveal that marriage between children of the same mother was taboo, although mention was made of cases of sibling love, for which the lovers suffered. We even have some examples in which they married. We also find many marriages between uncles and nieces, or aunts and nephews, prior to medieval times. Turning to the world of the imperial court, we find that consanguineous marriages occurred to a surprising degree up until the end of the Kamakura period, supporting the contention of Tsuda Sōkichi that the ancient *uji* were different from clans.[18] Tsuda contends that *uji* were actually political associations that were first formed among the ruling strata under the influence of the Chinese.

Under such conditions, women's and men's social positions would not be that unequal. The Chinese legal system was grafted onto this dual lineage situation. This is important because Chinese society developed a patriarchal structure early on, taking on a formal structure in which men were legally superior and patriliny and patriarchy were the rule. Formally and in legal framework, lineage relations were understood to descend from the father on a patrilineal principle.

17. In the Japanese text, Amino notes, "I myself am a product of a marriage between close relatives; my parents were cousins. My father's and mother's parents were also cousins. I have five brothers and sisters, and we sometimes note with relief that none of the potential negatives of consanguineous marriage have appeared in us."
18. *Uji* are conventionally translated as "clans," thus presenting the problem of translating the sentence as "ancient clans were different from clans." For this specific example I have left *uji* untranslated. See Tsuda Sōkichi, *Jōdai Nihon no shakai oyobi shisō* (Thought and Society in Ancient Japan) (Tokyo: Iwanami shoten, 1933).

When this system was grafted onto the society of the Japanese archipelago, the public obligations of commoners—taxes in kind and corvée labor taxes—were borne by men (adult males only), and the officials who determined policy were also strictly male. Meanwhile, women receded into the background, into the inner recesses of the palace in the case of the aristocracy. But this formal situation was vastly different from the actual conditions of society in Japan at that time, opening up a gap between appearance and reality.

The signs of friction produced by this gap are most easily found in those instances in which women made exceptional appearances in the formal system of the Ritsuryō state. For example, we occasionally find women designated as the head of the family in household registers. Similarly, in the eighth century there were a number of female emperors, which I believe was the result of the intervention of noblewomen of the inner palace in politics. While there are a variety of explanations for the appearance of these female emperors, I believe their rise to power was made possible by the fact that the formal gender principles of the Ritsuryō system—in which the public world was male and the inner, private world was female—had not yet completely permeated society. But that was only through the eighth century. At the beginning of the ninth, during the reign of Emperor Heizei, the Kusuko Incident led to significant changes.[19] Emperor Saga came to power as a result of this incident, establishing the dynasty of the Saga line. From that point on, the formal principles of the Ritsuryō system came to be more thoroughly implemented. After this incident, women in the inner palace were unable to publicly engage in politics; men came to the fore, and women receded into the background.

The fact that women seldom made an appearance in the official registries was also due to Ritsuryō ideology. For example, inspection reports were

19. The Kusuko Incident refers to a complicated series of events that occurred between 807 and 810. It began with the eradication of a branch of the Fujiwara clan when its scion was accused of conspiring against Emperor Heizei. The accusation came from a member of another branch of the Fujiwara clan, Fujiwara Nakanari, but it has been widely blamed on his sister, Fujiwara Kusuko, who held the highest post in the Office of the Women's Quarters of the imperial palace. Shortly after the plot, Emperor Heizei retired, citing health problems, and was succeeded by his younger brother, who became Emperor Saga. Nevertheless, Kusuko, who had the ear of Heizei, reportedly harbored ambitions to become empress. When Heizei recovered from his illness, she and others worked to get him reinstated to the throne. In response, Saga dismissed her from her post and demoted her brother, Nakanari. The following day Heizei and Kusuko left the capital and headed east to raise troops and retake the throne. Their uprising soon failed. Heizei took the tonsure and became a priest, Nakanari was executed, and Kusuko committed suicide.

The importance of this incident to Amino's argument is that its motive force was located in Kusuko and thus brought intense scrutiny to the political activities of women in the inner compiled for *shōen* estates and public lands until the eleventh century. These reports record the owner of each and every plot of agricultural land. When we consider the fact that women had the right to buy, sell, and transfer land, it should not be hard to find the names of women in the registries. However, apart from a limited number of exceptions, the owners in these registries were always listed as men.

Until recently, historians have taken the exclusive male presence in these registries at face value, concluding that Japanese society has been patriarchal since the archaic past. But exclusive male registration was in fact only a formal principle adopted as a result of the Ritsuryō system. As we saw in our discussion of the spread of writing, the world of Chinese characters (*kanji*) and public affairs was considered masculine. Yet the world of *hiragana* and the activities of women in the recesses of the private world were by no means insignificant. The truth is that writing had disseminated among women. Moreover, the unique women's literature that developed in the inner palace shows that women firmly maintained their own perspective. A hard and fast patriarchal system had merely been grafted onto a dual lineage society.

The transplanting of a patriarchal system into a society in which women's social status was by no means low produced conditions rare in world history. I believe this gap between formal appearance and actual practice was critical to the development of the women's literature of the Heian period. We cannot understand the genesis of this literature as long as we see it as having been produced in a context in which women were firmly under the control of a patriarchy. The same applies to understanding the meaning of the very public social activity earlier noted in women.

POLLUTION AND WOMEN

Just as women were being excluded from public life, a similar situation was developing in the Buddhist world. Takagi Yutaka claims that the first formal monks at the time of Buddhism's entry into Japan during the Nara period were probably women—nuns in other words.[20] In fact, there were many

---

palace. Saga's response, according to Amino, was to strive to make the formal principles of patriarchy the practical principle of governance.

20. Takagi Yutaka, *Bukkyōshi no naka no nyonin* (Women in the History of Buddhism) (Tokyo: Heibonsha, 1988).

female monks (*sōryo*) during the Nara period who had undergone formal ordination procedures.[21]

However, after the ninth century we find no female monks seated at the altar or receiving formal rites. By this time, women were completely excluded from the formal, state-recognized, Buddhist altar. This exclusion was closely connected to women's exclusion from politics and public society, but in the case of Buddhism it was argued that women's sexual being itself was polluted. As a result, the teachings of the Buddha came to be seen as being beyond the reach of women. Nevertheless, women's function as mothers, particularly as the mother of monks, was recognized as valuable; this was how Buddhism in the late Heian period classified women.

This relation between women and pollution presents us with the reason why discussions of women and nonhumans are inseparable. The so-called new Kamakura Buddhist sects that made the salvation of nonhumans a major goal also worked for the salvation of women as another group cast off by mainstream Buddhism. For example, the monks of the Ritsu sect were famous for their strenuous efforts toward the salvation of nonhumans. But Hosokawa Ryōichi has recently demonstrated that the Ritsu sect also built convents, thus providing a way for women to be welcomed into the religious association.[22] Unlike the Tendai and Shingon sects, which formally and systematically excluded women from receiving rites of ordination, the Ritsu sect made it possible for women to become monks (or nuns) by pledging before the Buddhas to observe the commandments. In this way, the monks of Ritsu turned what had previously been temples into convents. The Ji sect's founder, Ippen, also explicitly welcomed women into his group from the beginning. In the Ji sect, female monks took the character for the number one into their names, while male monks attached the first two characters of Amida Buddha's name, *ami*, to theirs. For example, Ji nuns with the character "one" in their names frequently appear in the fourteenth-century nobleman's diary known as *The Record of Moromori*. Likewise, *The Picture Scroll of the Holy Man Ippen* shows female and male monks traveling together, and the salvation of women is one

21. There is a specific term for nun (*ama*), but Amino insists on using the term *sōryo*, which is currently gendered male. This suggests that the English word *monk*, which is also gendered male, is not the best translation for the practice of this early period. In effect, Amino is talking about Buddhism before and during a gendered specialization of labor. As the following sentence suggests, *monk* (*sōryo*) was more a term of rank and accomplishment than gender.

22. Hosokawa Ryōichi, *Chūsei no risshū jiin to minshū* (Medieval Ritsu Sect Temples and the People) (Tokyo: Yoshikawa kōbunkan, 1987).

of its major themes. In essence, Ippen's Ji sect dealt with the issue of women's salvation in the same way that it dealt with the salvation of nonhumans. Another of the new Kamakura Buddhist sects, Shinran's True Pure Land sect, is famous for allowing monks to marry. This was unprecedented in the history of Buddhism in Japan. Meanwhile, the reader may recall my mention of the scene in *The Pictorial Biography of the Holy Man Hōnen* in which courtesans appeal to Hōnen for salvation. Without doubt, the salvation of women was a major issue for all of the new Buddhist sects of the Kamakura period.

But we can also read this trend against the grain, from the perspective of those who saw nonhumans and similar groups as highly polluted. *The Picture Book of Goblins* took Ippen to task by alleging that relations between men and women within his group were improper. On that point, *The Picture Book of Goblins* attacks Ippen's group as immoral.

Thus, there was a violent intellectual and religious confrontation over how to understand women's sexual difference, just as there was with the existence of nonhumans. It was a struggle, in other words, over the concept of pollution. This, in turn, was linked to the fundamental issue of evil. On the one hand, we have Shinran's doctrine of "the advantage of evil," in which the evil person is seen as the one most likely to be able to understand and embrace Amida Buddha's vow of unlimited compassion. On the other hand, the warrior government in Kamakura was engaged in the ever more urgent suppression of groups it had designated evil bandits (*akutō*).

Relatively speaking, women's social standing went into decline in the Muromachi and Warring States periods. Nevertheless, we still find many tradeswomen in the late-fifteenth-century picture scroll, *The Songs of Seventy-one Tradesmen* (fig. 54). Indeed, this scroll contains a surprising number of images of saleswomen and female artisans. But they appear in decreasing numbers in the popular "Scenes in and out of the Capital" (*Rakuchū rakugai*) paintings of the Momoyama period and the early Edo tradesmen's songs collections.

For example, fan selling had traditionally been a women's profession. We naturally find images of these women in *The Songs of Seventy-one Tradesmen* and even some images of them at their stands in the "Scenes in and out of the Capital." However, from the Edo period on, these jobs were often taken by men. Although this had been an artisanal field in which women were able to work in the public sphere, in the sixteenth and seventeenth centuries women were forced into the background even here.

Figure 54. Rice seller and bean seller, from *The Songs of Seventy-one Tradesmen*. Source: *Shichijû-Ichiban utaawase*, from the collection of the Tokyo National Museum.

THE DECLINE IN THE STATUS OF WOMEN

Discrimination against itinerant women and courtesans also came clearly to the fore during the Muromachi and Warring States periods. In one historical document from the Northern and Southern Courts period, we find that a courtesan house in Kyoto, called the Keiseiya[23] and run by the courtesans themselves, began to be popularly known as Hell's Corner. In the Muromachi period, we find increasing use of the epithets "hell's corner" and "worldly corner" in relation to courtesans. The discriminatory nuance in "hell's corner" is obvious. While the *worldly* of "worldly corner" comes from a cryptic

23. The term derives from an ancient Chinese story of a ruler who lost his kingdom because he was so enamored of a woman. It literally means "the house of the fallen castle." But *keisei* also came to serve as a euphemism for a beautiful woman. The name of the operation was thus understood more as "the house of beauties." That is the implication in Amino's description of the shift from Keiseiya to Hell's Corner.

word used in women's quarters, it, too, appears to have had a negative connotation. There is a great deal of corroborating evidence that courtesans came to be looked down upon during this period, and we have documents showing that men began to sell women into work as courtesans, or *keisei*, in the late Muromachi period.

This was entirely different from the way courtesans lived and worked prior to the Northern and Southern Courts period. In this change, we can discern the same kind of social stigmatization to which the nonhumans were subjected. Frois's observation that convents and nunneries were houses of prostitution may have been a reference to one extreme of the temples of the new Buddhist sects in this later period. The famous traveling Kumano Bikuni nuns were also said to be prostitutes.[24] The stigmatization directed at the Kumano Bikuni came to be directed more generally at traveling women of all kinds during late medieval times.

Things also changed for commoner women in the *shōen* estates. We still find a few examples of women involved in disputes over land ownership in the documents of Tara-no-shō in the Muromachi period, but conditions had changed dramatically compared to the situation before the Northern and Southern Courts era. It is not entirely clear why things changed so drastically, but after the fourteenth century women hardly ever appeared as the named parties to legal disputes in *shōen* and government states. The same was true in the world of the warriors. While the principle of male superiority went into decline when the Ritsuryō system broke down and women could once again make an unrestricted appearance in the secular world from the end of the Heian period into the Middle Ages, by the Muromachi period women's exclusion from center stage had been reinforced by a newly reconstituted patriarchal society.

It is likely that women were still quite active behind the scenes, but the principles of patriarchy took an even more thorough, systematic form in the Edo period. This is not to say that patriarchy had achieved total dominance. Once can still find Edo period documents that hint at more flexible conditions for women behind the scenes. For example, on the island of Manabe in Bitchū Province, we find what was, as far as we know, the only case of a village headwoman. Some have claimed that this was only possible

24. Kumano Bikuni were Edo period nuns who traveled to the famous Kumano Shrine (in present-day Wakayama Prefecture) to perform a series of rituals. On their return home, they sold amulets related to the Kumano Shrine. They also became known as singers of popular songs and as diviners. As Amino notes, they were eventually associated with prostitution.

Yamato Plain.[1] Through struggles and confrontations with the leaders of *uji* in northern Kyushu and the other regions of western Honshu, the Kinai *uji* gradually came to dominate most of western Japan and even made their power felt in the nearby eastern regions. As a whole, it was a society that was still "uncivilized," controlled by primitive animism and magical powers, as we can readily see in the large mounded tombs they built. We have been able to confirm a rank of *ōkimi* (great king), which later became that of the emperor, among the leaders of the Kinai region. But at the time many *uji* were still resisting, so the Kinai *uji* were unable to create a strong system. Conditions were not yet right for the system in itself to stably maintain the position of *ōkimi*.

Meanwhile, occasional exchanges took place across the sea and along the Korean Peninsula with societies on the Asian mainland. In China, there was already a well-established imperial system built upon a long history of civilization in the Sui and Tang dynasties. There was also movement, under the strong stimulus of the Chinese, toward the formation of government systems on the Korean Peninsula. It was within these tensions, in a society that was still extremely "soft," that the leaders of the Kinai *uji* began on their own initiative to adopt the "hard," rational, and civilized legal system of the Chinese mainland.[2]

There are many examples in world history of an uncivilized society adopting a civilized system under a variety of conditions. In the case of the Japanese islands, the choice of the *uji* leaders' decision to accept a world religion (Buddhism) and a governmental system based on Confucianism had an impact on the subsequent development of Japanese society that cannot be underestimated. It is also important that we recognize that this influence came to Japan via the sea, which functioned as both a transportation route and an obstacle to intercourse.

---

1. While *uji* is usually translated into English as "clan," Amino is apprehensive about the general tendency to understand it as referring to a familial organization in which all members are related by blood. In chapter nine, Amino took pains to argue that such was not the case in the archaic Japanese islands, that *uji* were instead largely political groupings that might be composed of several different bloodlines. So, while I have tried to minimize the number of Japanese words left in romanized form in this translation, *uji* appears to be one of those terms where leaving it in Japanese will help the reader distinguish the concept from the commonplace understanding of *clan*.

2. Amino used *hard* here to describe a society that has constructed or adopted a stable and encompassing system, while *soft* means a society without a strong enough system to predetermine and organize relationships of power.

The title of emperor for the ultimate head of the government was established in the process of forming the state. This is usually believed to have begun with the rule of Empress Suiko (592–628). Recently, however, the consensus among historians of the archaic Japanese islands is that the stable use of the title emperor as part of a state system began with the establishment of the Ritsuryō system and the Kiyomihara Codes around the time of Emperor Tenmu (673–86) or Empress Jitō (690–97).[3] Thus, if we are to view the past in strict accordance with this theory, we must state that there was no "Emperor" Yūryaku, Sushun, or even Tenji.[4] Although many textbooks still carelessly count emperors from the legendary Jinmu, or according to lineages developed in the Edo period, it is very important that we uphold a stricter standard.

Historians have traditionally dated the coining of the name Nihon (Japan) to around the reign of Empress Suiko. But recently it has been argued that it came into use around the time of Emperor Tenmu or Empress Jitō, when the Ritsuryō system was firmly established. In other words, it came into use in tandem with the title of emperor. This is an important point, for it forces us to recognize that there was no "Japan" or "Japanese people" before this time. In this sense, the people of the Jōmon and Yayoi periods were not Japanese, nor was Shōtoku Taishi.[5]

Whatever date we assign to the origin of the terms *tennō* and *Nihon*, the manner in which the still undeveloped society of the islands was linked to the highly civilized Chinese legal system determined the shape

3. The adoption of the Ritsuryō system was actually a drawn-out process of working and reworking legal and administrative codes. The very term *Ritsuryō* refers to laws and regulations for governmental organization (*ritsu*) and civil and criminal law (*ryō*). Overall, there were four sets of codes produced, each one superseding the previous set, which constituted the adoption of the Ritsuryō system: the Omi Codes of 668, the Kiyomihara Codes of 689, the Taihō Codes of 702, and Yōrō Codes of 718. The Yōrō Codes are the only set that is extant. See Karl F. Friday, *Hired Swords: The Rise of Private Warrior Power in Early Japan* (Stanford: Stanford University Press, 1992), 9.
4. Japanese imperial legend dates the beginning of the imperial line from Emperor Jinmu, grandson of the sun goddess Amaterasu, who supposedly reigned from 660 to 585 B.C. According to the legendary genealogy, the rulers Amino discounts as having been "emperors," in part because the title was not yet in use, were the twenty-first (Yūryaku, r. 457–79), the thirty-second (Sushun, r. 587–93), and the thirty-eighth (Tenji, r. 662–71). While most of those listed prior to Yūryaku in the imperial lineage are probably legendary, there is archaeological evidence for the existence of people who later generations knew as Yūryaku, Sushun, and Tenji.
5. Shōtoku Taishi (574–622), commonly called a "a prince of the imperial family," is credited in history and legend with important achievements in the creation of the imperial state as well as with the introduction of Buddhism to Japan. As Amino sees it, however, he lived before there was a "Japan," so it is incorrect to see him as a great Japanese. Since he predated the use of the title emperor, it is also anachronistic to call him a member of the imperial family.

and development of the state and society in Japan, including the emperors themselves, for centuries to come. To begin with, the Chinese legal system was built upon a foundation of Confucian ideology, particularly the theory of the Heavenly Mandate (the idea that the emperor attained his position through the will of Heaven) and the theory of dynastic succession (the idea that if the present emperor is not moral he will lose the Heavenly Mandate, which will then devolve upon a new imperial line; that is, a new dynastic succession would be established). When the nascent state in Japan adopted the Chinese legal system, however, attempts were made to exclude the ideas of the Heavenly Mandate and dynastic succession.

Yet the idea of the Heavenly Mandate could not be entirely erased, since the adoption of the legal system meant the acceptance of Confucianism. According to Hayakawa Shōhachi, documents from the period that record the oral statement of the emperor clearly contain ideas related to the theory of the Heavenly Mandate.[6] In one case discussed by Hayakawa, the Heavenly Mandate was used as a justification for explaining why the direct descendants of Tenmu and Jitō should become emperors, thereby excluding other people of "imperial" lineage from the succession. However, in the end it was the theory of Heavenly Descent that comprised the main pillar for supporting the imperial position. In other words, this was the theory that my generation, educated during World War II, was taught: that a descendant of the Sun Goddess came down from the Heavenly Sphere (Takamagahara) to the earth (the Japanese archipelago) and established the imperial seat. The Chinese theory of the Heavenly Mandate was only used to rationalize this myth.

But while the Chinese theory of the Heavenly Mandate was comparatively rational, the theory of Heavenly Descent was magico-religious in its characterization of imperial succession based on a lineage originating with the Sun Goddess. That is, it was supported by myths of an uncivilized society, myths that were utterly different from the universalistic and clearly conceptual premises of the Chinese conception of Heaven. Therefore, the theory of heavenly descent was distinctly different from the theory of the Heavenly Mandate.

6. This class of documents was known as *senmyō*. See Hayakawa Shōhachi, *Ritsuryō kokka* (The Ritsuryō State) (Tokyo: Shōgakkan, 1974).

But was the imperial lineage really unbroken, as the theory of Heavenly Descent would require? During his reign, Emperor Kanmu (r. 781–806), a descendant of the branch of the imperial clan founded by Emperor Tenji, massacred all the descendants of the Tenmu line, the bloodline that had ruled throughout the eighth century. This act can be read as the establishment of a new dynasty, and Emperor Kanmu further demonstrated the novelty of his rule by practicing Chinese-style imperial ceremonies unused by his predecessors. This was a way of claiming the legitimacy of his position in contrast to that of the Tenmu line. Even in this case, however, the theory of the Heavenly Mandate did not replace the theory of Heavenly Descent. After the ninth century, the Heavenly Manadate was no longer necessary to secure the legitimacy of the emperor. The theory would not reemerge until the imperial succession crisis in the early fourteenth century (I will return to this later).[7] The fact that the theory of the Heavenly Mandate was downplayed in the adoption of the Ritsuryō system is crucial to any account of the character of the early Japanese state.

The fact that the emperor had no family or *uji* name is also important for our understanding of the early Japanese state. This practice probably emerged around the time of the adoption of the title of emperor. As discussed earlier, archaic society in the Japanese islands was not organized along the lines of an exogamous clan system. Instead, before the establishment of the Ritsuryō system, *uji* were probably political groups established among the ruling strata. Before the Ritsuryō system, each of the *uji* possessed an *uji* name, such as Atai, Muraji, or Kimi. These names may also reflect a degree of influence from the Asian mainland, or they may have been respectful forms of address for the leaders of the *uji*.

Yoshida Takashi argues that the *ōkimi* had the *uji* name of Wa and that *ōkimi* referred to his or her rank before the adoption of the title of emperor.[8] According to the *History of the Sui*, an emissary from Wa came to the Sui court in China in 600. The emissary claimed that his king was of the Ame (this would correspond to the family name), his name was Tarashihiko, and his title was *ōkimi*. The way in which the emissary represented his king gives us a glimpse of the state of transition that led to the establishment of the title of emperor.

---

7. The crisis he refers to is the struggle between two imperial lineages that finally resulted in the split of the Northern and Southern Courts.
8. Yoshida Takashi, *Kodai kokka no ayumi* (The Path of the Archaic State) (Tokyo: Shōgakkan, 1988).

THE HISTORY OF THE NAME NIHON

Most likely, society in the archipelago was already loosely unified, with an *ōkimi* at the head of many *uji*, which were organized according to rank, even before the introduction of the Ritsuryō system. At that stage, the *ōkimi* probably had both *uji* and family names. But when the title of emperor was established, the emperor came to occupy a position in which he or she gave family names to all the people, beginning with the nobility (which was constituted by the heads of the most powerful *uji*). It is well known, for example, that Emperor Tenmu bestowed "many ranks" (*yakusa no kabane*) on the various *uji* and thus established an order of families. These *uji* names include such well-known *uji* as the Fujiwara, the Nakahara, the Minamoto, the Taira, and the Tachibana. At the same time, all commoners in the territories under the control of the state had *uji* and family names recorded in new family registries in imitation of the system on the Asian continent. This was done in such a way as to make it appear that the emperor had given them their names. But in the process of granting names the emperor lost both his *uji* and family names. In effect, there was no one who could grant an *uji* or family name to the emperor. This illustrates one way in which the emperor in Japan was distinct from the emperors and kings in China and Korea. It is possible for there to be a king without an *uji* or family name in a society without *uji* names, but there are very few examples of such in world history.

Jumping to the sixteenth century, we see that even Toyotomi Hideyoshi followed the ancient form of receiving his name from the emperor when he began to use the new name of Toyotomi. It became common in the Heian period to use place-names as surnames (so that almost all surnames today are place-names), but even those who fell in this category were given *uji* names when they were granted positions in the court by the emperor. For instance, during the Edo period a warlord named Satake received an honorary court position from the emperor. The documents announcing and recording his imperial office necessarily referred to him as possessing the *uji* name and court rank of Minamoto no Ason. That this practice continued even into the Edo period shows how deep its roots were.

These days, the search for family roots has become quite popular, but when surviving genealogies are used without being subjected to any critique of their historical production, everything seems to originate with the imperial family or the ancestral gods of the emperors. Genealogies have been structured in such a way that many Japanese naively came to believe that they were all descendants of the imperial family. But we must recognize that this structure originated in the establishment of the Ritsuryō state and the institutionalization of the imperial title.

These issues also have a bearing on the name of the country, Nihon, which is not a dynastic name, nor is it the name of the tribe of the person who established the dynasty. I believe that France, Prussia, and Deutschland are based on names of tribes rather than place-names like England. Apart from such dynastic names as Yuan, Ming, and Qing, it seems that the Chinese dynastic names derive from the name of the place where the founder of the dynasty was born. But Nihon is not that kind of name.

If we read the Chinese characters for Nihon with an alternative Japanese pronunciation, we have *hinomoto*, which means "the place where the sun rises." It means, in other words, the east. There have been many debates and much confusion since ancient times about the meaning of this name. If we depart from the proper reading of the characters themselves and read them as Yamato, as was occasionally done, then we have the place of origin of the dynasty itself (the Yamato Plain). But Yamato is usually written with other characters. Why the characters for Nihon came into use remains unclear, but in the last analysis the name is only comprehensible from the perspective of the Asian continent, as the eastern direction where the sun rises.

Therefore, we should begin by recognizing that this is a national name that is powerfully conscious of the Chinese empire on the Asian mainland. It also derives from the deep roots of sun worship in the archipelago, indicating that this was a country ruled by a "heavenly son" emperor whose mythical origins represented him as the child of the sun deity. This kind of national name was unusual even for countries in East Asia at the time.

In addition, since Nihon (alternatively read as *hinomoto*) also means "east," the location of its referent shifted over time. The ancient *Suwa daimyōjin engishi* (*The Origins of the Deity of Suwa*) records the existence of three groups, the Hinomoto-tō, the Watari-tō, and the Tōshi-tō, in the fourteenth century.[9] The fifteenth century saw the appearance of a person who dubbed himself the Great Generalissimo of Hinomoto. This man was

---

9. Hinomoto-tō can be rendered as the "Band of the East," the Watari-tō can be translated as the "Band of the Crossing," and the Tōshi-tō literally means "The Band of the Children of China." Suwa is in the southwestern region of the Kanto Plain, which was itself usually called "east."

the head of the Andō family, whose power base included the Oshima Peninsula of southern Hokkaido and the northernmost section of Honshu. Iwaki Hōga of Mutsu, who appears in the popular sixteenth-century sermon *Sanshō dayū* was also said to have taken the title Great Generalissimo of Hinomoto.[10] When in the sixteenth century the great merchants of Omi petitioned for the right to travel throughout all of Japan, from Kumano in the south to Sado in the north, their petition named the east Hinomoto (in this case, an alternate character was used for *moto*, one meaning "below"). For a final example, we may point to Toyotomi Hideyoshi's use of the term *hinomoto* to designate Oshū Province at the northern end of Honshu when he ordered the great land surveys.

In other words, the eastern border of the country of Nihon was generally called Hinomoto, or "the east," with the same characters being used to designate both the country, Nihon, and its eastern border, *hinomoto*. The location of *hinomoto* gradually shifted over time, moving further up the island of Honshu toward Hokkaido as population density increased in eastern regions such as Kanto.[11] Since Nihon was the name of the Ritsuryō state, which was centered in the Kinai region, Hokkaido, Tohoku, Okinawa, and southern Kyushu were not in it. If we remember that eastern Japan, which includes the Kanto Plain, was called Azuma-ebisu (Eastern Barbarians), we also have room to doubt whether the people there were considered "people of Nihon" (i.e., Japanese). As Tohoku and Kanto finally became part of the country of Nihon in the medieval era, *hinomoto* came to designate different areas, places outside of Nihon. As a result, there are different views of Nihon and the emperor in each region of the Japanese archipelago.

Since the point of departure for this discussion was the fact that the name of the emperor and the name of the country are deeply bound together, we may find that someday in the future, when the emperor is no longer seen as necessary, our descendants may reconsider whether or not to continue using the name "Nihon." What is important for the present is a recognition of the specific history that is tied to the name "Nihon."

---

10. Popular sermons (*sekkyō-bushi*), of which the *Sanshō dayū* was one of the most famous and enduring, were narrative tales set to musical or rhythmic accompaniment. The *Sanshō dayū* dates from the sixteenth century but has been given a second life in the modern era in children's stories and films.

11. While we tend to see northern Honshu as being "north," the Japanese spoke of Honshu as an island stretching west to east, so while not entirely accurate in geographical terms, the northern end of Honshu was imagined to be its eastern extremity.

TWO FACES OF THE EMPEROR

Under the Ritsuryō system, the emperor stood at the pinnacle of the council of the aristocracy, known as the Grand Council of State. This could be called Chinese-style imperial government. Under this system, the population was governed as "the people of the realm" (kōmin). The emperor stood at the pinnacle of the realm, and in a sense he was the essence of it.

On the other hand, the Ritsuryō state differed from its Chinese model in that its foundation was a system under which all paddy land was designated as state land and then formally distributed to the people. In turn, the government drew revenue from taxes on rice, craft production, and corvée labor. With its emphasis on distribution of paddy land, the state naturally placed rites related to the production of rice at the center of the system. The imperial accession rite, the daijōsai, for example, is in part a rice ritual.[12] On that point, then, the emperor clearly could be described as a king of rice.

But there is one other face to the emperor. As a system, it is not hard to understand the practice of making divine offerings, known in the Japanese islands as nie.[13] Originally, nie were offerings of the year's first produce made to the deities by people living on the coast and in the mountains. Prior to the Ritsuryō system, offerings of first produce were made to communal and uji leaders, who were placed in a position comparable to that of the deities. With the establishment of the Ritsuryō state, this kind of nie was given to the emperor, who then consumed the offerings. Native practice was thus institutionalized but not actually within the Ritsuryō system. Instead, we have recently come to understand that this practice existed outside the Ritsuryō system. Until recently, we have only found traces of this system of offerings in the text of the early-tenth-century Institutes of the Engi Period (Engishiki).[14] But in the excavation of Heijō Palace in the 1960s, archaeologists unearthed

12. The daijōsai is the accession ceremony that Japanese emperors perform upon taking the throne. Much of the ceremony remains secret, but it is clear that the soon to be emperor consumes rice and is supposedly imbued with the sacred spirit of his divine progenitors. There are two book-length, English-language studies on the ceremony, Robert S. Ellwood's, The Feast of Kingship: Accession Ceremonies in Ancient Japan (Tokyo: Sophia University, 1973); and Daniel Clarence Holtom, The Japanese Enthronement Ceremonies; With an Account of the Imperial Regalia (London: Kegan Paul International, 1996).
13. See chapter seven and Amino's description of offerings as financial capital (suiko) for further details.
14. The fifty-volume Engishiki was commissioned by Emperor Daigo in 905 and completed in 927. It was commissioned as a compilation of guidelines to and precedents for court etiquette and protocol, discussing and establishing the details of ceremonies, official duties, and so on.

a huge number of wooden placards related to *nie* offerings.[15] From this, we have come to understand that these offerings had considerable significance from the very beginning of the Ritsuryō system.

In receiving these offerings, the emperor was likened to a divinity. This fact clearly reveals that the emperor also possessed something of the character of "divine kingship," such as existed in the Incan empire or with certain African kings. In the Ritsuryō state, the people who actually made the offerings to the emperor as a divine king came to be directly associated with him by virtue of the fact that they shared the offerings with him. For this they acquired enormous special privileges. In the Nara period, people known literally as "slaves of the deities" (*kami no nuhi*) or "divine menials" (*shinsen*) possessed the same status as the earlier bearers of offerings.

The divine kingship role of the emperor, which differed from his role as the head of a Chinese-style imperial state, as stipulated in the Ritsuryō system, is most clearly seen in the system of offerings. Since the emperor had these two sides to him—as a primitive king and a civilized emperor—the Japanese Ritsuryō system was also characterized by a blend of "primitive" and "civilized" rituals and practices. In that sense, the *daijōsai* is not simply a rice festival; it also expresses the divine succession of an emperor who is considered to be a descendant of the gods.

What I am saying here is not so different from Inoue Mitsusada's argument about the dialectical relation between the Ritsuryō state and the clan system, or Ishimoda Shō's about the relationship between primary and secondary productive relations in the early state system.[16] However, I would express this situation in terms of the emperor's two faces—as the Ritsuryō Chinese-style emperor and the divine king of a primitive society.

THE SYSTEM OF TAXATION

The coexistence of the primitive and the civilized can also be observed in the Ritsuryō state's system of taxation. The Ritsuryō state exacted four kinds of

---

15. Heijō was the main imperial palace in Nara when it was the capital city. Among the most important archaeological findings was a large cache of wooden tablets with inscriptions that appear to have been used to mark offerings made to the emperor that originated in various regions.
16. Inoue Mitsusada, *Kodai kokka no kenkyū* (Studies in the Archaic State) (Tokyo: Iwanami shoten, 1985); Ishimoda Shō, *Nihon kodai kokkaron* (The Theory of the Archaic Japanese State) (Tokyo: Iwanami shoten, 1973).

taxes from the common people: rice (*sō*), labor (*yō*), crafts (*chō*), and miscellaneous (*zōyō*). According to the latest research, *sō* taxes were a type of first-harvest (*hatsuho*) offering that was not submitted to the capital but kept in provincial and country storehouses. In all likelihood, it was originally used as a kind of capital and loaned to people in the form of *suiko*, as discussed in chapter seven. In the fall, the rice was returned to the storehouses with interest. This interest rice, called "proper taxes" (*seizei*), covered regional government expenses. This tax system, then, was developed by systematizing customary practices based on the agricultural cycle, especially the production of rice. Thus, the tax system that took root in Japanese society took the form of "rice taxes."

Yō taxes were originally paid in the form of corvée labor, but they quickly became indistinguishable from *chō* taxes. *Chō* referred to local products, the specialties of every region. It was also called "tribute" (*mitsugi*), representing the institutionalization of submission rituals in which local specialties were offered to the local leader. *Chō* included a wide range of products, such as silk, cloth, salt, iron, and so on, but rice was almost never offered in this capacity. As had been the customary practice before the Ritsuryō state, commoners carried these goods directly to the capital at their own expense. Since rice was submitted as *sō* to provincial storehouses, the goods submitted as *yō* and *chō* supported the cost of operating the central government. The *zōyō* category, on the other hand, included labor for maintaining communal infrastructures, as well as military service.

My point is that these offerings were customary practices carried out at the local level, which were then institutionalized as offerings made to the state or the "realm" (*kō*). Over time, they gradually changed in name, becoming the *nengu* (yearly tribute), *kuji* (public matters), and *buyaku* (corvée labor) of the medieval era and the *nengu*, *komononari* (miscellaneous goods), and *kaeki* (corvée labor) of the early modern state. However, the way in which the customary practices of commoners were institutionalized as offerings to the state remained unchanged.

We can trace the long-term effects of this redirection of customary practice toward the state by observing the durability of the term *kō* (the realm, the public), which was used to identify the new state. Originally, "the realm" was pronounced *ōyake* and was written with the characters meaning "large house." This word referred to the residence and storehouses of the local leader, which were not, however, his private property. Instead, the word referred to the facilities of the community, with the leader as the representative of it. With the establishment of the Ritsyuryō state, the term *kuge* (literally, "house of the realm") came to be used in reference to the emperor. By the Middle Ages, the shogun was called *kubō* (the public person), and in the early modern era the shogunate and the regional lords were called *kōgi* (affairs of the realm). While the person or institution identified with the realm itself changed, the tax burdens established by the Ritsuryō state continued to be seen as service to the realm (whoever or whatever constituted it).

It is worth reminding ourselves that the realm was created by the Ritsuryō state but not through a simple imposition. By institutionalizing the existing customs of the commoners, the Ritsuryō system of taxation can be seen as having organized the subjective inclination of the commoners themselves. Of course, this institutionalization was backed up by force and resulted in a rather harsh expropriation of wealth. Yet it is important to note that the *particular form* of this first taxation system had a major impact on society in the Japanese islands for centuries thereafter.

Since the tax burden was established by systemizing the commoners' own customs, they tended to resist strenuously when the government deviated noticeably from prevailing forms. Over time, as commoner lives and forms of resistance changed, the tax system was also modified. But we should be careful to observe that in the many cases of commoner resistance to changes in the tax system, from ancient to early modern times, we almost never encounter an open appeal for the abolition of rice taxes. There were countless movements for the reduction of taxes but not for outright abolition. Of course, the commoners firmly believed that if the realm did not fulfill its proper function there was no need to submit yearly tribute. But that did not lead to an open call for the abolition of annual taxes since yearly tribute was not seen as a private payment for land but as a public tax.

In sum, this concept of the realm was the most enduring creation of the Ritsuryō state, in part because it was established upon a foundation of commoner freedom and creativity.[17] One further important result of this creation was that from the founding of the Ritsuryō state the emperor always stood at the pinnacle of the realm in one capacity or another.

---

17. By freedom and creativity Amino is suggesting that commoners had a kind of subjective investment in maintaining the system, since it made use of practices that were familiar. In a sense, Amino is assuming that those customary practices were developed by the people themselves and not simply forced upon them by earlier leaders. Readers may note that this is consistent with his general evaluation of ethnological data.

"THE SYSTEM OF PROFESSIONS":
THE PURVEYOR SYSTEM AND THE EMPEROR

At the beginning of the eighth century, when the Taihō Ritsuryō codes were written, the heads of the *uji* of the Kinai region (the future aristocracy of the imperial court) were still fairly powerful. Under the Ritsuryō system, the Daijōkan (the Grand Council of State, comparable to today's Cabinet), the highest department in the state, was composed of representatives of the most powerful *uji* in the Kinai region. This council could check the power of the emperor on a number of points. For example, without the agreement of the Grand Council of State, there could be no imperial succession. Moreover, it was the council that proposed the *daijōsai* ceremony as the rite of imperial succession. In this way, the *daijōsai* became something that the emperor could not perform of his own free will. The council's willingness to place restrictions on the emperor led to a great deal of tension between the two institutions.

The eighth century was a time of nearly continuous struggle and infighting over the imperial succession, both within the imperial family and among members of the aristocracy who constituted the Grand Council of State. Since the patriarchal principles of the Ritsuryō system had not yet thoroughly permeated society, this period also occasionally produced a female emperor. However, after Emperor Kanmu's coup against the Tenji line, and after Emperor Saga's suppression of the Heizei Insurrection led by Kusuko, it was no longer necessary to legitimize imperial rule using the ideology of the Heavenly Mandate.[18] With that question settled, friction between the emperor and the council also subsided. One can say, therefore, that it was during the ninth century that the imported legal system finally took root in the islands of Japan, at least in principle. In general, this was the period in which the culture of the Chinese Tang empire was in ascendance in Japan.

In the ninth century, however, the most powerful of the aristocratic *uji*—the Fujiwara—came to hold an overwhelming advantage in the noble councils. In addition, the emperor's pronouncements began to carry greater authority with the aristocracy. At the same time, government bureaus directly controlled by the emperor—the Sovereign's Private Office (Kuroudo

---

18. For details of the Heizei Insurrection, see chapter nine.

Dokoro) and the Imperial Police Agency (Kebiishi)—assumed much of the power that had previously been held by other departments of the government. As a related development, a system began to develop in the ninth century whereby particular *uji* possessed hereditary control of particular official posts or departments in the government. By the late tenth century, this had become the norm.[19] This had been common in western Japan (eastern Japan may have been different) before the formation of the Ritsuryō state, since particular functions had been hereditarily performed by particular kinship groups.[20] What became the norm by the late tenth century was a system that had in fact existed prior to the establishment of the Ritsuryō. In fact, we see the same kind of principle at work in the *iemoto* system of the Edo period.[21]

In other words, what we see is a historical tendency toward what I call a system of professions, in which particular functions were hereditarily controlled by particular *uji*. By the eleventh century, the imperial government was running entirely on such a contract system. To give a few concrete examples, the Bureau of Housekeeping (Kamonryō) was the agency in charge of cleaning and maintaining facilities for rites in the imperial palace. The head of this agency was always a member of the Nakahara *uji*. The top officer of the Grand Council of State's secretariat was always a member of the Ozuki *uji*, a lineage known for its possession of advanced mathematical and accounting skills. The Bureau of Divination was managed by the Daoist adepts of the Abe, and the Bureau of Medicine benefited from the superior medical skills of the Tanba and the Wake *uji*. As this system took hold, the relative statuses of the noble families became fixed.

The descendants of Fujiwara no Michinaga of the northern house of the Fujiwara clan held such a tight monopoly on the posts of regent (*sesshō*) and chief imperial adviser (*kanpaku*) that their line became known as the

19. This has been concretely demonstrated by Satō Shin'ichi in his famous study *Nihon no chūsei kokka* (The Medieval Japanese State) (Tokyo: Iwanami shoten, 1983).
20. Over time these functions had tended to become concentrated in the hands of particular families within these *uji*. The vast Fujiwara *uji* is a good example of this.
21. The *iemoto* system is a kinship-style procedure for the transmission and licensing of technical skills. In a typical case, a particular school of an art form (tea, acting, painting, and so on) is controlled by a group with a leader who is invested with the authority and status of a father (the head of the "family," or *ie*). The leader's control of the group aims to guarantee a certain consistency and standard of practice. Acquisition of skills involves submission to the group, through its leader, in a form of familial relation. Leadership of the group is understood to be hereditary, passing from father to son, but in practice it was not at all uncommon for a teacher to adopt the most talented student as his son so that leadership of the group would be constituted by both familial authority (through adoption) and skill.

Sekkan (regent-advisor) house.[22] The families that inherited the posts of grand counselor, minister of state, and general were known as the Seika (pure and brilliant) families. The Kanjōji line of the Fujiwara supplied officials for the secretariat, while members of certain other families could only rise as far as major counselor (essentially a second-in-command position). Therefore, even among the nobility official function was determined by family, not by talent. Moreover, working functionaries (as opposed to titular heads) also came to inherit their positions. This trend began in the ninth century, was common by the tenth, and was dominant by the eleventh.

At the top of this system of professions was the emperor. To put it in modern terminology, we might say that the emperor succeeded by heredity to the office of the emperor. That is, the functions that should be performed by an emperor could only be fulfilled by a member of the imperial family. It appears that on the whole this system contributed to a stable imperial succession. At the same time, however, it effected a real separation between the person who performed the functions of the emperor and the emperor himself. That is, the functions of the emperor came to be carried out by the Sekkan (regent-adviser) house as the representative of the emperor. In the latter half of the Heian era, retired emperors seized the practical functions of the emperor from the Sekkan family.

As a result, the government could continue to operate even if the emperor himself was just an infant. The same process occurred in the government agencies. A post, such as the head of the Bureau of Housekeeping, might formally be held by a son, but it might well be the father, who was accustomed to the job, who ran the office. This kind of situation was common. Therefore, the medieval relationship between the emperor and the retired emperor—the man who actually fulfilled the functions of the emperor—was based on a well-practiced norm and was not at all an anomaly.

The imperial state was supported by a land tax system that by the eleventh century had taken form as a system of *shōen* estates and imperial lands. Until recently, historians believed that *shōen* estates were similar to

22. By the early Heian period, the Fujiwara was an enormous *uji*—too large to function along the lines of *uji* self-interest—with which many readers may be familiar. For the sake of more specific identification, the Fujiwara *uji* was split into several layers of subdivision. The northern branch, to which Amino refers, was one of the higher-level subdivisions. That is why Amino specifies the descendants of Michinaga in the northern branch, a distinction that would rule out most members of that branch. For an explanation of *uji* and *uji* names, see Jeffrey Mass, "Identity, Personal Names, and Kamakura Society," in *Antiquity and Anachronism in Japanese History* (Stanford: Stanford University Press, 1992).

European manors; the term *shōen system* was coined to correspond with the European historical term *manorial system*. But the term *shōen*/imperial lands system was more appropriate for at least two reasons. First, while European manors were largely independent fiefs, the *shōen* in Japan were more along the lines of an administrative unit. Second, the imperial lands controlled by provincial governors had approximately the same total area as did the *shōen* estates. In any case, the hereditary system of professions I have described for the nobility and the central government permeated the land system as well. The administration of both *shōen* and imperial lands was carried out through various levels of offices such as the office of the owner (*ryōke shiki*), the office of the manager (*azukarisho shiki*), and the office of the lieutenant governor (*geshi shiki*), all of which were managed through subcontractors. In other words, it followed the model of the system of professions as a multilayered contracting system. If we return to my metaphor of the "two faces of the emperor," this whole system was an extension of the emperor as pinnacle of the Ritsuryō system. In the medieval era, the power to establish or revoke *shōen* estates was held by the Office of the Retired Emperor, that is, the person who controlled the office of the emperor. It was this "ruler of Heaven" who controlled the actual functions of the government.

The system of taxation under the *shōen*/imperial lands system was of course based on the rice paddy. It relied on the fact that the common people (designated "the many names") paid service, or tribute, to the realm in the form of rice, labor, and specialty products. Yet even as the *shōen*/imperial lands system was coming into being, it was paralleled by another system of administration for nonagricultural peoples, for such tradespeople as shrine and imperial purveyors. The majority of tradespeople, though not all, were shrine or imperial purveyors. As I mentioned earlier, shrine, temple, and imperial purveyors were called "slaves" and were in direct service to the deities and the emperor. Their institutionalization by the state was realized in the shrine and imperial purveyor system discussed in chapter eight.

In this parallel system, the emperor functioned in the other aspect of his position, as a sacred being. That is, this system was formed as an extension of the ancient practice of tribute being offered to the emperor by specially designated tribute bearers. Therefore, here as well the emperor was at the pinnacle of a system—just as he was at the top of the government's subcontracting system for official posts. The emperorship entered the medieval period with these two functions still intact.

BUDDHISM AND THE EMPEROR

One of the greatest changes effected by the establishment of the Ritsuryō state was brought about by the official promotion of Buddhism. The first of the Ritsuryō codes, the Yōrō Codes, created an institution called the Sōjō (Monks' Organization) and a special set of laws by means of which the government could rigidly control Buddhist temples and their inhabitants. However, with the construction of the Great Buddha in Nara,[23] the relation between the state and Buddhism changed dramatically, and the state became less able to control the Buddhist institutions. By the ninth century, the positions of relative power had been reversed such that Buddhist rituals, particularly those of the Tendai and Shingon sects, became firmly insinuated into the ceremonial practices of the imperial palace. In the tenth century, large Buddhist temples with connections to Shinto shrines began to wield a great deal of power. The changes were so sweeping that the emperor himself came to be called a "slave of the Buddhas."

How did the emperor and the native shrines react to this rise in Buddhist power? Recent studies have clearly shown that the authority of the emperor did not depend on a relationship with the native deities alone. From the beginning, imperial authority was also sustained by a deep, continuous relationship with Buddhism. In fact, apart from two or three exceptions, all emperors—from the first to be known as such (Empress Jitō, 690–97) to those of the Edo period—were cremated in accordance with Buddhist practice. From Emperor Shōmu (724–49) on, all had Buddhist funerals and were buried in Buddhist temples, not interred in a funerary mound as was common during the period immediately preceding the founding of the Ritsuryō state. The type of funeral we saw in 1989 when Emperor Shōwa died was actually invented for Emperor Meiji's funeral in the early twentieth century. Since modern imperial funeral rites were invented as a faux "revival" of funerals from the pre-Ritsuryō period, a time when the title of emperor had not yet come into use, it makes no sense to call this "an ancient tradition."

---

23. Construction of Tōdaiji and its enormous statue of the Buddha was begun in 745 at the command of Emperor Shōmu and completed in 751–52. For Amino, the scale of investment in time, money, and administrative energy in the construction of Tōdaiji marks a turning point in the relation between the state and Buddhism in Japan. For a good description of the importance of Tōdaiji in the early Ritsuryō state, see William H. Coaldrake's study of Japanese architecture, *Architecture and Authority in Japan* (London: Routledge, 1996), chap. 3.

While the links between the emperor and Buddhism are not fully understood, we have recently discovered that in the latter half of the thirteenth century the emperor performed an esoteric Buddhist baptismal rite (the *kanjō* rite) at his accession ceremonies.[24] We have verified that this esoteric ritual was performed at the accession of Emperor Fushimi (1288–98), and it is possible that something similar took place earlier. In any case, the strong link between Buddhist-style rituals and the emperor is worth renewed consideration. Reevaluating the significance of this relationship is likely to highlight important transformations in the existence of the emperor after the ninth century.

MULTIPLE STATES IN THE JAPANESE ARCHIPELAGO

In the ninth century, the power of the state, which was centered in the Kinai region and known as Nihon, became more and more precarious. Not only did its authority *not* extend to Hokkaido and Okinawa, but there are even some doubts as to how far it extended to eastern Honshu. The separation of eastern Japan from the ruling authority of the emperor had begun by the tenth century. The event that clearly signaled the beginning of this trend was the Tengyō Disturbance of the early tenth century.

The Tengyō Disturbance was actually two uprisings, one led by Taira no Masakado and the other by Fujiwara no Sumitomo.[25] Sumitomo is remembered for having led a rebellion of pirates in the western Inland Sea region, but we believe that he also forged an alliance with pirates from the kingdom of Silla on the southern end of the Korean Peninsula. In the end, he was unable to establish an independent state. Masakado, on the other hand, drove off the imperially appointed provincial governors of eight eastern provinces

24. The *kanjō* rite is a kind of Buddhist baptismal ceremony involving the application of water or oil to the forehead. The fact that a Buddhist rite is part of imperial succession rituals is significant for Amino because it suggests how much the emperor, as the post is historically known, was dependent upon the new system imported from China. This means that despite the continuation of what Amino calls "the magical face of the emperor," the emperorship never was a pure link to an unadulterated Japanese past.

25. As is often the case in Japanese history, the incidents that comprised the Tengyō Disturbance received their name from the years in which they took place, the Tengyō era (937–48). Fujiwara no Sumitomo's uprising was centered in the western region of the Inland Sea and was quickly suppressed in 941. Taira no Masakado's uprising was centered in the Kanto region in Shimōsa Province. Masakado captured the provincial headquarters of Shimōsa, Shimotsuke, Musashi, Izu, Sagami, Kōzuke, Kazusa, and Awa before his defeat in early 940.

and established a new state (even though it only lasted about three months). Masakado named himself the "new emperor" (*shinnō*), a title he claimed to have received from the Hachiman deity, Sugawara no Michizane.[26] He located his capital on the Shimōsa Peninsula, added the province of Izu to the traditional seven provinces of Kanto, and appointed his own provincial governors. As short-lived as it was, Masakado established a kingdom in Kanto that was completely separate from the monarchy in Kyoto. Indeed, its establishment had a decisive impact on the archipelago's subsequent history, one that long survived its brief existence. The "eastern provinces" were reclaimed by the Kyoto monarchy after Masakado's defeat, but from then on powerful local leaders operated as independent contractors in the delivery of goods to the capital. In other words, a system developed that largely bypassed the local organs of imperial rule that had been established elsewhere. Therefore, it is historically inaccurate to claim that there was just one state in the Japanese archipelago. It would be more accurate to recognize the existence of (and will to establish) multiple sovereign states in the islands.

Around the time of Sumitomo and Masakado's uprisings, the Abe, the Kiyohara, and finally the Oshū Fujiwara *uji* rose as independent powers in northern Honshu. Such was their independence of action that it is possible to view these *uji* as constituting a succession of states. Finally, at the end of the twelfth century, these states were superseded by the establishment of the Kamakura shogunate, which placed under its jurisdiction everything east of the provinces of Mikawa, Shinano, and Echigo.

Scholars are deeply divided in their evaluations of the Kamakura shogunate. One school of thought holds that the Kamakura shogunate was in fact an independent state and should thus be recognized as constituting a form of the medieval state in addition to the model of the imperial government in Kyoto. Another school holds that it was essentially a branch office of the monarchy in Kyoto that undertook military functions and was thus nothing more than another power center. In general, those scholars born in Tokyo (the east) hold with the first school, while scholars from Kyoto favor

26. Sugawara no Michizane (845–903) was an apt choice for Masakado for he was an important counselor in the late-ninth-century court whose efforts to curtail Fujiwara dominance led to his exile from Kyoto in 901. His death in exile in 903 was followed by a series of calamities in the capital, which were blamed on his wrath at having been wrongly accused. In order to appease his vengeful spirit, he was enshrined as the deity Tenman Tenjin. Not only was his association with Hachiman, the deity of war, propitious for an uprising, but his reputation for having been wronged by the court would have had an obvious appeal to the rebels.

the second. Scholars from Tohoku are allies of the scholars from the west, while those from Kyushu are allies of scholars in the east, a breakdown that reflects old regional animosities.[27]

To measure sovereignty, we should examine the functions of medieval government. On this basis, I believe the evidence suggests that there were two medieval states. During the Kamakura period, judgments in disputes over the boundaries between provinces were issued by two authorities since disputes at the provincial borders exceeded the authority of governors and could only be decided by an authority with greater power. If the dispute was in the east, the Kamakura shogunate handed down the decision; if the dispute was in the west, the decision came from the imperial government. Military and civilian governors in the provinces had the authority to adjudicate cases within provincial borders. The same regional breakdown was applicable in the case of barrier gates (a kind of checkpoint and tollbooth). The authority to establish a barrier on transportation routes (or to pass through a barrier unimpeded) was divided between eastern and western Japan, held by the political body with the highest authority in that region. In the east, this was the shogun, while in the west it was the emperor. The same could even be said for laws. Laws issued by the Kamakura shogunate after the Jōei Formulary (1232) are known as the New Kanto System.[28] Historians refer to the laws issued by the imperial government after 1232 as the New System for Noble Houses. In other words, both juridical and legislative authority was split.

27. The dispute over the location of Yamatai, the ancient country depicted in the fifth-century Chinese text *History of the Latter Han Dynasty*, also tends to reflect such regional identifications. The oldest recorded reference to the Japanese islands is found in another Chinese text, *The History of the Wei Dynasty*, which was compiled in 280 A.D. by Chen Shou, in a section on "Eastern Barbarians." The text refers to the people of Wa, composed of several countries, the most powerful of which was called Yamatai. The controversy over the location of Yamatai arose for several reasons. The text gives directions which, if followed precisely, would put one in the middle of the ocean south of Kyushu. Several of the listed stops along the way are clearly in Kyushu, but the name of the country resembles the name of the plain where the imperial family rose to prominence, Yamato. For those interested in establishing the antiquity of the imperial family, it is important that Yamatai refer to Yamato, thus demonstrating its preeminence from the beginning. Scholars from Kyushu tend to believe that Yamatai was located there, and they are supported by scholars from Tokyo. Kyoto scholars make the argument that Yamatai was located in Kinai. These are examples of how even today regional history affects us unconsciously. For a detailed discussion of the historical question and controversy, see William Wayne Farris, "The Lost Realm of Yamatai," in *Sacred Texts and Buried Treasures: Issues in the Historical Archaeology of Ancient Japan* (Honolulu: University of Hawai'i Press, 1998).

28. The Jōei Formulary (*Jōei shikimoku*) was a set of legal principles articulated by the Kamakura shogunate in 1232 that many historians assess as having represented a permanent recognition of dual polity in Japan, a split between the imperial court and the Kamakura shogunate. As Jeffrey Mass notes, it resulted not in a settlement of legal questions, but in a rapid increase in legislation dictat-

While there were points of contact between the two institutions, this division of authority implies that the Kamakura shogunate was a state. However, their differences went beyond questions of administrative jurisdiction. The Kamakura shogunate adopted organizing principles different from those of the imperial government. In Kamakura, it was the secular relationship between lord and vassal that supported the state, with the system of professions and the *shōen*/imperial lands system having little effect. This, at least, is how historians in eastern Japan see it.

If we take the perspective of scholars from the Kyoto region, however, the most salient point is that the shogun was appointed by the emperor. Moreover, the Kamakura shogunate measured time according to the year names of the imperial government, while its system of offices was incorporated as a part of the imperial government's system of offices. Kyoto scholars also point out that the Kamakura shogunate did not designate a new name for its "country."

Naturally, other arguments are made, but the points about year names, the system of officials, and the name of the country are extremely important. These are clearly indispensable items for a state. In fact, a number of times the shogunate used a different year name from that being used at the imperial court, even though there are no cases of it determining a year name on its own. The argument for overlap in official posts also has serious limitations. For example, even when Minamoto no Sanetomo, the third shogun of the Kamakura shogunate, accepted the post of minister of the right in the imperial government, he did not attend the nobles' councils. Likewise, when the shogunal regent became minister of the right quarter of Kyoto, he had nothing to do with the administration of the city. Although appointments to posts in the imperial government still had significance in the Kamakura period, the imperial offices granted to members of the shogunate were given in name only. As for the question of an independent name, Kanto, the general name of the region in which the shogunate was located, clearly functioned as a form of national name in distinguishing the shogunate from the imperial court.

ing how disputes of property and inheritance were to be settled. As such, it can be seen as a kind of declaration of independence, even as it acknowledged an authority (imperial) outside itself. For a translation of the Jōei Formulary, see John Carey Hall, "Japanese Feudal Laws: The Hojo Code of Judicature," *Transactions of the Asiatic Society of Japan* 334 (1906). For a fuller discussion of their significance, see Jeffrey Mass, *The Development of Kamakura Rule, 1180–1250* (Stanford: Stanford University Press, 1979), chapters four and five.

Thus, both sides have some basis for pressing their claims. While there is still much to learn, it is important to remember that the authority of the emperor did not extend to the east. In fact, after the Mongol invasion, the authority of the emperor did not even extend to Kyushu. Moreover, the right to conduct foreign relations was held by the shogunate. Finally, after the thirteenth century, succession to the office of the emperor was carried out according to the will of the shogunate, not the will of the imperial family or the Grand Council of State.

THE CRISIS OF THE IMPERIAL FAMILY

The reader should be aware that an important element of postwar historiography in Japan has been the reaction against prewar and wartime imperial-centered history. In that context, postwar history textbooks have almost entirely limited their discussion of the Kamakura period to the history of the warriors as a way of downgrading the importance of the emperor and his government. While this emphasis on local leaders and the functions fulfilled by warriors made an important contribution to resisting imperial history, one unexpected result was that the history of the imperial court and the nobility since the Kamakura period has been almost left blank.

Fortunately, progress is being made in filling in the gaps. Nevertheless, the textbooks still have nothing to say about the Kamakura era emperors after Emperor Go-Toba's loss to the shogunate in the Jōkyū Disturbance.[29] This silence notwithstanding, the emperor and the retired sovereign clearly wielded power in the imperial government and its effective territory during the Kamakura period. The rule of the regents or retired sovereigns, from the late Heian through the Kamakura periods, is usually portrayed as a time when the emperor was powerless. But I believe this view is an outright mistake. There were times when the imperial government was controlled by the

29. In greatly simplified terms, the Jōkyū Disturbance was a struggle between the imperial court in Kyoto, led by Emperor Go-Toba, and the Kamakura shogunate. Go-Toba declared war on the shogunate in 1221 and was militarily defeated one month later. The postwar settlement gave the shogunate greater rights to intervene in Kyoto court politics, which is why Amino suggests that the textbooks slight the emperors who ruled between Go-Toba (who initiated and lost the war) and Go-Daigo, who began the conflict that led to the fall of the shogunate. He insists that the claim that the emperors were powerless is a drastic misunderstanding of the relations between the shogunate and the court. It is, in other words, a mistaken equivalence of power with authority, categories that Amino argues should be considered separately.

emperor himself (*tennō shinsei*), and in the world of the nobility the person who controlled the office of the emperor still carried a great deal of weight.

As mentioned above, the imperial government issued its own set of laws, known to historians as the New System for Noble Houses, from the Kamakura to the Northern and Southern Courts period. These laws were not meaningless, for even after the imperial defeat in the Jōkyū Disturbance, the court still held actual power in western Honshu. It is precisely because the imperial court *still had power* that we can follow the trail of the shogunate's gradual encroachment on it. We should be careful not to equate the trail with the outcome. But the trail does point to something important: the imperial system entered a period of severe crisis from the late thirteenth to the fourteenth centuries, as its ruling authority and the right to determine the office of the emperor were gradually usurped by the shogunate.

One element in this story was of course the strong external pressure brought to bear on the "monarchy of the west" (the imperial court) by the "monarchy of the east" (the shogunate). But the decline in imperial power was not just due to external pressure. As the court faced pressure from the shogunate, its system for controlling the large temples and shrines broke down, and aristocratic families began to fracture. These internal crises eventually led to a major division within the imperial family, which manifested itself in the tense confrontation between the Daikakuji and Jimyōin lines of emperors.[30]

Emperor Fushimi, of the Jimyōin line, and Emperor Kameyama, of the Daikakuji line, had both made such strong efforts at the end of the thirteenth century to revive imperial rule that they were suspected by the shogunate of plotting an insurrection against shogunal authority. By the first decades of the fourteenth century, the sense of crisis pervading the imperial family led Go-Daigo (of the Daikakuji line) and his contemporary Jimyōin rival, the retired sovereign Hanazono, to argue that virtue, not simply lineage, should be the foundation of imperial succession. They argued that if the

---

30. The division in the imperial family arose from a series of succession disputes in the post-Jōkyū era. The shogunate exercised its right to determine the imperial succession, won in the Jōkyū Disturbance, by demanding the enthronement of Emperor Fushimi in 1297, against the wishes of the dominant retired sovereign Kameyama. A split within the imperial family ensued in which rival parties, centered on Emperor Kameyama (the Daikakuji line) and his nephew Emperor Fushimi (the Jimyōin line), struggled to place their own descendants on the throne. The shogunate's solution to the struggles was to institute a system of alternate succession, from Jimyōin to Daikakuji and back, with reigns of limited extension. It was Emperor Go-Daigo's attempt to end this system that sparked the civil war that toppled the Kamakura shogunate.

emperor lacked virtue, chaos would ensue and the monarchy would collapse. A persuasive argument could thus be made that Go-Daigo and Hanazono had thereby taken up the theory of Dynastic Succession, which had been dropped from the Chinese model of the emperor following the adoption of the Ritsuryō system. Go-Daigo clearly gambled on a "great insurrection" as a means of overcoming the crisis. In the end, he succeeded in toppling the Kamakura shogunate but not in restoring exclusive imperial rule.

However keenly the members of the imperial family may have felt this sense of crisis, there was a deeper pattern of social change underlying these events. The salient condition here was the continual and decisive decline in the "sacredness" of imperial authority, an authority that itself had been staked to the power of the deities (both native and Buddhist).

As I argued in chapter eight, I believe that around this time a major transformation took place in the relationship between nature and human society that shook the authority of the deities. The imperial family was forced to search for new support when its relationship with the deities no longer sufficed. That is why emperors Hanazono and Go-Daigo drew close to the Zen and Ritsu monks who rose with the tide of the new Kamakura Buddhist sects. Monks like Monkan (of the Ritsu sect but with deep roots in the esoteric Shingon sect) were for this reason well situated to gain imperial confidence and influence. Hanazono and Go-Daigo's interest in Song Neo-Confucianism had similar motivations, although Go-Daigo was more decisive in this matter. Both men attempted to mobilize new religions and new trends in foreign thought, under imperial leadership, to overcome the crisis in imperial authority.

But Go-Daigo did not limit himself to a search for a new religious authority. In the secular sphere, he mobilized shrine and imperial purveyors—as well as nonhumans—into a military force. He sought control of commercial forces and planned to issue his own money. He even attempted to create a new framework for governing all the *shōen* estates and imperial lands in the country, which was later institutionalized by the Muromachi shogunate. The new system taxed fief income (from yearly tribute) at a rate of 5 percent, while corvée labor was to be mobilized at a rate of one day for every ten *chō* of paddy land. Go-Daigo also sought to make the district a far more important administrative unit.[31]

---

31. For a detailed English-language study of Go-Daigo's career, see Andrew Edmund Goble, *Kemmu: Go-Daigo's Revolution* (Cambridge: Harvard University Press, 1996).

Go-Daigo thus groped his way toward a new system—centered upon an emperor with a new source of authority—that would completely transform society. Upon his failure, the imperial family fell into even more dire straits. The imperial clan split into a Southern Court in Yoshino that opposed the new Muromachi shogunate and a Northern Court in Kyoto that was supported by it. The Southern Court reached its low ebb when in 1348 it was driven out of its stronghold in Yoshino by Kō no Moronao, leader of the shogunal forces. Had Kō or the shogunate pursued the Sourthern Court until it was destroyed, it is likely that the imperial family would have disappeared. But since the shogunate failed to do that, the 1392 agreement to reunify the imperial clan after fifty-six years of fighting revived its chances of survival.

The criticism of the military class that emerged in the latter years of the Edo period could not look to an imperial family descended solely from the Northern Court as an alternative authority to the shogunates of the warriors. Because the Northern Court had collaborated with the warrior clans, it could not establish a truly independent existence. Only the Southern Court, with its legitimate history of resistance, could provide the emperor with the mantle of authority in a struggle against the military houses. That is why Emperor Meiji, himself a descendant of the Northern Court, acknowledged the legitimacy of the Southern Court when the question of historical legitimacy arose in the modern era.

But we may also approach this problem from another direction. We might ask why it was that the Muromachi shogunate was unable to destroy the Southern Court. For some reason, Kō no Moronao was held back. Therein lies another problem for us to consider.

AUTHORITY AND POWER

After the events that initiated the Northern and Southern Courts period, the next crisis faced by the imperial family came in the time of Ashikago Yoshimitsu, the third shogun of the Muromachi shogunate. In the early 1370s Prince Kaneyoshi, a son of Go-Daigo and the commander of the Southern Court forces in Kyushu, exchanged envoys with the Ming emperor in China, representing himself to the Ming as Yoshikane, of Japan.[32] The

---

32. Prince Kaneyoshi is more familiarly known as Kanenaga. That is how he appears in most indexes in the English-language literature.

Ming emperor sent an emissary in return, who conferred official recognition on Kaneyoshi's claim. Kaneyoshi's Headquarters of the Western Command (Seiseifu), located in the ancient city of Daizaifu in Kyushu, was relatively powerful at this time, and it seems that Kaneyoshi, unlike his father Go-Daigo, attempted to use that position of strength to establish an independent country in Kyushu. Yoshimitsu must surely have felt concern upon hearing of this.

Yoshimitsu rushed his close adviser Imagawa Ryōshun to Kyushu to negotiate with the Ming emissary while continuing to fight with Kaneyoshi. Negotiations with the Ming had to proceed under specific conditions: unless supplicants brought documents recognizing the superiority of the Ming, the emissary would not receive the petitioner. Since Yoshikane had brought the necessary documents and indicated his subservience to the Ming, he had received investment as the king of Japan. Yoshimitsu, held back by the court nobles of Kyoto, was not in a position to do the same so easily. However, Yoshimitsu ultimately pushed aside aristocratic concerns and submitted a petition to the Ming emperor, which he signed "Your servant, Minamoto Michiyoshi." Having thus indicated his submission, Yoshimitsu received investiture as the king of Japan in place of Kaneyoshi.

This chain of events returns us to the central problem of this chapter: the connection between the name of the country, Nihon, and the title of the ruler. That is, from Yoshimitsu's investiture to the end of the Muromachi period (with one exception, discussed below), the state that called itself Nihon was represented by the Ashikaga household of the Muromachi shogunate, which had taken the title "king of Nihon." Up to this point, Yoshimitsu had been working toward a compromise with the Southern Court of the imperial clan, which he hoped to absorb into the Northern Court. He was able to do this because he had complete control of the office of the emperor as well as "the ruler of the realm." When Yoshimitsu later made his son Yoshimochi shogun, he tried to make another son (Yoshitsugu) emperor and himself retired sovereign (*daijō tennō*). Had Yoshimitsu lived longer, he might have been able to realize his ambitions. In fact, after he died, some court nobles tried to have him posthumously designated retired sovereign. But his son Yoshimochi, feeling that Yoshimitsu had gone too far, squelched the plans for posthumous honors and then cut off relations with the Ming. Yoshimochi's actions ended the possibility that someone from outside the imperial family would become emperor, at least during the medieval era.[33]

The next crisis visited upon the imperial family came during the era of Oda Nobunaga. As we know from what Christian missionaries wrote about him, Nobunaga clearly had ambitions to become a deity himself. He received the imperial post of great minister of the right from the emperor but immediately resigned it, preferring to develop a new authority unencumbered by imperial restraints. There is no telling what might have happened had Nobunaga also lived longer. However, his ambitions were crushed when one of his generals, Akechi Mitsuhide, betrayed and killed him at the temple of Honnōji in Kyoto. The next warlord on the scene, Toyotomi Hideyoshi, adopted a different strategy, seeking to combine his power with the authority of the emperor to re-create the Japan of the Ritsuryō system.

The threats presented to the imperial family by the attempts of Ashikaga Yoshimitsu and Oda Nobunaga to usurp monarchical and divine power pose important dilemmas for our efforts to understand how the imperial family has survived to the present day. Most importantly, why is it that Yoshimochi and Hideyoshi chose different courses *after* the grandiose attempts of their predecessors Yoshimitsu and Nobunaga? I believe the answer to this question is related to the failure of monotheism to take root in Japan, particularly as a result of the suppression of the Ikkō sect and the Christians by the military powers. This may even require extending our inquiry into the continuing survival of nature worship among the Japanese.

We must remember that after the reign of Emperor Go-Daigo, the imperial family lost almost all political power, so much so that the office of emperor was stolen from them by Yoshimitsu at the end of the fourteenth century. But if we ask whether they were completely passive, we must admit that they were not. When the shogunate stripped Emperor Go-En'yu—the last of the emperors of the Northern Court—of the right to govern the capital, it obtained the right to levy taxes on the sake brewers and moneylenders of the city, one of the few rights that had remained to the imperial family. In the midst of this radical change, Go-En' yū did something remarkable. Believing that his main consort had carried on an illicit affair with Yoshimitsu,

---

33. Amino recommends a book by Imatani Akira on Ashikaga's flirtation with imperial rule: Imatani Akira, *Muromachi no ōken: Yoshimitsu no ōken sandatsu keikaku* (The Muromachi Kingship: Yoshimitsu's Plan to Usurp the Throne) (Tokyo: Chūō kōronsha, 1990).

Go-En'yū drew a sword in his own palace and struck her on the crown of her head in what came to be known as the "Bloodletting Incident." This action caused a huge commotion because it was unheard of for an emperor to strike a consort and draw blood within the palace. Go-En'yū was so distressed by the uproar caused by his attack that he threatened to retire to a mountain villa in Tanba and cut open his stomach.

The individual character of Emperor Go-En'yū himself was largely responsible for this incident. But in addition to personal instabilities one can discern an element of resistance against the shogunate in Go-En'yū's outburst. Neither were the emperors after Go-En'yū, from the Warring States through the Edo periods, simply submissive yes-men bending to the will of the shogunate, Emperor Go-Mizuno-o's resistance to the Tokugawa shogunate being the best-known case of imperial struggle.[34]

From the fifteenth century through the Edo period, the emperor retained the authority to designate and make promotions in court rank, even if in name only. Accordingly, court rank conferments and transcriptions of imperial edicts continued to be published in the Edo period. The actual determination of new reign names was carried out by the Tokugawa shogunate, but the decision remained the emperor's in form. Thus, even though the shogunate placed increasing limits on imperial power, the emperor continued to possess not just authority but a modicum of power. If he had not possessed some degree of power, I do not believe the kind of emperor system that developed after the Meiji Restoration would have been possible. Some argue that the emperor was completely stripped of power, but that argument has not yet passed beyond the realm of anecdotal evidence.

THE GREAT TRANSFORMATION

Historians have not yet sufficiently clarified the structure of authority in Japanese society after the fifteenth century. Neither Buddhism nor Shinto had any particular commanding authority, and Christianity had been completely suppressed. It would not be out of line to say that religion in general had no

---

34. Go-Mizuno-o attempted to resist the shogunal imposition of laws on the court and nobility by retiring from the throne and then working behind the scenes through the office of the retired emperor, a legacy of the Heian period, to control his four successors. While he is usually remembered as a patron of the arts, and certainly as a political maneuverer hopelessly struggling against the unstoppable rise of the Tokugawa shogunate, Amino's point is that the will to resist remained.

authority. Confucianism possessed great significance, but it is not yet clear how far it had disseminated to the masses. The emperor had something to do with this issue, but it is not at all clear what kind of influence he had on society at large.

If we shift our perspective, we find that there are many points in common between the structure of power in the Edo period and after the Meiji Restoration. The position of the emperor changed dramatically, but the structure of authority in and the composition of both eras show an unexpected number of continuities.

While I am not an Edo period specialist, it is obvious that in systemic terms, the Edo and modern periods must be considered separately. But when we look at the conditions of towns and villages from the Edo through the Meiji period, or when we consider the continuing problem of discrimination against *burakumin,* there are grounds to wonder whether things changed very much after all. We need to take a closer look at continuity in the structure of authority from the Edo period.

A key point in the structure of authority—and the emperor's function within that structure—in the Edo period is that consciousness of the "realm" was very strong among the masses. Yearly tribute (*nengu*) and other taxes (*kaeki*) as obligations to the realm (*kō*) kept such awareness alive for, as noted earlier, villager uprisings did not call for the abolition of yearly tribute. Of course, the idea of an obligation to the realm contained the seeds of a counterpart notion. That is, over time the idea developed that when the realm was not fulfilling its duties—acting as the realm should—then public obligations could be refused. I believe that this particular consciousness of the realm shaped the structure of the rule of the shogun and the *daimyō* and at the same time supported the continuing existence of the emperor.

Moreover, writing practices and family and *uji* names further fed into this consciousness. For example, components of official titles of the Ritsuryō system were widely used in villagers' names during the Edo period. It was common for villagers to have names with such elements as *saemon, uemon, hei, sakin, ukin, sakyō, ukyō, dayū,* and so on.[35] All came from Ritsuryō system guard titles. These official titles were first used as both pseudonyms[36] and actual names of villagers in the late Kamakura period, becoming common throughout the country by the Edo period. In some cases, one even

---

35. The result is names such as Jinzaemon, Yajibei, and so on.
36. Villagers in the Kamakura period could not use their real names in official correspondence, so they used pseudonyms.

AFTERWORD

Amino Yoshihiko

Amino Yoshihiko passed away in 2004, and in a manner befitting the passing of a monumental figure, publishers quickly reformatted previously published titles and issued books of recollections. As is typical of exceptionally prodigious Japanese authors, Amino's works were sorted, organized, and compiled into *Amino Yoshihiko chosakushū*, (The Works of Amino Yoshihiko). The publication has eighteen thematic volumes and one supplement (*bekkan*), each ending with explanatory notes by a scholar.[1] The collection as a whole helps us find our footing in surveying the vast intellectual territory Amino traveled in more than four hundred published titles over a period of more than half a century. In the tracks that Amino left in these works, we come to understand

---

1. Amino Yoshihiko, *Amino Yoshihiko chosakushū* (The Works of Amino Yoshihiko), 19 vols. (Tokyo: Iwanami shoten, 2007–2009). The volumes contain what the compilers deemed "researched" works (*kenkyūsho*), not general history.

how he approached sources, gained new insights, and shaped and reformulated ideas.

The broad scope of Amino's interpretation won him a readership among historians of all periods, who found "Amino-shigaku" (Amino historical study) interesting, highly relevant, and sometimes controversial. Amino wrote dense scholarly books with meticulous and intense analyses of sources, while also authoring easy-to-read digests of his findings and ideas. The present two volumes belong to the latter category of his output. Amino was a talented writer who delivered intricate new ideas with clarity and conviction. And the reading public swarmed to obtain his books, which were stacked high in an eye-catching "Amino corner" that extended from floor to ceiling in major bookstores.

In the English-language world as well, Amino's scholarship has appealed broadly to those of various interests and specialties. Interestingly, as I write this, it is primarily historians of modern, not medieval, Japan who have translated or written about Amino's works.[2] Considering that Amino's scholarly home is medieval, this is curious. Perhaps modernists feel a greater urgency to disseminate his ideas than do premodernists. Or, it may simply reflect the dearth of premodern historians in the English-language world. Whatever the case, I comment on some features of Amino's scholarly endeavor from the perspective of one premodern historian, and serve it as an Afterword to Alan Christy's masterful translation.

Amino began in the 1950s with what one might call a fairly conventional Marxist analysis of feudal Japan, and he moved in the 1960s and 1970s to new interpretations of medieval society and its legacy. During these years, he taught at a high school and held a post at Nagoya University and the Institute for the Study of Japanese Folk Culture. Amino was an indefatigable champion of textual and material evidence and an empathetic and imaginative spokesperson for the medieval population with a small voice and big strides. Yet his conceptualization of history was not limited to the medieval period or to the Japanese archipelago. He extended his ideas to encompass the entire trajectory of historical development, from prehistory to the present, and to a far wider space, including the sea and beyond. According to Amino,

---

2. For example, see the translation by Gavan McCormack, "Deconstructing 'Japan'," in *East Asian History* 3 (June 1992): 121–42. William Johnston, whom I cite below, is a clear exception.

his experience in lecturing on the entire history of Japan as a high school teacher required him to consider fundamental historical questions, such as the continuation of the imperial (*tennō*) institution, and nurtured his ability to "think big." The ethnographic methods (*minzokugaku*) that the Institute fostered influenced Amino's approach to material culture, while vigorous archaeological excavations in the sixties not only broadened the types of sources he could read but also added the important concrete material dimensions to his understanding of medieval peoples' livelihood and movements. His work at the Institute also led him to encounter hither-to unseen and, for him, eye-opening sources about commoners with nonagricultural livelihoods, such as *ukai* (cormorant fishermen) and *imoji* (metalsmiths).

In the late 1970s and 1980s, fresh waves of innovative work were streaming through the halls of research institutes. These waves came from many angles. The history of marginalized people regained force, especially with the discovery of new documents and the involvement of some scholars in the research related to the liberation movement. The history of women made a dramatic entry as a vital new field of investigation. Visual material, especially scrolls and portraits, won citizenship as a legitimate source of historical inquiry. In this trend, *chūseishi* (medieval history) became bracketed as a shining field with special attraction. Titillating titles, such as *Mato to ena: Chūseijin no sei to shi* (Target and Placenta: Medieval Life and Death) by Yokoi Kiyoshi[3] or *Sugata to shigusa no chūseishi: Ezu to emaki no fūkei kara* (Form and Gesture in Medieval History: From the Landscapes of Pictures and Picture Scrolls)[4] by Kuroda Hideo, flourished and caught the imagination of readers. Amino, of course, played a central role in this trend, inviting his own "Amino boom."

Needless to say, before the Amino boom struck, he already had published a number of significant works. For students studying the *shōen* (estate) system, then a core topic in this field, Amino's *Chūsei shōen no yōsō* (Medieval Estates in Transformation) on the Tara estate was a must along with dozens of other books on estate history. Published in 1966, it signified the culmination of fifteen years of research, during which he was active in the leftist movement and teaching at Kitazono High School.[5] He wrote spin-off

3. Yokoi Kiyoshi, *Mato to ena: Chūseijin no sei to shi* (Target and Placenta: Medieval Life and Death) (Tokyo: Heibonsha, 1988; first pub. in *Shakaishi kenkyū*, 1983).
4. Kuroda Hideo, *Sugata to shigusa no chūseishi: Ezu to emaki no fūkei kara* (Form and Gesture in Medieval History: From the Landscapes of Pictures and Picture Scrolls) (Tokyo: Heibonsha, 1986).
5. Amino Yoshihiko, *Chūsei no shōen no yōsō* (Medieval Estates in Transformation), Hanawa sensho 51 (Tokyo: Hanawa shobō, 1966). In *Amino Yoshihiko chosakushū*, bekkan, 3–17.

articles on the Tara estate, some important but little known. For example, one confirmed descent along both the maternal and paternal lines in early medieval Wakasa through a study of a genealogy, which marked, surprisingly, the years of death using Chinese era names.[6] In 1974, Amino published *Mōko shūrai*, or *Mongol Invasions*,[7] which features the rare use of an event for the book title, probably not his choice but the publisher's. The book begins with three puzzling words—*tsubute, bakuchi*, and *sai no kami* (rocks for stoning, gambling, and border gods)—and then discusses the rapidly transforming society and economy that developed around the time of the Mongol invasions. According to many, this book introduced the investigative and narrative style that would become quintessential Amino.[8]

For most English-language medievalists, this period marked a time of liberation from postwar scholarship, some of which had pained us with a largely inflexible theoretical construct. Many works dealing with the state, lordship, and landholding analyzed the material through the lens of a Marxian vocabulary and concepts that fitted the medieval world into a linear teleological framework of progress. They entertained questions associated with the timing, nature, and meaning of feudalism, a slippery entity that, we understood, had evolved out of "the Asian style dictatorial state structure" (*Ajia teki sensei kokka*) of the ancient Ritsuryō state. Commitment to dialectical materialism, class-based conflict, and a hope for a possible socialist future—a future devoid of the imperial institution and class disparities—explicitly or implicitly underlay most of the scholarly writing. Admittedly, this is an oversimplified description of the multidimensional and continuously shifting postwar decades in which, as Amino has described, historians were segmented into different theoretically driven factions, rivalries, and alliances.[9] Moreover, it would be unfair to ignore the large corpus of publica-

6. Amino Yoshihiko, "Chūsei ni okeru kon'in kankei no ichi kōsatsu: Wakasa Ichininomiya shamu keizu o chūshin ni" (An Observation of Medieval Marriage Relations: Focusing on the Genealogy of Wakasa Province Ichi and Ni no Miya Shrine Genealogy)," *Chihōshi kenkyū* 107 (October 1970): 1–24.

7. Amino Yoshihiko, *Mōko shūrai* (Mongol Invasions), *Nihon no rekishi*, vol. 10 (Tokyo: Shōgakkan, 1974).

8. Nakazawa Shin'ichi, *Boku no ojisan, Amino Yoshihiko no omoide* (Recalling My Uncle, Amino Yoshihiko) (Tokyo: Shūeisha, 2004), 55–60. Amino, *Mōko shūrai*, 16.

9. Amino segmented the postwar years into phases. The first phase includes the immediate postwar years through 1955. As of 1979, the second phase was still continuing, but the third was about to begin. In terms of historiography, the first phase began with the publication of Ishimoda Shō's *Chūseiteki sekai no keisei* (Formation of the Medieval Style World) (Tokyo: Itō shoten, 1946), which founded the field and set the course of study thereafter. The book is considered the most significant contribution to postwar medieval studies. Another exemplary writing of the era is *Chūsei shakai no kenkyū* (Study of the Medieval World) (Tokyo: Tōkyō daigaku shuppankai,

tions that do not fit the above description. Especially noteworthy are those on subjects that Amino would later expand or reformulate, including merchants, artisans, commerce, markets, coins, flow of goods, and the discriminated, by scholars such as Toyoda Takeshi, Kobata Atsushi, Hayashiya Tatsusaburō, Tanaka Takeo, Nagahara Keiji, Sasaki Gin'ya, and Takeuchi Rizō. Amino's own participation in the postwar scholarship began with two articles on the Tara estate, published in 1951 and 1952, which fit the teleological model of Marxist analysis. He later denounced them as shameful.[10] His book on the Tara estate, mentioned earlier, hardly employed Marxian terminology and took a decidedly narrative style to describe "the history of the people who lived on the stage of one small medieval estate," while noting the pattern of conflict along the vertical social axis nonetheless.[11] At any rate, the seminal change in the 1970s and 1980s was marked by the diminution of the debate over who held the means of production; whether or not a particular group of servants were serfs, slaves, or something else; how land levies defined the nature of control by the state and the estate lords; or what kind of landholding or what degree of exploitation in particular should be called feudal. The historical vocabulary no longer served the ends of historiography.

In this atmosphere, Amino was thrust into the limelight with the publication of *Muen, kugai, raku: Nihon chūsei no jiyū to heiwa* (Disconnectedness, Public Space, and Markets: Freedom and Peace in Medieval Japan).[12] Written in an easy writing style, the book revises the hitherto dark *chūsei* era, characterized by conflict and contradiction, into a bright and energetic space of self-determination and the movement of commoners. The puzzling title with three unfamiliar terms draws the reader to an imaginative world of the unknown. Open the first chapter, and another strange term, *engaccho*, jumps into view. Amino probes the meanings of these terms by placing them in context, examining associated terms, recalling words of similar sounds, and

1956) by Matsumoto Shinpachirō, whom Amino characterizes as an abstract thinker with a multidisciplinary and broad vision (Amino Yoshihiko, *Chūsei Tōji to Tōjiryō shōen* [The Medieval Tōji and Tōji Estates] [Tokyo: Tōkyō daigaku shuppankai, 1978], 3–63). Also mentioned in chapter 1, "Sengo rekishigaku no gojūnen" (Fifty Years of Postwar Historical Studies), in Amino Yoshihiko, *Rekishi to shite no sengo shigaku* (Historicizing Postwar History Writing) (Tokyo: Yōsensha, 2007; originally pub. Tokyo: Nihon editā sukūru shuppanbu, 2000), 21–68; idem, *Chūsei saikō: Rettō no chiiki to shakai* (Rethinking the Medieval: Region and Society of the Archipelago) (Tokyo: Nihon editā sukūru shuppanbu, 1986), 3–4, based on an interview conducted on April 2, 1979, and published in the newspaper, *Nihon dokusho shinbun*, no. 2000.
10. Amino, *Amino Yoshihiko chosakushū*, bekkan, 3–17.
11. Preface, p. 1, in Amino, *Chūsei shōen no yōsō*.
12. Amino Yoshihiko, *Muen, kugai, raku: Nihon chūsei no jiyū to heiwa* (Disconnectedness, Public Space, and Markets: Freedom and Peace in Medieval Japan) (Tokyo: Heibonsha, 1978).

consulting ethnographic wisdom. He constructs an image of a social and cultural space unfiltered by modern rational logic, and allows the reader to understand and empathize with the worldview and activities of commoners, who are detached from the reach of political authorities but linked to the sacred and profane, including the abstract and symbolic prestige of the *tennō*.[13]

By stating that English-language medievalists were rescued from the Marxian teleological paradigm, however, I do not imply that Amino and other authors of the 1970s and 1980s had abandoned Marxism. As William Johnston clarifies, although "skeptical toward what he saw as inflexible theory," Amino "never completely rejected a materialist view of historical change," and that his "views remained informed but not determined by theory."[14] In various interviews, Amino describes how he began rereading the works of Marx and Engels in 1953, after fallout from his activist movement, and observed how Marx's ideas transformed over time.[15] Marx's "The Eighteenth Brumaire of Louis Bonaparte, 1851–52" showed Amino the potential of forces that lay deeply beneath visible events, and "Letter to Vera Zasulich, 1851" influenced him to reconsider communes and communities in relation to medieval commoners on the Japanese archipelago. Nakazawa Shin'ichi explains what Marxism may have meant for Amino in the following way: Historical consciousness emerged when the Asiatic mode of production rose, but there existed a space for transcendental ideas, which remained outside the consciousness of history. The transcendental ideas did not vanish with the birth of history in the manner predicted by Hegel; they lived on. The "transcendental" for Amino was represented by the abstract and real space of asylum (*ajīru*) or sanctuary.[16]

13. A précis of this work can be found in Eiji Sakurai, "Foreword to 'Medieval Japanese Constructions of Peace and Liberty: *Muen, kugai,* and *raku,*'" translated by Gaynor Sekimori, *International Journal of Asian Studies* 4 (2007): 1–2. The translation of chapter 11 of the book by William Johnston, who is completing a translation of the entire book, follows Sakurai's "Foreword" in the same issue of the journal, pp. 3–14.
14. William Johnston, "From Feudal Fishing Villagers to an Archipelago's Peoples: The Historiographical Journey of Amino Yoshihiko," *Edwin O. Reischauer Institute of Japanese Studies Occasional Papers in Japanese Studies*, no. 2005-1 (March, 2005), 13.
15. His behavior around that time was considered odd. His affiliation with the Institute for the Study of Japanese Folk Culture invited a half-serious comment that he might have become an imperialist spy for the United States. Amino Yoshihiko, *Rettō no rekishi o kataru* (Talking about the History of the Archipelago), edited by Fujisawa, Amino san o Kakomu Kai (Tokyo: Hon no Mori, 1985), 101. Based on an interview in 1983.
16. Nakazawa Shin'ichi refers to Yoshimoto Takaaki's notion in order to explain Amino's ideas (*Boku no ojisan, Amino Yoshihiko* [My Uncle Amino Yoshihiko] [Tokyo: Shūeisha, 2004], 62–63, 141, 156). Amino, *Chūsei saikō: Rettō no chiiki to shakai,* 3–19. Amino concedes that, among all West European thinkers, Karl Marx is the one he respects the most (Amino, *Rekishi to shite no sengo shigaku,* 333).

The concept of asylum solved a number of historical and historiographical problems for Amino.[17] After intense involvement in the postwar Marxist movements and reading the historiography of the time, Amino felt uneasy about academic Marxism for various reasons. Especially after his study of sources on fishing villages at the Institute for the Study of Japanese Folk Culture, he felt critical of the nearly exclusive focus academic writings gave to the agricultural sector. For one thing, the heated debate over the pattern of feudal land rights and extraction ignored the question of the fundamental meaning of basic terms, such as *nengu* (dues or "annual tribute") and *kuji* (tax or "public matter"), both of which embodied a direct link to the symbolism of the emperor.[18] He also was unsure how to analyze "the folk" and "culture" from a Marxist perspective. Amino felt that he could uphold the spirit of Marx by examining the conceptual space of asylum (*ajīru*), concretely expressed by *kugai* and *raku,* historical terms appearing in sources. These were communal spaces of liberty (*jiyū*) frequented by people detached from the dominant structure of the land.

By linking the nonagricultural people to the space of detachment, he also could consider the resilience of the imperial institution, one of the most significant and little understood historical issues. The remarkable aspect of Amino's *ajīru* is that it existed in various places and forms, and hosted various people who were deeply rooted in the transcendental power close to *kami* as far back as in ancient sources. Under the Ritsuryō system, the populace with land allotments had the obligation to serve in the military as well as to pay other taxes and services, whereas the base people (*senmin, nuhi*) and artisans were exempt and "free" from taxes in return for service to the imperial court. When conscription was abandoned in the eighth century and the military came to be assumed by the warriors, the land-bound populace continued to pay taxes or their functional equivalent, estate dues (*nengu*) to various lords. However, in medieval times, artisans and merchants (*shokunin*) found spaces that were detached from such obligations. Analytically speaking, these commoners who occupied the spaces external to taxation were different from the Marxian "masses" who were entangled in power relations,

17. Amino broadly reformulated the notion of *ajīru*, or asylum, a concept Hiraizumi Kiyoshi focused on as early as in 1926 in his *Chūsei ni okeru shaji to shakai to no kankei* (The Relationship between Shrines, Temples, and Society in Medieval Times) (Tokyo: Shibundō, 1926). This link is mentioned by Nakazawa Shin'ichi (*Boku no ojisan, Amino Yoshihiko*, 68–70). It is noteworthy that, in other contexts as well, Amino frequently refers to prewar and wartime works, which typically engaged with sources in a meticulous positivist manner.
18. Amino, *Chūsei saikō: Rettō no chiiki to shakai*, 3–6, 8–9.

whereby "power" was understood and defined from a modern perspective. Those "masses" stood at one end of a conflict fought between the oppressor and the subordinated.[19] In contrast, Amino's untaxed people or folk possessed free will, which is the essence of a human desire, and these people contributed to the creation of free, unattached spaces, found in locations often considered sacred, mythical, or mysterious, such as temples, mountains, forests, and markets. In Amino's language, these were not the "productive" masses of Marx but instead nonagricultural people (hinōgyōmin) who were mostly mobile. But their lifestyle validated Marx's original idea that a free society can be built by people who have nothing to lose but iron chains.

In *Muen, kugai, raku* and other books, Amino insists on historicizing contemporary terminology. This, to me, is the foundation of what is called "the Amino-shigaku" (historical method), which he brought to the field, *bravely*, at the risk of becoming a "drop out."[20] Granted, this method is presumed necessary for any historical inquiry. But for uncovering undiluted and unfiltered meanings, the reality of the people who used the words, and ultimately the history itself, Amino is passionate, honest, and humble. The first section of the first chapter in his *Rekishi o kangaeru hinto* (Hints for Considering History) is titled, "History and Words." It begins: "Words that we use daily without thinking may contain meanings that may surprise us. We may understand the meanings of those words incorrectly if we assume we know them. In studying history, it is easy to encounter such occasions. We attribute the meaning that we understand today to historical terms. This should be corrected."[21] This critical attitude, as fundamental as it may be for any historian, guides Amino's works from the 1960s onward, leading to a discovery of fresh meanings in commonly used terms such as *hyakushō* and "Nihon," and eventually to broad arguments regarding the nature of the "Japanese" history, the Japanese state, and the position of *tennō*. Needless to

---

19. One of the earlier terms used for the commoners in Japanese historiography was *minshū*. In 1960, the Association for the Study of *Minshū* was formed. The members numbered more than a hundred as of 1975. They wrote on topics related to cultivators, people of the mountain, people of the sea, merchants, and artisans. They approached their subject with a concern to fit the people's productive capacity in Marxian terms. For example, see Chūsei Minshūshi Kenkyūkai, ed., *Chūsei no seijiteki shakai to minshūzō* (Medieval Society and Politics and the Image of the People) (Tokyo: San'ichi Shobō, 1976).
20. "Drop out" (*ochikobore*) is a term that Amino uses for himself often, especially in relationship to the change he experienced with the Marxist movement in 1953.
21. Amino Yoshihiko, *Rekishi o kangaeru hinto* (Hints for Considering History) (Tokyo: Shinchōsha, 2001), 11–12. He states that he learned this attitude from a senior scholar, Satō Shin'ichi, who emphasized in 1958 the need to critically examine historical vocabulary appearing in sources. Amino gives an example of *shihai* (control), a favorite term in Marxist writings, which he states had a meaning in medieval times different from the way we use it today.

say, Amino was not the only scholar who approached sources in this manner. One of the fascinating collections published in that era is a collaborative
work, *Kotoba no bunkashi: chūsei 1 to 4* (A Cultural History of Words), compiled by Amino Yoshihiko, Kasamatsu Hiroshi, Katsumata Shizuo, and Satō
Shin'ichi. It begins by asking: Have we not neglected the task to clarify the
historical usage of these sources?[22]

Despite or because of the huge popularity of *Muen, kugai, raku*, Amino
was soon faced with a storm of severe criticism. Ironically, while Amino won
global acclaim for his innovative scholarship, he also gained many academic
foes. Coming from every chronological segment of the Japanese historical
field, some challenged his interpretations that, to them, failed in the face of
hard evidence and logic. Some demanded precision in the meaning of terms
such as "liberty" (*jiyū*). Others asked what validity there was in dichotomiz-
ing the people into agriculturalists and *hi-nogyōmin* when most artisans or
the people of the sea also cultivated crops. Some criticized his assertion that
women's "sex" was liberated and "open" in the public space, for ignoring the
question of who possessed this "freedom" and what it would have meant for
women.[23] Still others accused him of embracing the *tennō-sei*, or the imperial system that the historical field had opposed for so long, in his discussion
of Nihon, emperors, and commoners. Generally, the new wave Amino represented was considered a "chaos in which disorder and distortion without
logic mingle and mix with new possibilities."[24] Instead of dismissing his critics, Amino took them seriously and sought to defend his position by clarify-
ing and substantiating his ideas through more exhaustive and meticulous
reading of sources. Consequently, in 1987, nine years after the first publication of *Muen, kugai, raku*, Amino published an expanded edition with
thirty new supplementary notes and four additional essays.[25] Whether or
not Amino was able to convert these critics, it is evident that he succeeded in
illuminating alternative ways to consider Japan's past, demonstrating imaginative methods for reading evidence and suggesting a critical outlook for
assessing the present.

22. Amino Yoshihiko, Kasamatsu Hiroshi, Katsumata Shizuo and Satō Shin'ichi, comps., *Kotoba no
    bunkashi: chūsei 1 to 4*, (Cultural History of Words) (Tokyo: Heibonsha, 1989), 3.
23. He later modified this stance by suggesting the possible danger awaiting itinerant women.
24. Mentioned by Ryūfuku Yoshitomo, review of *Genjitsu no naka no rekishigaku*, by Kuroda Toshio,
    Shigaku zasshi 87.7 (July 1978): 88.
25. Amino Yoshihiko, *Amino Yoshihiko chosakushū*, vol. 12: *Muen, kugai, raku* (Tokyo: Iwanami sho-
    ten, 2007), 487, 267–70. An English-language translation of the supplementary notes by William
    Johnston is available as "Medieval Japanese Constructions of Peace and Liberty: *Muen, kugai,* and
    raku, Supplementary Notes," *International Journal of Asian Studies* 4 (2007): 161–72.

Amid pros and cons, Amino occupied a premier position in medieval studies. Throughout his intellectual journey, Amino remained self-reflexive and malleable, and expressed frequently his debt to people who had inspired and influenced him, while remaining firm in his fundamental convictions. In addition to single-author monographs, Amino produced collaborative titles based on research and seminars with scholars of various disciplines. A partial list includes: medieval historians, such as Katsumata Shizuo, Ishii Susumu, Satō Shin'ichi, Kasamatsu Hiroshi, Imatani Akira, Fukuda Toyohiko, Yokoi Kiyoshi, and Sakurai Eiji; ethnologists, such as Akasaka Norio, Miyata Noboru, and Kamino Yoshiharu; feminist anthropologist Ueno Chizuko; and archaeologitst Mori Kōichi. Amino interviewed frequently and held lectures for both the academic and interested public. In 1997, Amino began a series of lectures titled, "Words in History," hosted by a publisher, and continued featuring these lectures and new articles in a journal called *Nami* (Waves). After twelve issues, in April, 2000, Amino found that he had lung cancer, and he was forced to terminate the series. The lectures are collected in the book *Rekishi o kangaeru hinto.* The book begins with a chapter titled, "'Nihon' to iu kokumei" (A Country Name Called "Nihon"). Perhaps it is significant that Amino chose "Nihon" as the first in his lecture series, "Words in History." His indictment that no other people on this globe know so little about the origin of their own country may not be true, but, for Amino, explication about "Nihon" clearly demanded the audience's and readers' attention.[26]

Facing the totality of Amino's work, one gets a sense of awe and admiration for its density and depth, not to speak of the output. The present translation of the two volumes, *Rekishi o yominaosu*, is a great beginning for the English-language readers to become familiar with Amino's scholarship. We thank Alan Christy for this translation, a difficult task that is an act of interpretation more than translation, and hope that this serves to enliven broad discussion of the people and history of the archipelago and the sea, as well as historical approaches and methods, in classrooms and research corridors.

26. Amino, *Rekishi o kangaeru hinto*, 14. Amino's last publication is *Nihon no chūsei 6: Toshi to shokunōmin no katsudō* (Japan's Medieval World, vol. 6: Cities and Activities of Artisans) (Tokyo: Chūō kōronsha, 2003), co-authored with Yokoi Kiyoshi.

INDEX

Page references to illustrations are in bold.

107; transition from late medieval, 117; warlords, types, 114n.22

Edo period class structure: farmers and other occupations, 99; meaning of the term *nōmin*, 15n.13, 97

Egami Namio, 41n.3

Eighteenth Brumaire of Louis Bonaparte, 1851–52, The (Marx), 282

Eiji Sakurai, 282n.13

Eison (monk), 166

elephant, transported, 93

elephant gift, 93

Emergence of Japanese Kingship, The (Piggott), 42n.5

Emishi, 50

Emishi people, 52

emonfu (Inner Palace Guards), 177

emperor (*tenno*), 48, 178n.14; and Buddhism, 261–62; deity personified, 178–79, 178–79n.14, 253–54; dual nature, 253–54; establishment of title, 250–51; female, 238; first, 247–48; funerals, 261; Heavenly Descent, 248–49; imperial history, 245–49, 279; slave of the Buddhas, 261

Emperor, Rice and Villages, The (Christy), xxxiii

emperor himself (*tennō shinsei*), 267

encompassing village. See *sōson* (encompassing village)

engaccho (game), 281–82

Engishiki (Institutes of the Engi Period) (Daigo), 253, 253n.14

enkiri-dera (relationship-ending temple), xx, 219, 219n.3

Enkyō (reign name), 130n.11

Enryakuji Shrine, 181

Enshū Sea, 46

entertainers and performers: artisan defined, 161n.18; dancers, female (*shirabyoshi*), 160, 235; female, 160, 235 (*see also* courtesans [*asobime*]); lacking Ritsuryō support, 176–77; *sarugaku*, 171n.2; singers, 243n.24; street performers (*hōka*), 167. *See also* festivals

entertainment: cost accounting of, 76; *utagaki* celebrations, 153, 221–23

epistolary style (*shosatsuyō monjo*), 132–33

Essays in Idleness (Yoshida Kenkō), 150–51

estate manager-contract system, 93

estate managers (*kumon*), 228

estates (*shō*). See *shōen* estates

estate system of taxation (*shōen-kōryōsei*), 24

eta disembowelers, 196

eta (greatly polluted), 195–97, 195n.28

eta warawa (greatly polluted) child, 192, 195–96, 195n.28, **196**, 213

Eternal Storehouse of Japan, The (Ihara Saikaku), 20

Ethnographic History of Pollution, An. See *Kegare no minzokushi*

etoki (picture scroll preachers), 77, 98n.2

etori (procurers of food for animals), 196–97

evil, 83–86, 241; beliefs differ among Buddhist sects, 101; represented by those pursuing money, 83; transformation at end of thirteenth century, 197

Evil Genta, 84

Evil Safu, 84

Evil Shichibei, 84

exchange rice (*kaemai*), 148

exclusionary policy, 103–4

Ezoana Tomb, 42–43, **43**

Ezo disturbances, 85–86

Ezo peoples, 175

F

family names, 273–74

family registries. *See* registered households (*gō*)

famines, 104–7; ninth century, 177

fan selling, 241

farmers (*nōmin*). See *nōmin* (farmers)

farming (*nō*), 99

farm village (*nōson*), 72

Farris, William Wayne, 26n.18, 41n.3, 136n.20, 264n.27

235–36. *See also* commerce;
    marketplaces
Meshino family of Osaka, 20
metal casters, 56, 71, 157, 274
metal smiths (*imoji*), 279
metori (taking a woman), 224–25
Middle Palace Guards (*hyōefu*), 177
migyōsho (instructions of nobles), 133
Mikawa: riots, 105
miko (walking shamans), 233
mikudarihan (letters of divorce), 219
Mikudarihan: Edo no ikon to joseitachi
    (Letters of Divorce: Women and
    Divorce in Edo Japan) (Takagi
    Tadashi), 219n.2
military governors (*shugo daimyō*), 164,
    227
military steward (*jitō*), 72, 113
millet, 35
Minamoto no Ason, 250
Minamoto no Sanetomo, 265
Minamoto no Yoritomo, 61, 113, 227
minshū (commoners), 284n.19
minzokugaku, 279
Mirror of Pastoral Life, A (*Nomori no
    kagami*), 88
miscellaneous tax (*zōyō*), 49, 255
mitsugi. *See* tribute
miuchibito (private vassals), 84
miumaya yoriudo. *See* imperial stable
    purveyors
Miura family, 114
Miwa, Ibaraki Prefecture, 46, 48
miyagomori (shamans, lower caste).
    See shamans, lower caste
Miyakawa Mushanojo, 227
Miyamoto Tsuneichi, xxxv, 10, 220, 220n.4,
    223, 244
Miyata estate, Tanba Province, 77
Miyata Noboru, 172n.4
mizunomi (landless villagers), 14
mizunomi (water drinkers), 14–17
modern era, early, 108
modernization, incomplete, xxviii
modern past / premodern past, xvii
Mogami River, Dewa Province, 49
mokkan. *See* wooden tablets
monarch of Kyoto, 110

monarchy of the east, xxiv, 110
monarchy of the west, xxiv
moneylenders (*dosō*). *See* financiers
money offerings (*jōbun*), 232
money worship, 151
Mongol invasion, 266
monjo shugi (principle of documents), 49,
    138
monks (*sōryo*), 240; attire, 160; as estate
    managers, 76; full time status, 78; of
    Kamakura period, 165–69; as land
    managers, 76, 84; lecture documents,
    130; as lenders and financiers, 78;
    and marriage, 241; social status of
    "slaves" and menials, 157–60; tax
    responsibility, 53; as traders and
    entrepreneurs, 89–92; women, 239–
    41, 240n.21, 243
Monks Organization (Sōjō), 261
Monogusa Tarō, 224–5
moshitsugi (the service desk), 110
moto (below), 252
motodori (topknot), 193
mōto (gate men), 14
mōto (landless villagers), 19–20
mountain ascetics (*yamabushi*), 76
mountain castles (*gusuku*), 95
mountain dwellers (*sanmin*), 4
mountain floats (*yamaboko*), 184
mountain tolls (*yamagoshi*), 82, 82n.4
mountain village. *See* sanson
mountain yeoman (*yamadachi*), 95
Mount Fugi, 105
Mount Hiei, 82, 182n.17, 227
muen (unconnected), 14. *See also*
    nonconnectedness
muen (world of nonrelations), xx
Muen, kugai, raku (*Disconnectedness,
    Public Space, and Markets*) (Amino
    Yoshihiko), xiii, xxx–xxxi, 152n.10,
    284, 285
muen no ba (site of disengagement), 152
muen no ba (unconnected spaces), xxxi
muensho (nonrelated spaces), 167
muen temples, 167. *See also* temples of
    disengagement
mulberries, 38, 40
Munakata Shrine, 63, 112, 114

206, 207; market scene, 154; notes on
wooden tablets (*mokkan*), 91; people
moving on a cart and a hut, 198;
rented ship from Kamakura period,
90
Picture Book of Hungry Ghosts, The.
See *Gaki sōshi*
Piggott, Joan R., 42n.5
pilgrimages (*okagemairi*), 223, 244
pillar culture, gigantic, 34, 36
Pillow Book of Sei Shonagon, The (Ivan
Morris, trans.), 131
pirates (*kaizoku*), 55, 81, 82, 262
pirates (*umi no ryōshu*), 55n.13, 82
planes of existence, 152–54, 153n.12;
childbirth, 233n.15; *muen* and *yūen*,
xx, 283–84; sacred places, 95, 186.
See also nonconnectedness
playgirls (*asobime*), 234. See also
courtesans
pledges (*rakusho kishō*), anonymous,
127–29
poetry, *waka*, 130
poetry contest picture scroll, 97–98, 161–
62, 164
political systems, hard and soft, 246
pollution, purifiers, 179–88, 193. See also
nonhumans (*hinin*)
pollution (*kegare*): associated with cattle,
187–88 (*see also* cow-herding children
[*ushikai-warawa*]); cause of
discrimination, 172; condition of evil,
83; contamination, xxvii; fear of, 197;
from killing and selling animals, 196–
97; through childbirth, 233n.15; and
women, 239–42; worker's character
negatively reflected in stigmatized
occupations, 98–99n.6, 173, 177–79
*Pollution and Purification. See Kegare to
oharae*
*Population Structure of Early Modern
Japan, The. See Kinsei Nihon no jinkō*
Portrait of the Medieval Japanese People, A.
See *Nihon chūsei no minshūzō*
port towns, 22, 62–63
post towns, 180–81
Power of Temples and Shrines, The.
See *Jisha seiryoku*

*Principles of the Scales, The. See Hakari no
honji*
prisoners, released (*hōmen*), 189–90;
differed but included in nonhuman
category, 189; hairstyles and clothing,
190, 191; as pictured in *Pictorial
Biography of the Holy Man Hōnen,
The*, 190, 191
Private Office (*kurododokoro*), of the
emperor, 187
private slaves (*shinuhi*), 158, 173
private *suiko* (*shisuiko*), 155
private vassals (*miuchibito*), 84
promissory note, official (*kirifu*), 57
proprietors' holdings, taxable value
(*kandaka*), 116
prostitution, 213, 243, 243n.24
Protestantism and the Spirit of Capitalism
(Weber), 168
province (*kuni*), 49
provincial governor, 65
provincial office (*kokuga*), 65
public service (*kūji*) tax category, 24, 71,
255
public slaves (*kunuhi*), 158, 173
pullers (*gōtei*), 55
puppeteers (*kugutsu*), 235
purifiers (*kiyome*), 188. See also
nonhumans (*hinin*)
purifying Hōnen's grave, 182

Q
Quarters, The (*shuku*), 180
Queen of Wa, The, 41

R
raibyō (leprosy), xxxv, 173, 183
rainbows, 152–53
raku (discriminated group), 216
Rakuchū rakugai ("Scenes in and out of
the Capital"), 241
rape, 224–25
realm (*kō*), 255
realm (*ōyake*), 255
Record of Moromori (diary), 240
Record of Myōhōji, A, 104, 105
Record of the Latter Ages of Japan, A.
See *Nihon kōki*

robes: of nonhumans, 187; of purveyor
groups, 158, 160
Rokurodan (Kitano Shrine riverside
dweller), 189
Rokushōji Temple, 62
Roman Catholic Church, 219n.3
Rongoshō (Comments on the Analects),
130
roof beam money, 89
rowers (*kandori*), 55
rural, xviii
ryōke shiki (office of the owner), 260
ryōko (tomb guards), 174
ryōmin. See good people, the (*ryōmin*)
Ryukyuan kingdom, 93
Ryukyus, 130–31

S

sacred places: commercial activities at
temples, 167–68; at death place of a
nonhuman, 186; first harvest rice
offerings at, 95
Sacred Texts and Buried Treasures (Farris),
26n.18, 41n.3, 136n.20, 264n.27
Saga, Emperor, 238–39n.19, 257
Sagami Province, 113–14
sailors, 29, 91
Saionji family, 85, 109–13; estate lands of,
111; hereditary directors of retired
emperors stables, 110; ship with coin
as ballast, 146–47; water
transportation, **111**
Saionji Kintsune, 112
salt, estate of, 66–69
salt manufacture, 34, 68
samurai, villages without, xviii
samurai-peasants-artisans-merchants (*shi-
nō-kō-shō*), 99
Sanbō ekotoba (Illustrations of the Three
Jewels) (Minamoto no Tamenori for
Princess Sonshi), 130n.10
sanctuary. *See* asylum
sankin kōtai (alternate attendance system),
115
sanmin (mountain dwellers), 4
Sannai Maruyama, Aomori City, 34, 36
Sano, Izumi, 22
Sanshū dayū (sermon), 252n.10

sanson (dispersed settlements), xxxvii
sanson (mountain village), 21–22
sarugaku, 171n.2
Sasaki Gin'ya, 281
Satake, 250
Satō Shin'ichi, 258n.19, 284n.21, 285
Satsuma, 118
Satsumon culture, 51
"Scenes in and out of the Capital."
See *Rakuchū rakugai*
scholarly research: post-World War II,
xxvii–xxix, 280–81
Scroll of Diseases, The (*Yamai no sōshi*),
231, **232**
seashell rings: Gohoura shell jewelry, 46,
48
sea slave (*kainu*), 29
seaweed (*konbu*), 77–78
seaweed (*nori*), 54
sedge hats (*ichimegasa*), **223**
segregated communities, 216
Seika (pure and brilliant families), 259
Seikai road, 49
Sekiguchi Hiroo, 28
Seki Temple dance hut, **88**
Sekiyama Naotarō, 5
Sekkan family, 61–62, 259
sekkyō-bushi (sermons), 252n.10
sen, use of character, 158
Sen (village headwomen), 244
Sendai, 114–15
sengenchō (town of one thousand
buildings), 136
seni kekachi (coin shortages), 104
seniority, 181
Senmaida (thousand-layered rice paddies),
17, **18**
senmyō (class of documents), 248, 248n.6
senshu manzai (felicitators), 77
senzu manzai (beggars), 98–99, 98n.1
sermons (*sekkyō-bushi*), 252n.10
Servants of the Four Posts, 190
service desk, the (*moshitsugi*), 110
service orders (*hōsho*), 133, 133n.15
sesshō. See regent
set aside coins (*bichikusen*), 150
settlements of the Ritsuryō state, xviii, 49
seven forms of written expression, 123n.1

sanson (dispersed settlements), xxxvii; sanson (mountain village), 21–22; script of written records kept by, 137–43; sengenchō (town of one thousand buildings), 136; shūson (concentrated village), xxxvii; sōson (encompassing village), xxxviii; urban settlements, xviii, 74–75; vs. towns, 141n.2; without samurai, xviii

Village Statistics for Fugeshi and Suzu Counties 1735, 17

virtuous men (tokujin), 81

virtuous people (yūtokujin), 151

vocation (shokuno), 233. See also trades, skilled

vows (kishōmon) to deity, 127

vows (kōmon) to deity, 127

vows to abstain from sex in certain areas of Kasuga Shrine, 221

W

wa (particle of speech), 127

Wa, kingdom of, xxiii; name changed to Nihon (Japan), 48; Queen of Wa, 41. See also Japan

wadō kaichin (coins, copper and silver). See coins, copper and silver

wage fields, 71n.3

Wajima, Noto Peninsula, 16–17, 22

wajin, the, 37, 53

waka poetry, 130

Wakasa Province, 14n.12, 280

Wakatsuru-nyō, 230

Wake uji, 258

wakō pirates, 101

walking shamans (miko), 233

wanderers (yūshu fushoku no tomogara), 82

wandering women (ukareme), 233

warlords (daimyō), 24n.17; types, 114n.22

Warring States period, 93, 101, 113; documents from, 125; new character to distinguish between post towns and nonhuman towns, 180–81; village tax accounting, 136n.18, 137

warriors, nonvassal, 134n.16

Wasurerareta Nihonjin (Forgotten Japanese: Encounters with Rural Life

and Folklore, The) (Miyamoto Tsuneichi), xxxv, 220n.4, 223, 244

Watanabe Makoto, 32, 33

water drinkers (mizunomi), 14–17

waterways, remains and artifacts along, 38–39

water well ceremonies, 188

Waves. See Nami

Way (dō), 163

Way of Household Instruction, A. See Teikin ōrai

wealth, symbols of, 149–52

Weber, Max, 168

Wei zhi wei ren chuan (Chinese text), 37, 38

wells, water, 188

whaling practices, 95

What Was the Edo Period? See Edo jidai to wa nanika: Nihon shijō no kinsei to kindai

widows, 227

women, 130–37, 222n.8, **223,** 233; abortion practices, 225–26; in bandit organizations, 83; child bearing, 233, 233n.15; divorce, xx, 218–20, 219n.3, 230–31; equality with men, 237–38; followers of Ippen, 87; land ownership, 230–31, 243; literacy, 123–24, 130–37, 244; merchants, 235–36; monks, 239–41, 240n.21, 243; and pollution, 239–42; professional groups, 233–36; property managers, 226–33; rape, 224–25; selling of, 243; sexual practices, 213, 220–26; social activities, 229–33; social status, 164, 213, 242–43; tax responsibility, 53; travel, 244, 285; as vassals, 227–28

women commanders (onna jitō), 228

women's literature, 239

women's professional groups: emergence, 233–36

Women's Quarters of the Palace, 234

wooden boxes (magemono), xxxviii, 157

wooden tablets (mokkan): of Akita Castle, 139; of the Heijō Palace, 26–27, 26n.18, 136–37, 136n.20, 138–39; of the Kusado Sengenchō excavation, 136, 136n.19; related to nie offerings,

ALAN S. CHRISTY, the translator and author of the Translator's Introduction, is an Associate Professor of History at the University of California, Santa Cruz. He was a member of Amino Yoshihiko's Tokikuni Family Research Project at the Institute for the Study of Japanese Folk Culture at Kanagawa University from 1991 to 1995. He has written on Japanese ethnography, Okinawa, and war memories and has translated Japanese scholarship on the same.

HITOMI TONOMURA, author of the Preface and Afterword, is Professor of History and Women's Studies at the University of Michigan. Her areas of study include war and violence, commerce and merchants, and gender and sexuality. Her next book will examine the gendered meanings associated with warfare and the war-prone society of medieval Japan. Her publications include *Community and Commerce in Late Medieval Japan: Sō Villages of Tokuchin-ho,* and *Women and Class in Japanese History,* as well as numerous articles.